Bonnie Stern's
CUISINART®
COOKBOOK

A Weil Company/Madison Press Book

First Edition 1984
Reprinted 1985

Canadian Cataloguing in Publication Data

Stern, Bonnie, 1947-
  Bonnie Stern's Cuisinart cookbook

Includes index.
ISBN 0-00-217273-9

1. Food processor cookery. I. Title. II. Title:
Cuisinart cookbook.

TX840.F6S83 1984   641.5'89   C84-098378-6

Design: Rod Della Vedova
Photography: S.C. Dean
Food styling: Margaret Fraser
Illustrations: Annette Tatchell
Editorial: Shelley Tanaka

This special edition has been produced for Weil Company
Limited, 79 - 81 Torbarrie Road, Downsview, Ontario, Canada
M3L 1G5.

Produced by
Madison Press Books
40 Madison Avenue
Toronto, Ontario
Canada M5R 2S1

Typesetting by Cybergraphics Co. Inc.

Printed and bound in Canada by
T. H. Best Printing Company Limited

Front Cover: *Pistachio Roulade (see page 178).*

For the two men in my life:
my husband, Raymond, who has unselfishly dedicated
his taste buds for the sole purpose of my culinary research;
and my young son, Mark,
whose taste buds are just developing.

Foreword

I'm immensely pleased and proud that Canada's Cuisinart® food processor cookbook has been written by Bonnie Stern. Bonnie is a friend of long standing and an excellent teacher of cooking. She was one of the first North American food authorities to recognize the many uses of the processor and to sense that its applications may well be boundless.

This handsome volume presents more than 140 original recipes, many of them representing the rich culinary diversity of Canada's peoples. Bonnie's skill, care and wide knowledge of cooking distinguish every recipe. I'm certain Bonnie Stern's book will gain all the success it so richly merits.

Bon appétit and good eating!

Carl G. Sontheimer
President, Cuisinarts® Inc.
Greenwich, Connecticut

Contents

Acknowledgments

Whenever I think about who encouraged my love of food and influenced my sense of taste, I come up with a never-ending list of people. My mother probably helped me the most. She not only always allowed me into her kitchen, but she also trusted me and didn't criticize even when I was very young. And then, after I dirtied every pot in the house, she did what all cooks dream of — she washed the dishes.

When I began my professional cooking training I could not believe how much there was to learn. The wonderful chefs at George Brown College — especially Jacques Marie, Klaus Savodny and Willi Brand — opened up a whole new world for me. Then I expanded my knowledge by taking courses with such experts as Simone Beck, Julie Dannenbaum, Ann Willan, Marcella Hazan, Jacques Pépin, Nina Simonds, Giuliano Bugialli and Elizabeth Andoh. And even now, I still can't believe how much there is to learn.

When I opened the cooking school many of my friends, relatives and colleagues encouraged me and shared their recipes, especially Ed Weil, Bob and Gail Bailey, Joel and Linda Rose, Gwen Fargeon, Ann Sharr, Ellen Freedman, Lillian Kaplun, Monda Rosenberg, Marg Fraser, Andrea Iceruk, Ruby Ure, Patti and Earl Linzon and Jani and Wayne Krangle.

I also owe a great deal to the media. You may think you have something terrific to offer people, but people have to know you are there. My thanks to Monda Rosenberg, Jim White, Kathy Brooks, Nanci Lugsdin, Judy Brandow, Ken Larone, Judy Webb, Peter Pacini, Jane Rodmell and everyone else who helped make my school so well known.

I'm also grateful to Ed Weil and Carl Sontheimer, who changed my cooking habits forever by introducing me to the Cuisinart®.

And thanks to all my students who keep coming back for seconds. Their questions, comments, praises and criticisms keep me on the right track — to know what courses to offer and what information to include in my articles and books.

Most of all, I have to thank my wonderful staff at the cooking school — Maureen Lollar, Linda Stephen, Julie Lewis and Sadie Darby. They are my best and toughest critics, helping and encouraging me constantly. Without them nothing would be possible, including this book.

Introduction

When I first opened the **Bonnie Stern School of Cooking** in 1973, Canadians were just beginning to recognize cooking as an art. Throughout the seventies, as people began to travel more, they became more discriminating about restaurants and looked for more variety in food. As a result, the interest in food and cooking techniques grew. To keep up with this enthusiasm, we have had to expand from one room and three students to a school that now includes two classrooms, a test kitchen and a cookware shop. We now offer a wide range of courses, both demonstration and participation, on a variety of techniques and cuisines and frequently feature distinguished guest teachers such as Jacques Pépin, Giuliano Bugialli, Marcella Hazan and Madeleine Kamman.

At the school we try to offer students much more than just interesting and delicious recipes. Our courses focus on food preparation techniques and general cooking principles. We stress the importance of using fresh, high-quality ingredients and the correct use of the tools and equipment that will give students the best results and help make cooking a joy rather than a chore.

The Cuisinart® food processor is one of the best labor-saving kitchen tools available to cooks today. It is rapidly becoming a standard appliance as more and more home cooks discover that it saves time, energy and encourages them to try more complex dishes. We have been giving food processor cooking courses since the machine was first introduced to Canada in 1975, and the increasing popularity of these classes is proof that the **Cuisinart® food processor** is not just another trendy gourmet gadget – it's a knife that's here to stay. But, as with any other basic kitchen tool, it takes experience and knowledge to get the most effective results. This book should help you get the most out of your food processor – the more you use it, the more you will learn about its potential.

After fifteen years in the food business, I still love food – I love cooking it, eating it, writing about it and most of all teaching people about it. I hope that by using this book you will be able to share my enthusiasm about food, and learn to enjoy cooking and entertaining even more.

Delicious wishes,

Bonnie Stern
Toronto, 1984

Cuisinart® Food Processors

Which model should you choose?

There are four current sizes of **Cuisinart®** available – the DLC-X series, DLC-7 series, DLC-8 series and DLC-10 series. These vary in price, capacity, power and extra accessories.

All **Cuisinart®** models consist of the motor base and the following:

> **Work bowl** with built-in handle.
> **Work bowl cover** with large feed tube.
> **Large pusher** and sleeve assembly (attached).
> **Small pusher** for small feed tube.
> **Serrated metal blade** for chopping, mincing, mixing and pureeing.
> **Medium shredding disc** for grating cheese and coconut, and for shredding vegetables.
> **Medium slicing disc** for slicing vegetables, fruit, etc.
> **Plastic blade** for kneading bread dough.

> **Spatula** for scraping down the sides of the bowl.
> **Cleaning tool** for cleaning metal and plastic blades.
> **Instruction/recipe book.**

Your **Cuisinart®** also has many optional attachments, including slicing discs that range in thickness from 1 mm to 8 mm, fine and medium shredding discs, a funnel to make it easier to add ingredients through the feed tube, and a disc holder for storing the discs, etc. Two of my favorite optional attachments are the French-fry cut and julienne discs, with which you can make matchstick French fries or some julienned fruits and vegetables.

Important: Read the instruction book **completely** and **carefully** before operating your machine.

DLC-10 series

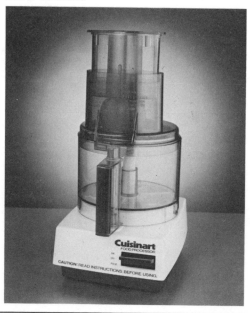

DLC-8 series

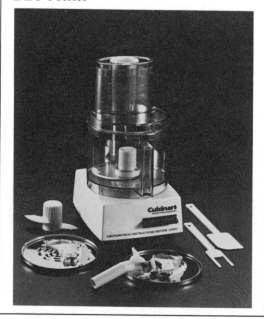

CUISINART® FOOD PROCESSORS
COMPARISON CHART

| MODEL | WORK BOWL DIAMETER | BREAD DOUGH | MEAT/ FISH | (INSIDE MEASURMENTS) | | SMALL FEED TUBE DIAMETER | NOTES |
| | | | | LARGE FEED TUBE | | | |
				LENGTH	WIDTH		
DLC-10 series	6⅜ in/16 cm	2 lb/1 kg (3 to 4½ cups/ 750 mL to 1L flour)	¾ lb/ 375 g	4¼ in/ 11.5 cm	2½ in/ 6.5 cm	2 in/5 cm	
DLC-8 series	6⅝ in/17 cm	3 lb/ 1.5 kg (4½ to 6 cups/1 to 1.5 L flour)	1¼ lb/ 625 g	4¼ in/ 11.5 cm	2¾ in/ 7 cm	2 in/5 cm	A pasta-making attachment is available.
DLC-7 series	7 in/18 cm	4 lb/2 kg (6 to 8 cups/1.5 to 2 L flour)	2 lb/ 1 kg	4¼ in/ 11.5 cm	2¾ in/ 7 cm	2 in/5 cm	A pasta-making attachment is available.
DLC-X series	8 in/20 cm	5 lb/ 2.5 kg (10 to 12 cups/2.5 to 3 L flour)	3 lb/ 1.5 kg	4¾ in/ 13 cm	3¹⁄₁₆ in/ 8 cm	2 in/5 cm	This model comes with three slicing discs – thin, medium and thick.

DLC-7 series

DLC-X series

Important Safety Notes

1. Read instruction book carefully before using machine.
2. Do not try to outwit the safety features of the machine. Do not operate machine if work bowl and cover are not properly in place. And do not use work bowl cover with the large feed tube if the sleeve assembly has become detached from the pusher.
3. Keep machine and blades out of the reach of children.
4. Keep machine unplugged when not in use, and do not store in an "on" position.
5. Do not immerse machine base in water.
6. Blades are very sharp, so handle carefully and store in a safe place.
7. Do not leave blades in soapy dishwater where they cannot be seen easily.
8. Do not place blades on machine base unless bowl is properly in place.
9. Make sure blades have stopped rotating before removing lid. Never try to stop blades manually.
10. Always use pusher to push foods through for slicing or shredding. Never use fingers.

Cuisinart® Tips

1. Keep machine on counter ready for action!
2. Store machine with cover upside down so that air can circulate around bowl and lid.
3. When cleaning blades, do not forget about the hollow area underneath the blades. Use the special two-pronged cleaner that comes with the machine for cleaning this area.
4. When slicing, pack feed tube tightly for best results.
5. If possible, wash blades, work bowl and cover immediately after using to make cleaning easier.
6. When processing hot soups or sauces, remove the small pusher from the cover. Otherwise the pusher may pop out because of hot air pressure when the mixture is processed.

A Note on Metric:

All the recipes in this book are given in both imperial and metric measurements. Follow a recipe in either imperial or metric, but do not try to use both and do not try to convert recipes yourself. Comparing the imperial and metric parts of a recipe can be confusing because the conversions are not always consistent or exact. In this book, 1 cup is replaced by 250 mL and each recipe is adjusted accordingly. So don't worry if the conversions do not follow a conversion table exactly. In some recipes, for example, ¼ cup is replaced by 50 mL and in some recipes 3 tbsp is replaced by 50 mL. But both will work because of the balance of the conversions of the other ingredients.

If you wish to follow the recipes in metric, buy a set of metric measures. They are worth the investment.

Note: At the time this book was written, most foods were packaged in imperial sizes, with metric equivalents given on the labels. However, some foods (e.g. pasta) are now being packaged in standard metric sizes (a sign that it will soon be easier for us to work in metric rather than imperial). In most cases, however, the slight variation will not affect the outcome of these recipes.

Food Hints

Bouquet garni: A bouquet garni is a spice bag that is used for flavoring stocks, soups, sauces and stews. You can buy them commercially, but they are very easy to make and if you make them yourself you can alter the flavors to suit the dish. I usually use a double thickness of cheesecloth and kitchen twine to make these pouches. Cut the cheesecloth into 5-in/13-cm squares. In the middle, for an all-purpose bouquet garni, place 5 whole peppercorns, a few sprigs of fresh parsley, 1 bay leaf, 2 whole cloves, 1 tsp/5 mL dried thyme and tie into a little pouch with the twine. The flavor can be altered by adding a clove of garlic, fresh or dried rosemary, basil or oregano.

Breadcrumbs: There are two basic types of breadcrumbs, and both can be made in the Cuisinart®. The breadcrumbs you normally buy in the store are dried breadcrumbs. These are made from bread that has been toasted or completely dried out. Because of the lack of moisture these crumbs keep indefinitely without refrigeration or freezing. Soft breadcrumbs are made from bread that is still moist. These breadcrumbs have a lighter texture when used for toppings on casseroles, and breading meats and fish. However, because they are still moist they can go moldy quickly, so once they are made they should be stored in the freezer. I usually keep them in plastic bags and use them directly from the freezer — they are so fine that they defrost in a minute.

To make the dry breadcrumbs, toast or dry out the bread, cut into 2-in/5-cm pieces and add to work bowl fitted with metal blade. Process on/off at first and then run continuously until crumbs are as fine as you wish.

When making fresh breadcrumbs, I usually process the crusts and the white parts of the bread separately. I use the crust crumbs for toppings on casseroles, etc., because they brown faster. For breading foods that are going to be cooked on direct heat, I use the inside crumbs as they do not burn as easily. Cut the bread into 2-in/5-cm pieces and add to work bowl fitted with metal blade (work bowl can be filled over half full). Process on/off and then continuously until crumbs are as fine as you wish. One slice of bread makes approximately ¼ cup/50 mL soft breadcrumbs.

Butter: I think butter is one of the most delicious foods used in cooking. Although **margarine**, **shortening** and **oil** can replace butter in most recipes, nothing can compare to the flavor of butter. The calories in fats are almost identical, so unless oil or shortening is specifically called for in a recipe, for my calories, I like to use butter.

Unless otherwise specified, the butter used in these recipes is unsalted butter. This is a purer butter that burns less easily when cooking on direct heat. It can be used for greasing cake and cookie pans without worrying about burning and it also controls the salt in recipes. I think it is well worth the difference in price.

Clarified butter is unsalted butter with the milk solids and other impurities removed. It burns even less easily than unsalted butter because it is the milk solids, salt and impurities that cause butter to burn so much faster than oils. To make clarified butter, melt 1 lb/454 g unsalted butter and allow it to sit about 30 minutes. Skim off any froth that may appear on the surface and discard. Then refrigerate for a few hours. The oil in the butter will rise to the surface and solidify and the milk solids will sink and remain liquid on the bottom. When the butterfat is hard on the top, run a knife around the outside edge and lift up the firm butter. Rinse off any milk adhering to the bottom. The remaining milk can be used in breads, soups, etc., but I usually discard it. The fat accounts for about 85 percent of the original volume of butter.

Clarified butter will keep for a few months because the milk has been removed, and it is the milk that sours butter. I keep it in the refrigerator. Use clarified butter for baking only if the recipe calls for it – it does not have the full dairy flavor of butter. If a recipe calls for clarified butter you can use instead half unsalted butter for flavor and half vegetable oil to help prevent burning.

Compound butters are butters that are flavored with other ingredients. They serve two purposes. They act as a garnish because they are usually served in neat slices that decorate the foods. And they act as a flavorful sauce when they melt. See Index for the compound butters included in this book.

Cabbage: Cabbage is one of the most difficult vegetables to chop or slice perfectly with the Cuisinart®. That's because the cabbage itself is not in perfect layers. To compound the problem, I have also found that just about everyone likes their cabbage for cole slaw cut differently. In the end I have decided that it is best to chop the cabbage. That way you get the most even pieces.

To chop cabbage, cut the cabbage into wedges, cut out the core, and cut the wedges into 3 or 4 pieces – the pieces should be about 2 in/5 cm wide. Fit work bowl with metal blade and add 4 to 6 pieces, depending on the size of your machine. If you try to put too much in at one time, the cabbage will not be evenly chopped. Process on/off with 3 to 5 pulses. Remove from work bowl. Continue to process in batches.

If you want to slice the cabbage, cut into wedges as explained above, and remove any large, leafy layers on the outside – process these separately, as they will not slice as well with the firmer center part of the cabbage. Cut a flat piece off the top and bottom of each wedge (or so that it will fit the height of the feed tube). Pack the large feed tube tightly with these wedges and then slice using the thin or medium slicer. The leafy layers can be rolled up tightly and stacked upright in the small feed tube for slicing.

Cheese: There are many different cheeses with various textures and they should be handled differently. If you want to grate any semihard (Cheddar or Swiss) or semisoft cheese (Gouda), use the shredding disc. Remove rind and use cold cheese. While grating, apply light to medium pressure on the pusher. If you are grating a softer cheese such as Mozzarella, make sure the cheese is very cold and apply a very light pressure on the pusher. (Mozzarella cheese should only be grated, not sliced.) Never use firm pressure when grating or slicing cheese. Any cheese that is softer than Mozzarella should not be grated or sliced, but it can be creamed with the metal blade for spreads or dips.

Hard cheeses such as **Parmesan** or **Romano** present their own problems. If you use the metal blade to chop the cheese it does not melt as smoothly as when you grate it. But when it is grated it does not look like the grated cheese you buy. But I still prefer it grated. These hard cheeses should always be processed at room temperature. The rind must be removed and the cheese cut into approximately 2-in/5-cm chunks for easier handling. If the cheese is so hard that it cannot be cut with a kitchen knife, do **not** process it in the machine as it may ruin your blades. If you buy the good quality Parmesan cheese (Parmigiano Reggiano), it should have a delicious, sweet taste that is not too salty and not at all dry or soapy. It should work well in the Cuisinart® and add a wonderful flavor to your foods. There are other good Parmesan cheeses, but always taste the cheese before buying it.

Although you can grate large batches of cheese at one time, I do not like to grate more than I'll need for a week or two. It goes moldy faster once it has been grated and if you freeze it, it tends to dry out (4 oz/125 g Parmesan cheese will equal approximately 1 cup/250 mL when grated).

Chocolate: Although the recipes in the book call for either **bittersweet** or **semisweet** chocolate, I prefer to use bittersweet. Bittersweet chocolate isn't quite as sweet as semisweet, but it is definitely not bitter. I usually use Swiss or Belgian chocolate. It is only slightly more expensive than domestic pure chocolate. Often when a recipe calls for chocolate chips, I make my own by chopping this excellent European chocolate with the metal blade and then sifting out the chocolate dust (to use another time when I need melted chocolate). It really does make a difference if you love chocolate.

Cocoa: In these recipes I use Dutch-processed cocoa. It is darker in color, richer in flavor and less acidy than regular cocoa. Look for a label that says "Dutch processed" or "alkali added."

Cream: If a recipe in this book calls for cream without specifying the fat content, then you can use any cream available. However, if the recipe calls for **whipping cream**, use that specific cream as some recipes simply will not work properly if a cream with a lesser fat content is used. Some sauces will not thicken properly if a cream with less than 30 percent fat is used, and cream will not whip unless whipping cream is used. Sometimes this high-fat content cream is refered to as heavy cream.

When whipping cream is called for, you can sometimes substitute **crème fraîche**. It is not as sweet as whipping cream or as sour as sour cream, but it is delicious in its own right. This can be bought commercially in some areas, but it is quite easy to make. Here are two recipes for crème fraîche – try them both and see which you prefer. 1) Combine 2 cups/500 mL whipping cream with 1 cup/250 mL sour cream and mix well. Cover with plastic wrap and allow to rest at room temperature 16 to 24 hours. Refrigerate 12 hours before using. 2) Combine 1 cup/250 mL whipping cream with 2 tsp/10 mL buttermilk and mix well. Cover with plastic wrap and allow to rest at room temperature for 16 to 24 hours or until thickened. Refrigerate 12 hours.

It is possible to whip cream in the Cuisinart® but it does not whip as lightly as with a whisk or electric mixer. If you are going to use the cream for a garnish or if volume is not essential then the Cuisinart® works beautifully. Make sure the cream is very cold and if it is particularly hot in your kitchen, chill the work bowl and metal blade as well. With the bowl fitted with the metal blade and the machine running, add the cream through the feed tube and process until thickened. Do not over-process or the cream will become butter. If this happens, drain it and use as butter – it is too expensive to discard. I do not like to whip more than 1½ cups/375 mL in the DLC-10; 2 cups/500 mL in the DLC-8; 3 cups/750 mL in the DLC-7; and 4 cups/1 L in the DLC-X.

Egg whites: Until recently it seemed impossible to whip egg whites easily and successfully in the Cuisinart®. But Abby Mandel, foremost Cuisinart® recipe developer in the U.S., found a way. She places the egg whites in a clean, dry work bowl fitted with the metal blade, runs the machine for about 8 seconds and then adds a mixture of 1 tbsp/15 mL each of water and vinegar through the feed tube. The egg whites are then processed about 1½ minutes longer or until they hold their shape. This amount of water/vinegar mixture works for anywhere between 3 and 7 egg whites. If you have no other way to beat egg whites and/or wish to use your Cuisinart® for everything, this is a great technique. However, I still feel that whites whipped traditionally whip to a greater volume. Also, although in many cases the flavor of the vinegar will bake out or disappear, it sometimes is slightly noticeable in more delicate mixtures.

Eggs: Unless otherwise stated, all the recipes in this book use large eggs. If a recipe calls for an egg at room temperature, just run it under warm water for five minutes.

Flour: Use the type of flour specified in recipes. Although there are ways to substitute one flour for another, the texture of the finished product is rarely the same. When measuring flour, dip the dry measure into the canister or bag of flour and bring out an overflowing amount. Sweep a knife evenly over the edge, leveling off the flour. Never shake the measuring cup to level the flour. **All-purpose flour** does not need sifting because it has been presifted, but if, for example, a recipe calls for all-purpose flour mixed with other dry ingredients, I might sift them together to blend them evenly. But I would sift **after** I had measured the flour, as sifting before would lighten the flour and the measurement would be different. If a recipe calls for "sifted flour," then sift before measuring, but if a recipe calls for "flour sifted," sift after measuring. If the recipe does not specify sifting but you wish to sift, sift after measuring. I usually sift icing sugar, cocoa and cake flour as they tend to lump.

Dried fruit: Dried fruits such as **dates**, **apricots**, **prunes** and **raisins** are very hard to process in the Cuisinart® because they are sticky. If I just have a few to chop I usually use kitchen shears. The best way to do them in the machine, however, is with the metal blade using on/off pulses, with some of the flour that is in the recipe to try to reduce the gumminess. Use approximately 1 cup/250 mL flour for 1 cup /250 mL fruit.

Garlic: I always use fresh garlic. It is easily available so there is no excuse for using garlic powder or garlic salt, which often have a bitter flavor and become stronger with age. But fresh garlic has a sweet and natural taste that is not at all bitter. If the garlic is left uncooked, then the garlic flavor will be quite strong, but if the food is cooked with the garlic, even though the recipe may call for lots of garlic, the taste will be sweet and mild. The longer the garlic is cooked, the sweeter and milder it becomes.

To peel a clove of garlic easily, place one on the counter. Place the flat edge of a knife on top and hit it with your fist carefully but firmly. The garlic will be smashed and the peel will come off very easily. If you have only one or two cloves to chop in the machine, add them through the feed tube with the machine running (bowl should be clean and dry). If you have many cloves to chop simply add them to the work bowl fitted with the metal blade and process on/off until chopped. Scrape down sides of bowl if necessary.

Ginger root: Fresh ginger root used to be difficult to find, but it is now quite common. If you have trouble finding it, look in Chinese, Indian or West Indian markets. If you want to store it indefinitely, peel the root and keep it in a jar of brandy, sherry or grain spirit (unflavored drinking alcohol purchased at liquor stores). But usually I just buy what I need and store it in a cool, dry place (I find that it gets stringy when frozen). Simply peel it before using and chop as for garlic.

Herbs: I try to use **fresh herbs** whenever possible, but they are sometimes difficult to find. Fresh parsley, dill and green onions are usually available. In the summer, basil, thyme, oregano, chervil, marjoram and many others are available. If a recipe in this book calls for a fresh herb, it means that it should be fresh. Otherwise recipes refer to dried herbs. When substituting **dried herbs** for fresh, use one third of the amount of fresh herbs called for.

I am usually very generous when using fresh herbs but am very careful when using dried ones as they are so much stronger. When I chop fresh herbs in the Cuisinart® I usually include some parsley as herbs tend to chop better when parsley is included. I remove the tough, large stems and just chop the leaves all together using on/off pulses. Fresh herbs chopped this way can be frozen by spreading them on cookie sheets, freezing and then packaging them in small bags. Freezing them in this way prevents the leaves from sticking together, so they can usually be used directly from the freezer. You can also preserve them by covering the chopped herbs with olive oil and refrigerating or freezing them this way.

Mushrooms: Mushrooms absorb liquid easily. Therefore the best way to clean them is to wipe them clean with wet paper towels. If they are so dirty that this is not enough, place them in a colander and rinse them under cold running water (do not let them soak in water for any length of time). Pat dry with paper towels.

If you want to chop mushrooms in the Cuisinart® you have two choices. You can add a few at a time to the work bowl fitted with the metal blade and chop using on/off pulses. But if you try to chop too many at one time, they can become very watery and lose their texture completely. An easier way, if you want them finely chopped, is to use the shredding disc. This way the pieces are all the same size and you do not have to keep emptying the work bowl.

If you want mushrooms to be sliced perfectly, remember to place them in the feed tube perfectly. Even though it takes longer, if I want to be very careful about getting even slices, I use the smaller feed tube which gives me more control. Lay the mushrooms on their sides and alternate sides of the tube with each batch.

Nutmeg: Because the taste of freshly ground nutmeg is so superior to pre-ground nutmeg, I always try to grind it fresh for each recipe. There are many different nutmeg grinders on the market, but you can also use the finest side of a four-sided grater.

Nuts: Nuts have a high oil content and can turn rancid easily, so buy them in small quantities from a store that has a high turnover. If you buy nuts in larger quantities, store them in the freezer.

To obtain the best flavor from the nuts, toast them lightly before using. Do this by preheating the oven to 350°F/180°C. Spread the nuts in one layer on a cookie sheet and bake 10 minutes or until lightly toasted. Cool before using.

To chop nuts in the machine, fit a clean, dry work bowl with the metal blade and process with on/off pulses until nuts are chopped. If you want to grind the nuts into a flour for cakes, etc., it is best to use some of the sugar or flour from the recipe with the nuts to stop them from turning into a nut paste or butter. But be careful to check their progress often so you can stop in time. Nuts can also be grated with the shredding disc although sometimes pieces fall into the bowl between the blade and the bowl.

Nut butters are made by processing the plain nuts continuously until they turn into a paste. If you accidently overprocess the nuts when grinding them, simply add some sugar and liqueur, roll them into balls and dip them into melted chocolate. Then serve them as truffles!

Hazelnuts: Just as this book was going to press, I learned a great trick from Darlene Byers, a friend in California. To remove skins from hazelnuts easily, just after removing toasted nuts from oven place nuts in Cuisinart® fitted with plastic blade. Pulse on/off 5 or 6 times, and skins will fly off. Lift out nuts and shake in a coarse strainer to sift out remaining bits of skin.

Oil: There are many different oils used in cooking, and they all taste different. Unless a recipe calls for a specific oil, I usually use **corn oil**, but many people prefer peanut or safflower oil for everyday use. When I want a stronger taste I use **olive oil**, but I am careful to use a good quality olive oil that tastes fresh and fruity like olives, not greasy or strong. I look for extra-virgin or first-pressed olive oil. Although it may be more expensive, I think the price is worth it. These oils are made from the first pressing of the olives and have the sweetest, fruitiest flavor. Sometimes I mix half olive and half corn oil for a milder taste or less expensive product.

Onions: Although the Cuisinart® can reduce your tears when handling onions, it cannot always stop them completely. It is the juice from the onions that causes the tears, so be sure to use a very sharp knife when trimming and peeling them. Although I usually store onions in a cool, dry place, I refrigerate what I will be needing for a week (if onions are stored in the refrigerator for too long, eventually they will go rotten). When onions are cold the juices run less and I cry less.

To chop onions in the Cuisinart®, peel them and cut them into quarters. Do not overfill the work bowl. Chop with the metal blade using on/off pulses. To slice the onions, pack them (flat edge down) tightly in the feed tube.

Oriental ingredients: The oriental ingredients called for in these recipes are available in Chinese or Japanese grocery stores, and in some large cities are even available in certain supermarkets. If there is no such store in your area, investigate the possibility of buying ingredients from your local Chinese restaurant.

Sake or **mirin** can be used where Chinese cooking wines are called for. **Sake** is a Japanese drinking wine available in liquor stores. **Mirin** (sweet rice wine for cooking) is available at Chinese and Japanese grocery stores. Gin, vodka or whiskey can also be used.

Parchment paper: Although parchment paper is hard to find in some places, you will soon not want to use anything else. Look for it in cookware shops and European delicatessens.

Parchment paper prevents sticking. Buy **silicone parchment paper** and use it for baking anything that normally sticks. If I want extra butter flavor, or if the mixture is something that sticks very badly, then I'll butter the paper with unsalted butter, but usually it isn't necessary. If you use waxed paper or foil instead, however, it should always be buttered.

Parsley: There are three types of parsley generally available. The most common type is the **curly parsley**, which is available almost everywhere. It is bright green, crisp, has a nice flavor and is perfect for garnishing.

Italian parsley has a large, flat leaf

and a stronger flavor than curly parsley. If it is available I prefer it. Curly parsley and Italian parsley are generally interchangeable. Italian parsley can be found in better vegetable stores and Italian markets.

The third type of parsley is really quite different and cannot be substituted for the others. It is known by three names – **Chinese parsley**, **fresh coriander** or **cilantro**. It looks similar to Italian parsley but the leaf is rounder and more jagged. It is used in Chinese cooking and can usually be found in Chinese markets (ask for Chinese parsley); it is also used in East Indian recipes and can sometimes be found in stores that specialize in curry spices, etc. (ask for fresh coriander). And it is used in Mexican and West Indian cooking and can sometimes be found in Mexican or West Indian markets (ask for cilantro). There really is no substitute for the flavor of this herb. Therefore if you can't find it, omit it.

To chop parsley in the Cuisinart®, cut off the stems and chop the leaves using on/off pulses. You can chop the stems separately if you wish to use them. They are usually much stronger and sometimes slightly bitter, but if they taste good use them in stocks, etc.

Peel: Chopped or grated citrus peel is a great flavor to add to desserts, baked goods and some savory dishes. Sometimes it is refered to as **"zest."** It sometimes even adds a slight flavor of liqueur to the finished dish. Grated citrus peel is easy to freeze if you want to chop a large batch at a time (spread on a cookie sheet and when frozen, pack into small bags). For a large batch, peel the fruit with a vegetable peeler, trying not to get too much of the white pith under the peel. Fit work bowl with the metal blade. Pat peel dry and add to work bowl. Chop with on/off pulses until finely chopped.

If you only have the peel of one or two lemons or oranges it is more difficult to chop. Chopping it with the sugar in the recipes makes it much easier. Pat the peel dry and, with the machine running, add to a clean, completely dry work bowl through the feed tube. Add some of the sugar from the recipe and continue to process until finely chopped. Scrape down the sides of work bowl if necessary.

Pepper: All the recipes in this book call for freshly ground pepper. Preground spices lose so much flavor so quickly after they have been processed that you actually need less freshly ground pepper. You'll pay for your pepper grinder in no time!

Black pepper is slightly stronger than the white and I like it the best, but sometimes a more delicate flavor or lighter color is needed and that's when white pepper is used. White pepper is actually black pepper with the outer husks removed. **Green peppercorns**, on the other hand, are unripe peppercorn berries and are usually purchased in cans or jars. I rinse them off and then crush them into dips, sauces, marinades, etc. They are not as strong as the dried peppercorns and can actually be eaten whole. They are also available freeze-dried (freeze-dried peppercorns can be ground).

Potatoes: When the Cuisinart® was first introduced, **mashed potatoes** always came out like glue. If you really want to use your Cuisinart® for making mashed potatoes, the best way is as follows. Cook potatoes and pat dry. Grate cooked potatoes with the shredding disc and then use the metal blade to combine them quickly with other ingredients such as eggs, cream, cheese, mustard, etc. But mix **very** briefly using on/off pulses!

When processing raw potatoes with the metal blade also be careful not to overprocess. Do not try to chop too many potatoes at once and process on/

off just until potatoes are chopped.

When pureeing soups that contain potatoes, use some liquid when pureeing the vegetables and be sure not to overprocess.

Spinach: Cooked spinach can be very watery, and its excess liquid can throw off the balance of a recipe. If spinach is purchased frozen, simply defrost it and wring out any excess liquid in a tea towel. If you buy fresh spinach, clean it well in several changes of water and then discard any tough stems. Place the spinach in a large pot with just the water clinging to the leaves. Cover and cook until wilted – just a few minutes. Cool and then wring out in a tea towel. Do not be dismayed that a whole package of fresh spinach will reduce to a large handful of cooked spinach.

Stocks: Stocks are the bases for soups, sauces, stews and many other dishes. Therefore well-made, home-cooked stocks are a great addition to a well-stocked larder. There are recipes for homemade stocks on pages 45 to 47. Substitutes are available in the form of bouillon cubes and canned stock. I prefer the cans, but whichever you use, be sure to dilute it at least according to package directions. In some cases you might dilute it even further if you are going to be using it in recipes calling for many other flavorful ingredients.

One of the biggest differences between homemade and commercial stocks is the salt content. When I prepare stocks I use very little or no salt at all so that I can add salt later according to the recipe. If you are using commercial products, do not salt until after the recipe is finished and you have tasted it. Homemade stocks can also be frozen – check the individual recipes.

Sugar: Unless otherwise specified, recipes calling for sugar refer to **granulated, white sugar**. Other sugars are available, however. If a recipe refers to **cas-** **tor**, **barberry**, or **fruit sugar**, it is calling for a sugar that is finer than granulated, usually because it dissolves more easily. It is available commercially but can easily be made by placing sugar in a clean work bowl fitted with the metal blade and processing it for 10 to 20 seconds. Make sure you measure it after processing, as the sugar becomes lighter.

Icing sugar is sometimes called **confectioners sugar** or **powdered sugar**. It is easily available commercially. It is used in whipping cream and icings as it contains cornstarch and thickens better than regular sugar. It should be sifted before using as it tends to lump.

Brown sugar contains molasses and has a very different flavor. It gets hard easily and should not be processed in the Cuisinart® to soften it because it could warp the blade. To soften brown sugar, simply put a piece of bread or a slice of apple in your sugar canister overnight.

Tomatoes: To **peel** tomatoes easily cut out the core and cut a cross in the other end. Place in boiling water for one minute, rinse with cold water and the peel will come off easily. To remove seeds, cut the tomato in half crosswise and squeeze gently. The seeds will ooze out. If you want to slice tomatoes in the Cuisinart®, use very firm tomatoes that will fit into the large feed tube. Slice off a piece on the bottom so the tomato will sit evenly on the slicing disc and slice using gentle pressure. If a recipe calls for **canned tomatoes**, I prefer to use plum tomatoes as I find their flavor generally less bitter and more consistent.

Vanilla: Vanilla is actually the pod of the climbing orchid. Pure vanilla extract adds a wonderful flavor to baked goods and desserts. It also helps bring out other flavors in the dish. I find that artificial extracts have unpleasant aftertastes, and although pure vanilla is sometimes more expensive, if you are taking the time and trouble to prepare your own desserts, it is worth the difference in price.

I also flavor my sugar with vanilla by placing a vanilla bean (cut in quarters) in my sugar canister. I use the sugar for all purposes — it has a lovely, faint vanilla flavor.

Yeast: There are two types of yeast you can buy for baking bread — **cake yeast** and **dry yeast**. Cake yeast is harder to find, but I prefer it as it has a yeasty flavor and aroma and also seems to make bread rise more quickly. It is perishable, so keep it refrigerated and use it in a few days or freeze it. One cake of yeast is comparable to an envelope or 1 tbsp/15 mL of dry yeast.

To use it simply stir the yeast into the small amount of warm water called for at the beginning of the recipe and proceed as directed.

Dry yeast is easily available. Check the expiry date. It comes premeasured in small envelopes or you can buy it less expensively in larger quantities.

When I use dry yeast I always like to proof it (make sure that it is still active) before beginning a yeast bread recipe. Dissolve the yeast in some sugared warm water and if the yeast bubbles up and increases in volume it is safe to use. If nothing happens after 10 minutes, either the yeast is inactive or the water you used to dissolve the yeast was too hot. Test another batch, but if it still doesn't work, buy fresh yeast.

Garnishes and Serving Suggestions

"Garnishing" can mean many different things, but the result should be that the food will look as good as it tastes. Sometimes no garnish is required because the food itself looks so attractive. If you plan a menu well and, for example, serve a meat main course with different-colored vegetables, that may be all you need. And some stir-fried dishes have so many beautiful colors that extra garnishes would not only be superfluous, but they might even ruin the look of the dish.

But it's good to have a few garnishes in the back of your mind, and if something just doesn't look quite right, or needs a finishing touch, you won't be left without ideas. One of the most important things to remember, however, is never to over-garnish. If you use large serving dishes or if a recipe is especially bland looking, you may be tempted to put every garnish you have ever learned on the same dish. Resist the temptation and keep it simple.

Another way to decide on a garnish is to use an ingredient that is in the dish, such as onions, lemons or tomatoes. Flavors that are in the recipe can be brought out by using a garnish. The garnish will also tell the diner what to expect. If you prepare a shrimp and scallop mousse, it is appropriate to have it garnished with shrimps and/or scallops. But if you have a smoked salmon mousse it would be more appropriate to garnish it with smoked salmon roses (by twisting strips of smoked salmon into a flower shape) than to use shrimps or scallops. Some of the photographs in this book may give you some presentation ideas. In addition, here are a few interesting garnishes to add to your collection.

Tomato Roses: A flower made from the peel of a tomato is one of the prettiest garnishes and one of the easiest to make once you learn how. With a little practice you can make one in less than a minute. It is also possible to make cherry tomato roses but start with big ones and when you feel secure move on to the tiny ones. And the first time you try to make one, buy more than one tomato!

Start with a large, firm, red tomato. Leaving the base attached, start to peel the tomato in one piece (I like to use a sharp, serrated knife) that is approximately 1 in/2.5 cm wide. When the tomato is half peeled, break the piece off. Curl this strip around the base to form the outside of the rose and set it aside. Begin to peel the tomato again where you left off but this time make the strip slightly narrower – approximately ¾ in/2 cm. When the rest of the tomato is peeled, curl this strip as tightly as possible and drop it into the center of the rose. (Sometimes when you are making cherry tomato roses the tomatoes are too small to make two strips of peel. Just peel them all in one piece and twirl.) Cover with plastic wrap and refrigerate until ready to serve. Large tomato roses can be used on serving platters for a decoration. Cherry tomato roses are better on individual servings.

Tomato or Lemon Cups: These attractive cups can be used as containers for sauces such as mayonnaise. They can be made from lemons, oranges, tomatoes or from a larger fruit such as cantaloupe to use as a container for fruit salad.

You can make these cups free form by using a small paring knife that has a blade approximately ¾ in/2 cm wide, or you can make them slightly more professional looking by using a special V-shaped knife. You do not even have to hollow out the fruit – it looks attractive just with the zigzagged edge. But if you want to use it as a container then just hollow it out with a grapefruit knife or spoon.

Start with a firm tomato or lemon. Cut a thin slice from the top and bottom of the fruit so that each half will stand up evenly on each end. With your paring knife cut V-shaped wedges around the circumference of the fruit. Very gently pull the two halves apart. If you have the V-shaped knife, just poke it into the middle of the fruit and travel around the circumference. If you want to hollow out the fruit for a basket, use a grapefruit knife or spoon and dig out the pulp gently. Dry thoroughly with paper towels.

Note: I do not usually cut tomatoes this way when I am filling them and then baking them. With the jagged edge, they seem to wilt more easily than the ones that are cut straight across.

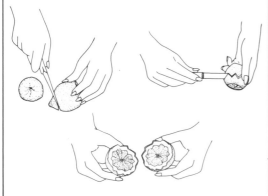

Lemon Twists: Lemon twists are a very pretty, easy garnish to make for all fish or seafood dishes, as well as any others that contain lemon. If you want to make them extra pretty you can decorate the lemon first by using a gadget called a "stripper" that removes pieces of the peel evenly, so that when you cut the lemon into slices, the slices have a fluted edge. If you have the stripper, remove strips of peel all around the lemon from top to bottom. Then cut the lemon into slices crosswise. Each slice should be approximately ⅛ in/3 mm thick. Remove seeds.

Cut a slit from the center of each slice through to the outside edge. Twist one edge of the slice in one direction and the other edge in the other direction. Arrange on serving plate. You can also place a sprig of fresh parsley or dill beside the twist.

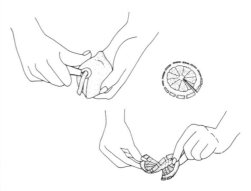

Scallion Brushes: Scallion brushes are the "brushes" used during the Peking duck ceremony to brush the sweet bean paste or hoisin sauce onto the Mandarin pancakes. But they can be used as a garnish on any recipe containing green onions.

Cut the root base off the end of a green onion. Cut about a 2-in/5-cm length that includes the white portion. Hold the center of the piece between your thumb and index finger. With a small, sharp paring knife that has a blade about ½ in/1 cm wide, cut through the stalk on one side of your finger and pull the knife to the end. Turn the onion and cut again. Repeat two more times. Do the same with the other half of the onion. The center of the onion should be left intact. Place the onion in a bowl of ice water and after a few hours the ends will curl.

This can also be done with leeks. Just make more slits so that the end pieces will be thin enough to curl in the cold water.

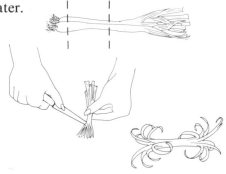

Carrot Flowers: Carrots can be cut this way to use as a garnish, to use in stir-fried dishes so that you find a flower here and there in among your other vegetables, or even just when preparing sliced carrots as a vegetable dish.

Peel carrots and trim off ends. For easy handling, cut carrots into 4-in/10-cm lengths. With a sharp paring knife, cut V-shaped slits down the length of the carrot, almost through to the core. Do this three or five times around the circumference of the carrot, depending on the thickness (if you go too deep to the core, the carrot may break in half, so be careful.) Then slice the carrots crosswise.

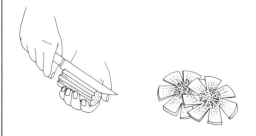

Chocolate Leaves: There are many chocolate garnishes, but chocolate leaves are among the loveliest. I like to use rose leaves, but other non-poisonous flower or tree leaves will work as well.

Pat leaves very dry. Arrange them with the underside facing up – this is the side you will spread with chocolate because the veins of the leaves are more pronounced.

For approximately 25 medium-sized rose leaves, melt 4 oz/125 g bittersweet or semisweet chocolate in the microwave, oven or on top of a double boiler. With a knife, spread the underside of each leaf with a thin coat of chocolate and arrange on a cookie sheet. Try not to allow the chocolate to run onto the other side of the leaf or the leaf may stick when you are trying to remove it from the chocolate. Freeze leaves for about 30 minutes.

Remove the leaves from the freezer one at a time and, from the stem end, gently pull off the real leaf one at a time (the chocolate on the leaves is very thin and melts quickly).

These look beautiful on any chocolate dessert, mousse, ice cream or cake.

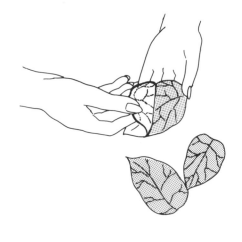

Appetizers, Hors d'oeuvres, Dips and Spreads

I always like to serve a special treat at the beginning of a meal. Even if I do not have the time to prepare a first course that can be served at the table, I like to start with a little appetizer of some kind that will tantalize and wake up the palate. The Smoked Trout Dip (page 27), Smoked Salmon Butter (page 32) or Marinated Goat Cheese (page 42), for example, take only a few minutes to prepare but taste as if you have spent hours making them.

If you have more time, and/or the meal is more formal, there are many delicious recipes that can be served as a sit-down first course. A cold appetizer or soup can be ready at each place setting when guests come to the table–a lovely and inviting start to any meal.

Don't forget about presentation–appetizers lend themselves easily to imaginative garnishing. In many of the recipes, such as the Scallop and Shrimp Mousse (page 26) or the White Snapper Terrine (page 28), I have suggested garnishing possibilities, but see pages 22 to 24 for other ideas. Although I believe that taste is more important than looks, I have also learned over the years that it is very easy to make food look beautiful. And remember that appetizers set the tone for the rest of the meal, so you should try to make an impressive start.

Scallop and Shrimp Mousse with Chive Mayonnaise

Before the food processor became an everyday appliance, it was rare that home cooks prepared fish mousses, terrines or quenelles. The technique was tedious to say the least. These mixtures are now very easy to prepare and are wonderfully light and delicate when made in the Cuisinart®. Although I usually bake this in a loaf pan and serve it in slices, it can be made into quenelles by chilling the mixture thoroughly, shaping it into small ovals and poaching them in boiling water for 4 or 5 minutes. This can also be baked in a ring-mold pan and served as a light lunch, brunch or supper dish with vegetables in the center. I like it served hot with a hollandaise or beurre blanc (see page 28), or cold with this mayonnaise. (If you are allergic to shellfish or cannot eat shrimps or scallops, use 1½ lb/750 g raw salmon or other firm-fleshed fish.)

1 lb	raw scallops	500 g	½ tsp	salt (or more to taste)	2 mL
8 oz	raw shrimps (weight after shelling)	250 g	¼ tsp	freshly ground pepper	1 mL
2	egg whites, cold	2	pinch	cayenne pepper	pinch
1½ cups	whipping cream, cold	375 mL	1¼ cups	corn or vegetable oil	300 mL
1 tsp	salt	5 mL	¼ cup	snipped chives or green onions	50 mL
pinch	freshly ground pepper	pinch	½ cup	sour cream	125 mL
pinch	freshly ground nutmeg	pinch			

Chive Mayonnaise:

1	egg, room temperature	1
	Juice of 1 lemon (¼ cup/50 mL)	
1 tsp	dry mustard	5 mL

Garnish:

Lemon twists or cherry tomato roses or green onion brushes or chopped chives (pages 22 to 24)

**Makes 1 small loaf (8 in x 4 in/1 L)
Serves 8 to 12**

1. Preheat oven to 350°F/180°C. Butter a medium-sized loaf pan and line with a strip of parchment paper (see diagram).

2. Fit work bowl with metal blade. Pat scallops and shrimps dry and if they are large cut into approximately 1-in/2.5-cm pieces. Add shrimps and scallops to work bowl and process with 5 or 6 on/off pulses until coarsely chopped. Add egg whites and puree until smooth.

3. Pour cream through the feed tube slowly, with machine running. Stop once or twice to scrape down bowl. Continue until all cream is added but do not overprocess or mixture will become too stiff and buttery. Add salt, pepper and nutmeg and blend in quickly.

4. Spoon mixture into prepared pan and spread evenly. Cover surface of mixture directly with a piece of buttered parchment paper. Place loaf

pan in a water bath (a larger pan of boiling water that comes halfway up the sides of loaf pan). Bake 35 to 40 minutes or until top feels firm when pressed gently. Remove from oven and cool on rack. This can be served warm (cool about 20 minutes and then turn out of pan) or cold (refrigerate and turn out of pan when thoroughly chilled).

5. Prepare Chive Mayonnaise.

6. To serve, spoon circle of mayonnaise on individual plates. Slice mousse ½ in/1 cm thick and place slice in center of circle. Garnish with one of suggested garnishes.

Chive Mayonnaise:

1. Fit clean work bowl with metal blade. Add egg, lemon juice, mustard, salt, pepper, cayenne and ¼ cup/50 mL oil. Blend 3 or 4 seconds. Add remaining oil slowly through the feed tube while the machine is running. The more oil you add the thicker the mayonnaise will become. (If the mayonnaise does not thicken, see page 123.)

2. Add chives or green onions and blend 5 or 6 seconds. Blend in sour cream. Taste and add salt if necessary.

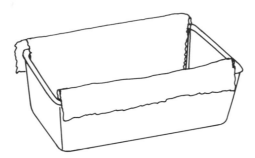

Smoked Trout Dip

Any smoked fish can be used to make this spread or dip. It can be used as a spread on French or black bread. Individual Belgian endive leaves make marvelous little cups for dipping.

2	smoked trout (approximately 8 oz/250 g each)	2
½ cup	mayonnaise, homemade (see page 123) or commercial	125 mL
2 tbsp	lemon juice	25 mL
1 tsp	white horseradish (or more to taste)	5 mL
¼ tsp	freshly ground pepper	1 mL

Makes 1½ cups/375 mL

1. Skin the trout and remove bones carefully. Break meat up into small pieces. Fit work bowl with metal blade and add trout.

2. Process with 4 or 5 on/off pulses until trout is coarsely chopped.

3. Add mayonnaise, lemon juice and horseradish and process until mixture is relatively smooth. Add pepper and taste. Add salt only if necessary.

Note: In some fish stores it is possible to buy smoked trout fillets, in which case you will only need 8 oz/250 g fish in total.

White Snapper Terrine with Beurre Blanc

This is a beautiful appetizer to look at and it tastes wonderful. It's very mild and even those who think they don't like fish are won over by its delicate flavor. Try to use the freshest fish possible. If you can't find white snapper, you could use salmon, pike, red snapper, lake trout or any medium-fat fish that is firm-fleshed. You can serve this dish hot with the sauce suggested below, or cold with a plain or flavored mayonnaise (see page 123).

½ cup	pistachio nuts, toasted	125 mL	**Beurre Blanc:**		
1½ lb	raw white snapper fillets, cold	750 g	1 cup	fish stock or mild chicken stock, homemade (see pages 47 and 46) or commercial	250 mL
3 tbsp	Cognac or brandy	50 mL	½ tsp	dried tarragon	2 mL
2	egg whites, cold	2	1 cup	whipping cream	250 mL
1½ cups	whipping cream	375 mL	⅓ cup	unsalted butter	75 mL
1½ tsp	salt	7 mL	**Garnish:**		
¼ tsp	freshly ground pepper	1 mL	8 to 12	sprigs fresh parsley	8 to 12
pinch	ground ginger	pinch	8 to 12	cherry tomato roses	8 to 12
pinch	ground nutmeg	pinch	3 tbsp	black caviar (lumpfish)	50 mL
2 tbsp	chopped black truffles, optional	25 mL	**Serves 8 to 12**		

1. Preheat oven to 350°F/180°C. Butter a 9-in x 5-in/2-L loaf pan and line with parchment paper (see diagram for Scallop and Shrimp Mousse, page 27). Butter paper.

2. Fit work bowl with metal blade. Add pistachio nuts and chop with 3 or 4 on/off pulses. Remove from work bowl and reserve.

3. Cut fish into 1-in/2.5-cm cubes. Pat dry if necessary. Add to work bowl and process with 8 to 12 on/off pulses until fish is finely chopped. Add Cognac and egg whites and puree.

4. With machine running, add cream slowly through the feed tube. Scrape down sides of bowl once or twice. Do not overprocess. Add salt, pepper, ginger and nutmeg. Process until blended. With a spatula stir in nuts and truffles.

5. Transfer mixture to prepared pan and cover with a piece of buttered parchment paper. Place in a larger pan filled with boiling water that comes halfway up sides of loaf pan. Bake 30 to 40 minutes or until mousse mixture feels firm to the touch. Allow to rest 5 minutes before inverting onto serving platter. If serving cold, refrigerate before turning out of pan.

6. Prepare Beurre Blanc.

7. Before inverting terrine, add to Beurre Blanc sauce any liquid that has accumulated on top of terrine.

8. To serve, place a circle of sauce on each plate. Cut a slice of terrine and place in center of plate. Place a dab of caviar on each slice and garnish with a sprig of parsley and a tomato rose.

Beurre Blanc (White Butter Sauce):

1. Place fish stock and tarragon in a small saucepan and cook over high heat until reduced to about 2 tbsp/ 25 mL.

2. Add whipping cream and reduce again to about ½ cup/125 mL. Add butter and cook until melted. Keep warm until ready to serve.

Moules Marinières

Mussels have become one of the most popular items on restaurant menus and yet not that many people prepare them at home. Try it — it's easy, delicious and very inexpensive. Some people prefer the taste of wild mussels, which are slightly less expensive than cultured mussels, but they are more difficult to clean. Although I usually serve this as an appetizer, it also makes a great light supper or luncheon dish. Serve with lots of bread and have empty bowls on the table for the shells.

6 lb	cultured or wild mussels	3 kg	¼ cup	unsalted butter	50 mL
	Large handful fresh parsley		1	bay leaf	1
	Handful fresh basil, if available (do not substitute dried)		1 tsp	dried thyme	5 mL
			1 tsp	dried tarragon (if you are not using fresh basil)	5 mL
4	cloves garlic, peeled	4		Salt and freshly ground black pepper to taste	
2	shallots, peeled	2			
2	onions, peeled and quartered	2	1½ cups	dry white wine	375 mL
			Serves 6 to 8		

1. Scrub mussels well and pull off beards. Discard any mussels that will not close tightly when tapped or any that have broken shells. Reserve.

2. Fit work bowl with metal blade. Add parsley and basil. Chop with 5 or 6 on/off pulses until coarsely chopped. Remove and reserve.

3. With machine running, drop garlic and shallots through feed tube and process until chopped. Add onions and chop with 5 or 6 on/off pulses until coarsely chopped.

4. Melt butter in a Dutch oven. Add onion-garlic-shallot mixture. Cook until fragrant but do not brown.

5. Add mussels, all herbs, salt, pepper and wine. Bring to a boil, cover, reduce heat and cook 5 minutes or until mussels have opened. Serve approximately 1 lb/500 g mussels per person in a large bowl.

Note: Sometimes mussels are very sandy. If that is the case simply strain the juices through cheesecloth and pour the strained juices over the mussels before serving. You really cannot remove the sand from the mussels themselves.

Gefilte Fish

Every Jewish family has its favorite recipe for gefilte fish. I jokingly call it "Jewish quenelles." This cooking method defies every rule of French cooking and yet the dish comes out tasting wonderful. Not only is it festive, Jewish holiday food, it is a great low-calorie meal all year round.

There are many different ways to prepare gefilte fish, but one of the most spectacular presentations I've heard of is from one of my coworkers, Julie Lewis. Her Romanian grandmother, Bianca Lefton, bones and removes the flesh of the fish leaving the skin intact. She makes the minced fish mixture and restuffs the skin perfectly. It is then baked and served as a whole fish. My family's version, which follows, isn't nearly as elegant but it is as delicious. At least for my taste. After all, it is a family affair.

2 lb	fish heads, bones, etc.	1 kg
5	onions, peeled	5
3	carrots, peeled and trimmed	3
16 cups	water	4 L
4 tsp	salt (divided)	20 mL
2 tsp	freshly ground pepper (divided)	10 mL

3 lb	fish fillets (combination of whitefish and pickerel)	1.5 kg
2 tbsp	sugar	25 mL
3	eggs	3
¾ cup	ice water	175 mL
3 tbsp	matzah meal or dry breadcrumbs	50 mL

Makes approximately 12 pieces

1. Place fish bones, etc., in a large pot. Fit work bowl with medium slicing disc. Cut onions to fit large or small feed tube and slice onions. Add to pot with fish bones.

2. Slice carrots through small feed tube and add to onions in pot. Add water, 2 tsp/10 mL salt and 1 tsp/ 5 mL pepper. Bring mixture to a boil while preparing the fish.

3. Cut fish fillets into 2-in/5-cm pieces. Refit work bowl with metal blade. In 3 batches, grind the fish by placing it in the work bowl and chopping with 8 to 10 on/off pulses or until finely chopped. Transfer each batch of fish to a large bowl as it is processed. Mix together. (If you have the DLC-7 you can do this in 2 batches and if you have the DLC-X you can do this in 1 batch.)

4. Add remaining ingredients to work bowl and blend together briefly. Stir into fish and combine well. Moisten hands and shape fish into 12 patties. Place in large pot with fish bones and vegetables.

5. Lower heat, cover the pot and simmer gently 1½ hours. Uncover and cook 30 minutes longer.

6. Remove fish from pot and strain 3 cups/750 mL stock over top (freeze the rest to use as fish stock). Arrange some of the cooked carrots from the stock on top of fish for a garnish. Chill. Serve with red horseradish.

Note: Some people like the juices to gel when the stock gets cold. If you do, after removing the fish from the pot, reduce the juices down to 3 cups/750 mL and then strain over the fish. If the stock is strong and you began with lots of bones, it should gel.

Shrimp Toasts

Dim sum has become very popular lunch-hour fare in many Chinese restaurants. "Dim sum" actually means "dots on the heart," or little bites of pleasure, which is certainly just what they are. There are so many dim sum snacks — some are boiled, some are baked, some are steamed and some are deep-fried. They are all wonderful and delicious. These shrimp toasts make a great appetizer even for a non-oriental meal. Although anything deep-fried tastes best hot from the pan, these can be made ahead and reheated briefly at 400° F/200° C.

12	slices white sandwich bread	12	2 tbsp	cornstarch	25 mL
4	water chestnuts	4	1 tsp	oriental sesame oil	5 mL
1	green onion, cut into 2-in/5-cm lengths	1	1 tsp	salt	5 mL
1 lb	raw shrimps, shelled and deveined	500 g		Fresh Chinese parsley, optional	
1 tsp	rice wine or vodka	5 mL	4 cups	peanut oil or other vegetable oil	1 L
1	large egg white	1		Hot chili sauce for dipping, optional	
¼ cup	ice water	50 mL			
1	piece ginger root, size of a quarter and 1 in/2.5 cm thick, peeled and coarsely chopped	1			

Makes 48 squares

1. Trim crusts from bread and use crusts for breadcrumbs (see page 13). Allow bread to dry while preparing shrimp mixture.
2. Fit work bowl with metal blade. Add water chestnuts and green onion and chop using 3 or 4 quick on/off pulses. Add shrimp and chop using on/off pulses until finely minced. Blend in rice wine and egg white.
3. Add ginger to ice water. Squeeze ginger to extract juice. Strain water and stir in cornstarch, sesame oil and salt. Blend into shrimp mixture.
4. Spread an equal amount of shrimp paste on each piece of bread. Cut each slice of bread into quarters. Top each piece with a leaf of Chinese parsley if available.
5. Place oil in a wok or other suitable pot for deep-frying and heat to about 375°F/190°C. Add toasts, about 8 at a time, with shrimp side **down** first. Cook 1 to 2 minutes, turn and cook 1 to 2 minutes longer. Drain on paper towels. Repeat until all toasts are cooked. Serve immediately with hot chili sauce for dipping.

Smoked Salmon Butter

Smoked salmon is one of Canada's finest but also most expensive delicacies. This recipe is a great way to use up leftover slices or imperfect pieces or ends that you may have been able to buy at a good price. This butter is a delicious mixture that can be spread or piped onto French or pumpernickel bread, into mushroom caps, Belgian endive leaves or barely cooked snow peas.

8 oz	smoked salmon	250 g		2 tbsp	fresh lemon juice	25 mL
1 cup	unsalted butter, left at room temperature for 30 minutes	250 mL				

Makes approximately 2 cups/500 mL

1. Cut smoked salmon into small pieces. Fit work bowl with metal blade and add salmon. Chop into very small pieces using 5 or 6 on/off pulses.
2. Cut butter into even-sized small cubes. Add to salmon and process with 5 or 6 on/off pulses until butter is in tiny cubes. Add lemon juice and continue blending until a smooth mixture is formed (add some freshly ground pepper if you like).

Canapés:

Cut pumpernickel or French bread into 1½-in/4-cm rounds or squares and pipe or spoon some of salmon mixture on them. Decorate with a sprig of dill or, for a glistening effect, a tiny dab of black lumpfish caviar, red salmon caviar, or Canadian whitefish (pale yellow) caviar. Makes about 16 to 20 canapes.

Stuffed Mushrooms:

Wipe mushrooms clean with wet paper towels. Cut out stems and use for another purpose. Pipe mixture into caps and swirl. Use mushroom caps that are all the same size — about 1 in/2.5 cm in diameter. Makes about 24 mushroom caps.

Belgian Endive Cups:

Belgian endive leaves make natural cups to use for dips or to fill. You can pipe the mixture all along the leaf for a 3-bite appetizer that is quite substantial, or you could just pipe a round of the salmon mixture into the larger end. Makes about 12 large appetizers or 24 smaller ones.

Stuffed Snow Peas:

The bright color and interesting shape of the snow peas make this a beautiful appetizer. Clean snow peas and cook in boiling water for 30 seconds. Stop cooking by rinsing with cold water. Pat dry and slit 1 side open. Pipe salmon mixture into peas (see diagram). Makes about 24.

Scallop and Shrimp Mousse with Chive Mayonnaise (see page 26).

Empanaditas

Empanaditas are little empanadas. And empanadas are turnovers. These are the perfect size to serve as spicy appetizers with cocktails. They also freeze well, both baked and unbaked. Freeze them unwrapped, in a single layer on cookie sheets. When they are frozen, pack gently into plastic freeze bags or containers. Reheat or bake directly from the frozen state at 400° F/200° C.

Pastry:		
1 cup	all-purpose flour	250 mL
½ cup	unsalted butter, cold	125 mL
4 oz	cream cheese, cold	125 g
Filling:		
4 oz	old Cheddar cheese, cold	125 g
3	green onions, cut into 1-in/2.5-cm pieces	3
⅓ cup	pitted black olives	75 mL

2 tbsp	Jalapeno peppers (canned)	25 mL
1 tsp	chili powder	5 mL
1 tsp	oregano	5 mL
½ tsp	salt	2 mL
Glaze:		
1	egg	1
2 tbsp	cream or milk	25 mL

Makes 30 to 36

1. To prepare pastry, fit work bowl with metal blade. Add flour. Cut butter and cheese into 1-in/2.5-cm cubes and add butter to flour. Process using 10 to 15 on/off pulses until butter is in tiny bits.

2. Add cheese cubes and process with 8 to 10 on/off pulses. Then process continuously until mixture is completely moistened but has not yet formed a ball.

3. Remove from work bowl and form ball with your hands. Wrap in plastic wrap and refrigerate at least 30 minutes.

4. To make filling, fit work bowl with shredding disc. Cut Cheddar to fit small feed tube and grate. Remove and reserve.

5. Refit work bowl with metal blade. Add onions and chop with 6 or 7 on/off pulses until onions are finely chopped. Add drained olives and chop with 5 or 6 on/off pulses.

6. Add peppers, cheese and seasonings and process on/off until everything is well mixed.

7. Preheat oven to 375°F/190°C. Line 2 cookie sheets with parchment paper or butter well.

8. Divide dough in half and roll out each half to ⅛ in/3 mm. Cut with a 2-in/5-cm round cookie cutter. Reroll scraps of dough (if you have trouble rerolling, allow dough to rest for 10 minutes first). You should have between 30 and 36 rounds. Place a small spoonful of filling on ½ of each round. Do not overfill.

9. To make glaze, combine egg and cream. Brush half the outside edges of the dough so that edges will stick together. Fold pastry over filling to form a semicircle. Pinch edges. Arrange on cookie sheets. Brush tops with remaining glaze.

10. Bake 20 to 25 minutes or until golden. Serve hot or cold.

Seafood Soup with Garlic and Ginger (see page 59).

Pasta Primavera

In the last few years vegetable sauces for pasta have become very popular. This recipe (meaning "springtime") can be made in many different ways but this is my favorite. The sauce can be made ahead of time and then be reheated just when the pasta is cooking. You can use the dried commercial fettucine or linguine, pasta from one of the fresh pasta shops that have opened up all over the country, or you can make your own (see pages 111 and 112). Serve this as an elegant appetizer or as a main course. If you can't find fresh asparagus, simply omit it. Sliced mushrooms, broccoli or cauliflower florets can also be used.

1 lb	asparagus	500 g		Salt and freshly ground black pepper to taste		
2	cloves garlic	2				
	Handful fresh parsley			1 cup	whipping cream	250 mL
	Handful fresh dill			1 lb	fettucine or linguine	500 g
1	leek, white part only	1		½ cup	unsalted butter, cut into bits	125 mL
1	green pepper	1		1 cup	grated Parmesan cheese (if using freshly grated Parmesan, grate cheese before proceeding with rest of recipe — see page 14)	250 mL
1	red pepper	1				
1	rib celery	1				
1	carrot, peeled and trimmed	1				
1	zucchini	1				
¼ cup	unsalted butter	50 mL		Serves 6 to 8 as an appetizer		

1. Wash asparagus well. Cut off tough stems and peel stalks about 2 in/ 5 cm from the bottom. Bring a skillet of water to the boil and cook asparagus lying flat in the boiling water 3 to 5 minutes, depending on the thickness of the stalks. Remove from water. Cut off tips and reserve for garnish. Cut stalks in half, crosswise (each half should be approximately 3 in/7 cm long) and cut each half into 2 to 4 slices, lengthwise. Reserve.

2. Fit work bowl with metal blade. With machine running, drop garlic through the feed tube and chop. Remove and reserve. Add parsley and dill and chop with 5 or 6 on/off pulses. Remove and reserve.

3. Refit work bowl with medium or thin slicing disc. Cut the white part of the leek in half lengthwise. Then cut across so that the leek fits into the large feed tube. Lay the leek lengthwise in feed tube. Slice. Remove from work bowl and reserve.

4. Cut red and green peppers in half and remove ribs and seeds. Cut into chunks. Pack in small feed tube and slice. Repeat until all peppers are sliced. Remove and reserve.

5. Refit work bowl with shredding or julienne disc. Cut celery to fit lengthwise in large feed tube and process. Repeat with carrot and zucchini. Remove and reserve with peppers.

6. Melt butter in a skillet and add garlic and leeks. Cook until fragrant and leek begins to wilt.

7. Add peppers, celery, carrot and zucchini. Cook 5 to 8 minutes or until vegetables have wilted. Add asparagus and some salt and pepper. Cook 2 minutes.

8. Add cream and bring to a boil. Cook a few minutes or until cream thickens a little. Add half the herbs. Remove from heat.

9. Bring a large pot of salted water to the boil. Cook pasta. Generally, cook dried pasta 10 to 12 minutes, pasta from the "fresh" pasta shops 5 to 6 minutes and homemade pasta that has just been made 1 to 3 minutes.

10. Place the butter bits in serving dish. Reheat sauce. When pasta is ready, drain well. Do **not** rinse. Add pasta to bowl with butter.

11. Pour sauce over the pasta. Sprinkle with cheese and remaining fresh herbs. Toss well until sauce coats the pasta. Taste and season.

12. To serve, place asparagus tips on each serving. Serve immediately.

Pasta with Lemon and Garlic Sauce

This is a light and lovely dish that is suitable as an appetizer but also as a side dish with a plain roast, chicken or salmon steaks.

	Peel of 1 lemon				
1 tsp	salt	5 mL	1 lb	linguine	500 g
2	cloves garlic, peeled	2	2 tbsp	lemon juice	25 mL
¼ cup	unsalted butter	50 mL	1 cup	grated Parmesan	250 mL
1 cup	whipping cream	250 mL		cheese (if using freshly grated Parmesan, grate cheese before proceeding with rest of recipe – see page 14)	
¼ tsp	freshly ground pepper	1 mL			
¼ tsp	freshly ground nutmeg	1 mL			

Serves 8 as an appetizer

1. Fit work bowl with metal blade. Cut lemon peel into 1-in/2.5-cm pieces and dry. Drop through feed tube with machine running. Add salt and process continuously until peel is chopped.

2. Add garlic and process until finely chopped. Scrape down sides of bowl if necessary.

3. Melt butter in skillet over medium-low heat and add garlic mixture. Cook gently until very fragrant. Add cream, pepper and nutmeg and warm gently. If not serving immediately remove from heat and reheat when pasta is cooked.

4. Bring a large pot of salted water to the boil. Just before serving add linguine. If pasta is dried, cook 10 to 12 minutes. If you have purchased the pasta at a pasta shop, cook 5 to 6 minutes, and if the pasta has been freshly made, cook approximately 1 to 3 minutes, after the water comes to the boil.

5. Reheat sauce. Drain pasta well. Toss with sauce, lemon juice and cheese. Taste and season with salt and pepper.

Baked Mushroom Tartlets

These are like miniature quiches. It's hard to stop eating them — and you shouldn't. My diet theory is if there is good food around, eat it, and when there isn't, don't eat. It is all the junk we eat that adds the weight, not wonderful little treats like these. These tarts are also delicious cold. They can be made ahead and reheated or can be frozen and reheated.

Pastry:		
1 cup	flour	250 mL
½ cup	unsalted butter, cold	125 mL
4 oz	cream cheese, cold	125 g
Filling:		
3 oz	Swiss cheese, cold	100 g
8 oz	mushrooms, cleaned and trimmed	250 g
	Handful fresh parsley	
1	onion, peeled and quartered	1

3 tbsp	unsalted butter	50 mL
3	eggs	3
1 cup	sour cream	250 mL
1 tsp	dried tarragon	5 mL
1 tsp	salt	5 mL
¼ tsp	freshly ground pepper	1 mL
¼ tsp	freshly ground nutmeg	1 mL

Makes 24 tarts (2 in/5 cm)

1. To prepare pastry, fit work bowl with metal blade. Add flour. Cut butter and cheese into 1-in/2.5-cm cubes and add butter to flour. Process with 10 to 15 on/off pulses until the butter is in tiny bits.
2. Add cheese cubes and process with 10 on/off pulses. Then process continuously until mixture is moist and almost forms a ball of dough.
3. Remove from work bowl and gather into a ball. Wrap and refrigerate at least 30 minutes.
4. For the filling, wipe work bowl dry and refit with shredding disc. Cut cheese to fit small feed tube and grate. Remove and reserve. Place mushrooms in small feed tube and grate. Remove and reserve.
5. Refit work bowl with metal blade. Add parsley and chop with 5 or 6 on/off pulses. Remove and reserve. Add onions to work bowl still fitted with metal blade. Chop finely with 6 to 8 on/off pulses.
6. Heat butter in a skillet and add onions. Cook until tender and fragrant. Add mushrooms and cook until mixture is dry. Remove from skillet and cool.
7. Wipe work bowl dry and refit with metal blade. Add eggs, sour cream and seasonings and blend using on/off pulses. Reserve.
8. Preheat oven to 425°F/220°C. Divide dough in half and roll out each half thinly. Cut out circles of dough to fit 2-in/5-cm tart pans and press dough in firmly. Reroll scraps of dough so that you have 24 tarts. Prick dough with a fork and bake in hot oven for 5 minutes. Remove from oven and prick if there are any air bubbles.

9. Turn oven down to 350°F/180°C. Spoon a little of the mushroom mixture into the bottom of each tart. Sprinkle with a little cheese and then parsley. Spoon in custard mixture until almost full. Bake 15 to 20 minutes. Cool 10 minutes before serving.

Note: Although it takes more time, an excellent way to prebake small tart shells is to line each raw shell with a paper muffin cup. Partially fill with pie weights or beans and bake 5 minutes. Remove weights and papers and continue with step 9.

Pasta with Hazelnut Sauce

This is similar to Fettucine Alfredo but has a delicious twist — chopped toasted hazelnuts. The recipe is from my friend and colleague Mary Risley who owns a great cooking school in San Francisco — The Tante Marie School of Cooking. Be sure to toast the hazelnuts for maximum flavor. You can use homemade fettucine noodles, dried pasta or fresh noodles from a pasta shop.

6 oz	shelled hazelnuts	175 g		cheese before proceeding with rest of recipe — see page 14)	
⅓ cup	unsalted butter	75 mL			
1 lb	fettucine noodles	500 g			
1 cup	whipping cream, hot	250 mL		Salt and freshly ground black pepper to taste	
1 cup	grated Parmesan cheese (if using freshly grated Parmesan, grate	250 mL			

Serves 6 to 8

1. Preheat oven to 350°F/180°C. Spread hazelnuts on a cookie sheet and bake 10 to 15 minutes until lightly browned. To remove skins, see Food Hints, page 18. Do not worry if all the skin does not come off.
2. Fit work bowl with metal blade. Add hazelnuts and chop using 6 to 10 on/off pulses or until finely chopped. Do not overchop or nuts may become pasty.
3. Place half the nuts in a large, shallow bowl and reserve the remaining nuts. Cut butter into small pieces and add to hazelnuts in the bowl.
4. Bring a large pot of water to a boil. Add 2 tsp/10 mL salt. Add pasta and cook until tender — about 1 to 3 minutes for homemade pasta, 5 to 6 minutes for fresh store-bought pasta and 8 to 10 minutes for dried. Drain well and shake out any excess water.
5. Add pasta to bowl with butter and nuts. Pour hot cream over pasta and sprinkle with cheese. Season with salt and pepper to taste. Toss until sauce coats pasta well.
6. Serve sprinkled with remaining nuts.

Artichoke Frittata

A frittata is something between a baked omelet and a crustless quiche. It can be assembled ahead and then baked just before serving, or it can be baked ahead and reheated. Cold, it makes a delicious appetizer, cut into bite-sized squares. Leftovers can be made into sandwiches. There are many variations (see Vegetable Frittata on page 39).

8 oz	Swiss or Cheddar cheese	250 g	5	eggs	5
	Handful fresh parsley or basil		1 tsp	salt	5 mL
3	green onions, cut in 2-in/5-cm lengths	3	¼ tsp	freshly ground pepper	1 mL
2	6-oz/170-mL jars marinated artichokes	2	¼ tsp	Tabasco sauce	1 mL
½ cup	pitted black olives	125 mL	½ cup	water	125 mL
2	slices French or Italian bread	2			

Serves 6 to 8 as an appetizer

1. Fit work bowl with shredding disc. Cut cheese into cubes to fit feed tube and process until all cheese is grated. Remove cheese to a large bowl and reserve.

2. Refit work bowl with metal blade. Add parsley or basil and green onions. Process with 5 or 6 on/off pulses or until herbs are chopped. Reserve with cheese.

3. Drain artichokes and olives and add to work bowl still fitted with metal blade. Chop coarsely with 5 or 6 on/off pulses. Remove vegetables to bowl with cheese.

4. Cut bread up into cubes and add to work bowl still fitted with metal blade. Process with 3 or 4 on/off pulses or until bread is in crumbs. Reserve with other ingredients.

5. Place eggs and remaining ingredients in work bowl still fitted with metal blade and blend together. Stir eggs into all other ingredients in large bowl. Mix together until thoroughly blended.

6. Butter a 9-in square/2.5-L pan or equivalent and pour in egg mixture. Bake in a preheated 350°F/180°C for 30 to 40 minutes or until set. Allow to cool 10 minutes before serving. Cut into squares.

Vegetable Frittata

A traditional Italian frittata is usually cooked in a skillet and then either flipped and finished on top of the stove or transferred to the oven to finish the uncooked top side under the broiler. This version is cooked totally in the oven and can be made completely in advance. If you have leftover cooked vegetables, they can be diced and added to the frittata in place of or in addition to the onion-pepper mixture. Just make sure that any vegetable included is cooked (either previously or with the onions) and that you do not have more than 2 cups/500 mL cooked vegetables in total.

8 oz	old Cheddar cheese	250 g	2	cloves garlic, peeled	2
8 oz	mushrooms, cleaned	250 g	3 tbsp	unsalted butter	50 mL
1	green pepper	1	5	eggs	5
1	red pepper	1	½ cup	sour cream or unflavored yogurt	125 mL
3	slices French or Italian bread	3	1 tsp	salt	5 mL
	Handful fresh parsley		¼ tsp	freshly ground pepper	1 mL
	Handful fresh dill or basil				
2	onions, peeled and quartered	2			

Serves 6 to 8 as an appetizer

1. Fit work bowl with shredding disc. Grate Cheddar cheese and transfer to a mixing bowl.
2. Refit work bowl with medium or thin slicing disc. Slice mushrooms. Reserve. Cut green and red peppers into quarters, discarding ribs and seeds. Fit tightly into small feed tube. Slice. Repeat until all peppers are sliced. Reserve with mushrooms.
3. Refit work bowl with metal blade. Break bread up into chunks and add to work bowl. Process bread into crumbs by running machine 5 to 10 seconds. Add crumbs to cheese.
4. Add parsley and dill or basil to work bowl and chop using a few on/off pulses. Transfer to cheese mixture and stir everything together.
5. Add onions and garlic to work bowl fitted with metal blade. Process until coarsely chopped with 3 on/off pulses.
6. Melt butter in skillet and add onions and garlic. Cook until tender and fragrant, about 5 minutes.
7. Add mushrooms and peppers to onions and continue cooking until tender – about 5 minutes longer. Cook until all liquid from mushrooms has evaporated.
8. Add eggs, sour cream and salt and pepper to work bowl still fitted with metal blade. Blend together. In a large bowl combine the cheese mixture, the vegetable mixture and the eggs.
9. Butter a 9-in square/2.5-L baking dish or equivalent and pour in egg mixture. Bake in a preheated 350°F/180°C oven for 30 to 40 minutes or until frittata is golden brown and set. Cool 10 minutes before serving.

Chicken Liver Terrine

There are times when I think if I ever see another pâté or terrine again I will surely die. And then a really delicious version will come along and I start loving them all over again. You can serve this creamy terrine plain or garnish it with vegetable flowers and the aspic below.

1	clove garlic, peeled	1
3	onions, peeled and quartered	3
¼ cup	unsalted butter	50 mL
1½ lb	chicken livers, halved and trimmed	750 g
1 tsp	salt	5 mL
¼ tsp	freshly ground pepper	1 mL
1 tsp	thyme	5 mL
1 tsp	curry powder	5 mL
1 tsp	crushed green peppercorns	5 mL
¼ cup	dry sherry or Port	50 mL
¼ cup	Cognac or brandy	50 mL

¾ cup	whipping cream	175 mL
Aspic and Garnish:		
1 cup	clear beef or chicken stock, homemade (see pages 45 and 46) or commercial	250 mL
2 tbsp	Cognac or brandy	25 mL
1	envelope unflavored gelatin	1
	Green onions, leeks, cucumber or zucchini; carrots or pimento-stuffed green olives	

Serves 8 to 12

1. Preheat oven to 350°F/180°C. Butter an attractive 8-in square/1.5-L baking dish.
2. Fit work bowl with metal blade. Drop garlic through the feed tube while the machine is running and process until finely chopped. Add onions and chop using 4 or 5 on/off pulses.
3. Melt half of the butter in a skillet. Cook onions and garlic until tender and fragrant but do not brown. Remove from pan and reserve. Melt remaining butter in pan and add livers. Cook until livers are tender and cooked through but still a light pink inside. Do not wash skillet yet.

4. Wipe work bowl clean and refit with metal blade. Add onions, livers and seasonings (except liqueurs and cream) to work bowl. Add sherry and Cognac to pan in which livers were cooked, turn heat to medium high and deglaze the pan by scraping all the flavorful bits of meat from the bottom into the liquid. Reduce liquid slightly and add to livers in work bowl. Puree mixture until smooth. Add cream and blend in. Taste and adjust seasoning with salt and pepper if necessary.
5. Spread mixture into prepared pan and cover with a piece of buttered parchment paper or waxed paper. Do not worry if mixture is very runny. Bake 30 minutes or until set. Cool completely.

Aspic and Garnish:

1. To prepare aspic, combine stock and brandy in a small saucepan and sprinkle gelatin over the top. Let stand 5 minutes. Heat gently until gelatin has dissolved completely.

2. Strain mixture if it isn't clear. Allow to cool at room temperature. If it sets before you are ready to use it, reheat gently.

3. Cook green part of leeks or green onions until barely tender. Cut into long strips for stems. Make carrot flowers (see page 24) or slice olives in circles. With a vegetable peeler, peel strips of cucumber or zucchini peel and trim to resemble leaves.

4. Decorate top of terrine with vegetable flowers. Press decoration into surface of liver. When aspic is cool and barely beginning to set, pour it over the flowers. Refrigerate until set. Serve from baking dish and spread on crackers.

Chopped Chicken Livers

This is the "pâté" that many Jewish children grow up on. When I was little my mother always used to render the chicken fat herself and use it in the recipe along with the grebenes (cracklings) that result. But now that people are so concerned with saturated fats and cholesterol, even my mother uses oil most of the time.

When preparing this you have a choice as to which blade to use — if you like the mixture very creamy and spreadable you can use the metal blade all the way. If you like the mixture slightly drier and more crumbly, as my mother does, use the shredding disc as described below.

2	onions, peeled and quartered	2	4	hard-cooked eggs	4
¼ cup	vegetable oil or chicken fat	50 mL	1 tsp	salt (or more to taste)	5 mL
1 lb	chicken livers, trimmed and halved	500 g	¼ tsp	freshly ground pepper	1 mL
			Serves 8 to 10		

1. Fit work bowl with metal blade. Add onions and chop with 5 or 6 on/off pulses until coarsely chopped.

2. Heat 2 tbsp/25 mL oil in a skillet and cook onions until lightly browned, tender and fragrant. Remove oil and onions from the pan and reserve.

3. Add another 2 tbsp/25 mL oil to pan and cook livers until browned on the outside and cooked on the inside. This should take about 15 minutes. Cool completely.

4. Refit work bowl with shredding disc. Place eggs in small feed tube and grate. Add cold livers and grate. Transfer eggs and livers to a mixing bowl and add onions and enough cooked onion oil to make the mixture hold together. Add salt and pepper, taste and adjust seasoning if necessary.

Marinated Goat Cheese

The first time I traveled to France, I remember being amazed at the number of cheeses of every kind. Not only were there hundreds of cow's milk cheeses, there were many goat cheeses as well. These are just beginning to become popular with North Americans. There are delicious goat cheeses now being made in California and Quebec.

If you are unsure about goat cheese, try it prepared this way first. The marinade mellows it considerably. And if you have a fussy guest, make sure you call it "chevre." Serve it as an appetizer with some of the marinade and allow guests to spread it themselves on French bread. You can also use other semisoft cheeses or even pieces of cream cheese in this recipe. I like to use a semisoft, creamy goat cheese without a rind, but if you can only find the cheese with a rind, just cut it off.

1	clove garlic, peeled	1	1 tsp	dried thyme	5 mL
1	shallot, peeled	1	1	bay leaf	1
10	whole black peppercorns	10	⅓ cup	pitted black olives	75 mL
¼ tsp	hot, red pepper flakes	1 mL	1½ cups	olive oil (see page 18)	375 mL
1 tsp	dried rosemary	5 mL	8 oz	goat cheese	250 g

Serves 6 to 8

1. Fit work bowl with metal blade. With machine running, drop garlic and shallot through feed tube and chop coarsely. Add peppercorns, red pepper flakes, rosemary, thyme, bay leaf and olives to work bowl. Process with 3 or 4 on/off pulses, or until olives are barely chopped. Add oil and process just to blend.

2. Cut cheese into 4 pieces and place in a jar or bowl. Add marinade. Coat cheese well. Marinate a few days in the refrigerator (oil will become cloudy but clears at room temperature) or overnight at room temperature. Serve with French bread.

Note: After a few days in the marinade, the peppercorns soften and become edible.

Italian Vegetable Dip

Although vegetables cut into long, julienne strips look great when served with a dip, many people do not like the idea that guests can redip their vegetables after biting part of them off. One-bite vegetables really are a better idea. You can slice carrots, zucchini or cucumber into rounds with the medium or thick slicing disc, or cut green beans, pieces of fennel root, etc., into smallish cubes. Or, if you really don't mind your guests redipping their vegetables, try using Belgian endive leaves for something different — they are almost perfect cup shapes. This dip can also be used as a creamy salad dressing.

1	clove garlic, peeled	1	dash	Tabasco sauce	dash
3	green onions, cut into 2-in/5-cm lengths	3	1 cup	mayonnaise, homemade (see page 123) or commercial	250 mL
	Handful fresh parsley		¾ cup	thick sour cream or unflavored yogurt	175 mL
4	anchovy fillets, drained and cut in half	4		Salt and freshly ground black pepper to taste	
3 tbsp	lemon juice	50 mL			

Makes approximately 2 cups/500 mL

1. Fit work bowl with metal blade. With machine running, drop garlic through feed tube and process until chopped. Add green onions and parsley and chop with 4 or 5 on/off pulses until finely minced. Add anchovies and chop a few more times.

2. Add lemon juice, Tabasco sauce, mayonnaise and blend thoroughly. Quickly blend in sour cream or yogurt. Do not overblend once sour cream has been added, or dip will be runny. Taste and add salt and pepper if necessary.

3. Refrigerate dip at least a few hours or overnight to blend flavors.

Stocks and Soups

Soups can fill many different needs. Hot soups are warm and comforting and can take the chill out of a cold winter night. A hearty soup can fill you up when you're hungry and with homemade bread or muffins can serve as a complete meal. A smooth and silky cream soup can be an elegant appetizer for a sophisticated dinner – in Far Eastern countries soups are even served for dessert. Cold soups are refreshing and can be made from fruits as well as vegetables.

The Cuisinart® is invaluable when it comes to preparing soups. If the soup is chunky you can chop or slice the vegetables for it in the machine. If you want the soup to be a puree, you can also use the machine to blend it as smooth as you wish after it is cooked.

Good stocks are the basis for good soups. They may seem time consuming to prepare, but when you study the recipes you will see that although the cooking time may be lengthy, stocks actually require little preparation time. I think it is worthwhile to prepare your own stocks. It's a good way to use up scraps of vegetables, bones from beef and chicken, and heads and tails from fish. When you prepare your own stocks you can also control the salt content of your soups and other dishes to a much greater degree. But I do realize that not everyone has the time or inclination to make homemade stocks, so I have suggested substitutes in the individual recipes.

Beef Stock

Although beef stock is easy to prepare, it does take much longer than chicken or fish stock. The darker the bones and meat are browned, the browner the stock, so be patient if you want a rich-colored stock (although it rarely gets quite as dark as the commercial variety).

4 lb	raw beef soup bones (shank, short ribs, etc.)	2 kg	1 tbsp	tomato paste	15 mL
1 lb	stewing beef, cut up into 2-in/5-cm pieces	500 g	5 qt	cold water	5 L
			2	bay leaves	2
2	onions, peeled and quartered	2	1 tsp	dried thyme	5 mL
2	carrots, cut into 2-in/5-cm lengths	2	5	whole black peppercorns	5
2	ribs celery, cut into 2-in/5-cm lengths	2		Half handful fresh parsley	
2	leeks, white part only, well washed and cut into 2-in/5-cm lengths	2			

Makes approximately 5 qt/5 L

1. Preheat oven to 425°F/220°C. Pat bones and meat dry and place in large roasting pan or on cookie sheet. Place in oven and allow meat and bones to brown well. This may take from 1 to 3 hours. Do not allow them to burn.

2. Meanwhile chop vegetables coarsely by fitting work bowl with metal blade. Process one vegetable at a time with a few on/off pulses. When meat has browned, spread bones and meat with tomato paste and arrange vegetables around and on meat. Return to oven for 30 minutes to 1 hour to brown again. (Watch it closely as tomato paste tends to burn easily.)

3. Transfer meat and vegetables to a large stock pot and discard any fat in pan. Place pan on heat and add 1 cup/250 mL water and deglaze. Add to stock pot. Add remaining water — more if necessary to cover bones and vegetables by about 2 in/5 cm.

4. Bring to a boil, skim off any scum that forms on the surface and reduce heat to a simmer.

5. Make a bouquet garni (spice bag) by wrapping bay leaves, thyme, peppercorns and parsley in cheesecloth and tying with string. Add to stock.

6. Cover stock pot and simmer gently 4 to 5 hours. Strain stock and discard bones, meat and vegetables. If you are not freezing the stock, cool and then refrigerate. The fat will rise to the surface and solidify — just use stock under fat but do not remove fat as it helps to preserve the stock. If you are freezing stock, remove fat before freezing.

Chicken Stock

Although you can always use commercial chicken stock in recipes, the flavor of homemade stock is far nicer. I usually prepare it completely salt free so that I can season whatever I'm preparing without worrying about oversalting. The difference between chicken soup and chicken stock, to me, is that soup is meant to be eaten on its own and therefore must be very strong and rich in chicken flavor. Stock is meant to be used in the preparation of other dishes, and therefore does not have to have quite as dominating a flavor. You can get more mileage, so to speak, when preparing a stock from one chicken than if you are making soup.

If you do not have enough room in your freezer for quantities of chicken stock, you can prepare it very strong, freeze it in ice cube trays, pack it into plastic bags and then dilute with water almost like homemade bouillon cubes. Just be sure to label the ice cubes or you may have some very strange mixed drinks!

3 lb	raw chicken or chicken wings, backs and necks (or more)	1.5 kg	1	bay leaf	1
5 qt	cold water	5 L	1 tsp	dried thyme	5 mL
2	onions, peeled and quartered	2	3	whole cloves	3
1	carrot, cut into 2-in/5-cm lengths	1	5	whole black peppercorns	5
2	ribs celery, cut into 2-in/5-cm lengths	2		Half handful fresh parsley	
2	leeks, white part only, well washed and cut into 2-in/5-cm lengths	2			

Makes approximately 5 qt/5 L

1. Cut chicken up into 8 to 10 pieces and place in a stock pot. Add cold water and bring to boil. A scum (white froth) will rise to the surface. Be sure to skim it off.
2. Fit work bowl with metal blade. Add onions and process on/off with a few pulses. Remove from bowl and reserve.
3. Add carrots to work bowl still fitted with metal blade and chop coarsely with a few on/off pulses. Reserve with onions. Add the celery and leeks to the work bowl and chop as above.
4. After skimming the scum off the broth, add the vegetables. Reduce heat to a bare simmer.
5. Make a bouquet garni (spice bag) by wrapping bay leaf, thyme, cloves, peppercorns and parsley in cheesecloth and tying with string. Add to broth.
6. Cover and simmer stock gently approximately 1½ hours. Do not cook longer than 2 hours.
7. Strain stock. (Although fat can be skimmed from the surface of hot stock, it is easier to chill the stock overnight first, as the fat will rise to

the surface and solidify.) Although most of the flavor has been drawn out of the chicken and vegetables, the chicken meat can be used for sandwiches or salads if you don't want to throw it away. The stock will keep about 1 week in the refrigerator. If you are not freezing it, allow the fat that rises to the surface to stay on, as this helps preserve the stock. Use what you need from under the fat layer. If you are going to freeze the stock, however, the fat is unnecessary so remove it before freezing.

Note: Do not use liver or giblets in the stock as it tends to discolor it. I do put in the necks, skin and fat, however.

Fish Stock

The reason for making your own fish stock is simple — there are no commercial substitutes. Bottled clam juice is too strong and salty, Japanese Dashi has too strong a smoky flavor for French and Italian recipes, and fish stores that sell their own fish stock usually make it with any kind of fish heads and bones available rather than lean, white-fleshed fish which makes the nicest stock.

3 lb	lean, white-fleshed fish heads, tail and bones	1.5 kg	1	bay leaf	1
			½ tsp	dried thyme	2 mL
5 qt	cold water	5 L	5	whole white peppercorns	5
2	onions, peeled and quartered	2			
			3	sprigs fresh parsley	3
1	carrot, cut into 2-in/5-cm lengths	1	2	whole cloves	2
			½ cup	dry white wine	125 mL
2	ribs celery, cut into 2-in/5-cm lengths	2			
2	leeks, white part only, well washed and cut into 2-in/5-cm lengths	2	**Makes approximately 5 qt/5 L**		

1. Place heads, tails and bones in a stock pot. Add cold water and bring to a boil. Skim off any scum that rises to the surface and reduce heat.
2. Chop vegetables coarsely by fitting work bowl with metal blade. Chop each vegetable separately by processing with a few on/off pulses. Add vegetables to stock.
3. Make a bouquet garni (spice bag) by wrapping bay leaf, thyme, peppercorns, parsley and cloves in cheesecloth and tying securely with string. Add to stock with wine. Cover and cook 30 minutes. Do not cook longer as stock can become bitter. Strain stock and refrigerate or freeze.

Cream of Lettuce Soup

This unusual soup can be prepared all year round although the very idea of a lettuce soup lends itself to springtime. It is also good served cold. Use lettuce like Romaine that has a slight bite to it and is not too sweet. Although you can simply chop the lettuce with the metal blade for this soup, it is good to practice the "chiffonade" technique.

3	shallots, peeled	3	1 qt	chicken stock, homemade (see page 46) or commercial, hot	1 L
3 tbsp	unsalted butter	50 mL			
2	heads Romaine lettuce, well washed	2			
6 oz	spinach, well washed and trimmed	175 g	1 tsp	salt (or more to taste)	5 mL
½ tsp	dried tarragon or 1 tbsp/15 mL fresh	2 mL	¼ tsp	freshly ground pepper	1 mL
3 tbsp	unsalted butter	50 mL	1 cup	cream	250 mL
3 tbsp	flour	50 mL			

Serves 8

1. Fit work bowl with metal blade. With machine running, drop shallots through the feed tube and process until finely chopped. But do not overprocess or shallots could become bitter.

2. Melt 3 tbsp/50 mL butter in a large, deep skillet and add shallots. Cook gently until tender and fragrant but do not brown.

3. Arrange approximately 4 lettuce leaves on top of each other and roll up tightly. Refit work bowl with thin or medium slicing disc. Stand up one roll in small feed tube and slice. Or, make a few rolls and stand them up in large feed tube until very tightly packed and slice all at once. Repeat with remaining lettuce.

4. Reserve approximately 1 cup/ 250 mL shredded lettuce for the garnish and add remaining lettuce "chiffonade" to the butter and shallots. Add spinach. Add tarragon. Cook until lettuce and spinach wilt. Do not brown.

5. Meanwhile, in a large saucepan, melt remaining 3 tbsp/50 mL butter and whisk in flour. Cook, whisking constantly until mixture is cooked and smells something like shortbread. Mixture can be slightly golden but should not brown. Whisk in hot stock and bring to a boil. Add lettuce and spinach mixture and reduce heat to low. Simmer gently about 10 minutes. Add salt to taste and pepper.

6. Refit work bowl with metal blade. Lift or strain vegetables from broth. Add vegetables to work bowl in 1 or 2 batches and puree. Stir puree back into soup broth and return to heat.

7. Add cream and heat soup thoroughly. Taste and adjust seasoning with salt and pepper if necessary. Garnish with shredded lettuce. Serve immediately.

Note: If radicchio, the Italian red lettuce, is available, you could garnish the soup with shreds of it for a wonderful contrast in color.

Cream of Leek and Fennel Soup

Fennel is a delicious vegetable with a unique anise flavor. It has always been very popular in Italian cuisine and is slowly becoming widely accepted. It can be used for dips along with carrots and celery and is sometimes served in salads. The flavor is slightly stronger when raw. To use fennel bulbs, cut off the ribs and discard. Reserve some of the dill-like feathery greens for a garnish. Trim the bulb and chop. If fennel is not available, substitute celery in this recipe.

This soup also freezes well. For a low-calorie variation, omit the cream and use 3 cups/750 mL stock.

2	leeks, white and light green parts only	2	1 tsp	salt (less if commercial stock is used)	5 mL
2	bulbs fennel, trimmed (approximately 1 lb/500 g)	2	¼ tsp	freshly ground pepper	1 mL
3 tbsp	unsalted butter	50 mL	1 cup	whipping cream	250 mL
1	28-oz/796-mL can plum tomatoes	1	**Garnish:**	Sprigs fresh fennel or chopped green onions	
2 cups	chicken stock, homemade (see page 46) or commercial	500 mL			

Serves 6 to 8

1. Cut leeks in half lengthwise and wash well under cold running water. Cut fennel bulbs into quarters lengthwise. Fit machine with the medium slicing disc and slice leeks and fennel through small feed tube using medium pressure.

2. Melt butter in a large saucepan and cook leeks and fennel until fragrant and wilted but without browning – about 10 minutes.

3. Add tomatoes with the juices. Break tomatoes up with a wooden spoon. Add chicken stock, salt and pepper and bring to a boil. Reduce heat, cover pot and cook until vegetables are very tender.

4. Strain or lift vegetables from the stock. With the machine fitted with the metal blade, puree vegetables. If you have the DLC-7 or DLC-X, this can be done in 1 batch. With the DLC-8 and the DLC-10, do this in 2 batches.

5. Return mixture to the broth and heat. Add cream and stir well. Reheat thoroughly. Season to taste.

6. Serve hot garnished with fennel sprigs or green onions or serve cold, chilling the soup thoroughly overnight in the refrigerator.

49

Cream of Mushroom Soup with Wild Mushrooms

While in Italy studying "la buona cucina" with Marcella Hazan, I learned about the incredible flavor of wild mushrooms. Fresh wild mushrooms are not usually readily available, but the dried variety can be a wonderful addition to soups, stews, rice dishes and pastas. Italian delicatessens sell the famous dried Porcini mushrooms, but other kinds of dried mushrooms are available at specialty stores and would work well. Although you can leave the dried wild mushrooms out completely, the flavor they add raises this soup from a conventional cream of mushroom to an outstanding start to any meal.

1	½-oz/15-g package dried, wild mushrooms	1	⅓ cup	all-purpose flour	75 mL
1 cup	warm water	250 mL	3 cups	chicken stock, homemade (see page 46) or commercial	750 mL
1½ lb	fresh mushrooms, cleaned	750 g	1 cup	whipping cream	250 mL
1	onion, peeled	1		Salt and freshly ground black pepper to taste	
1	clove garlic, peeled	1			
3 tbsp	unsalted butter	50 mL			

Serves 6

1. Place dried mushrooms in a bowl and pour warm water over them. Allow to rest 20 to 30 minutes until they are reconstituted.
2. Meanwhile, fit machine with medium slicing disc. Place fresh mushrooms in feed tube and, exerting gentle pressure, slice all the mushrooms. Remove to a bowl and reserve. Set aside about 20 of the nicest slices for a garnish.
3. Without washing bowl, refit machine with metal blade. Cut onion into eighths and add to work bowl. Add clove of garlic. Chop vegetables using on/off technique until coarsely chopped.
4. Heat butter in a large saucepan or small Dutch oven. Add onion mixture and cook gently until onions and garlic are tender and fragrant but do not brown.
5. Meanwhile drain wild mushrooms through a cheesecloth-lined sieve, reserving liquid. Rinse mushrooms of any remaining sand and chop coarsely. Add to onion mixture. Combine reserved liquid with chicken stock.
6. Add flour to the onion mixture and cook, stirring, about 5 minutes but do not brown. Add stock (chicken and mushroom) and bring to a boil. Add sliced mushrooms (except the ones reserved for the garnish), reduce heat and simmer gently 20 to 25 minutes.
7. Fit metal blade in clean work bowl. Strain or lift mushrooms and onions out of broth and puree in 1 or 2 batches depending on the size of your machine. Return everything to the pot, add the cream and heat thoroughly. Taste and season.
8. Serve hot, garnished with a few raw mushroom slices.

Cream of Broccoli Soup with Curry

In most large cities, fresh dill is available year round, but in summer when it grows easily you can chop and freeze it for future use (see page 17). If you don't have fresh or frozen dill, simply substitute ½ tsp/2 mL dried dill. The fresh parsley gives the soup a fresh herb flavor. The curry powder does not add a strong taste, but makes the soup extra special. This soup can be served hot or cold. It also freezes well.

3	leeks, white and light green parts only	3	1 tsp	salt (less if commercial chicken stock is used)	5 mL
1	large bunch broccoli (approximately 1½ lb/750 g)	1	¼ tsp	freshly ground pepper	1 mL
3 tbsp	unsalted butter	50 mL	¼ tsp	freshly ground nutmeg	1 mL
1 tbsp	curry powder	15 mL	¾ cup	whipping cream, optional	175 mL
	Handful fresh parsley				
	Handful fresh dill				
4 cups	chicken stock, homemade (see page 46) or commercial	1 L	Serves 6 to 8		

1. Cut leeks in half lengthwise and rinse thoroughly under cold running water. Trim broccoli stalks and, if they are very large and tough, peel partway up the stems. Cut off the florets and reserve.

2. Fit machine with medium slicing disc and slice leeks and broccoli stems upright through small feed tube using medium pressure.

3. Melt butter in a large saucepan and cook leeks until fragrant and wilted. Add curry powder and cook 2 minutes longer. Add broccoli and combine well.

4. Meanwhile, without cleaning work bowl, refit machine with metal blade. Add parsley and dill and chop using on/off technique until finely chopped. Add to vegetables along with broccoli florets and chicken stock, salt, pepper and nutmeg. Bring to a boil, reduce heat, cover and simmer gently for about 6 minutes.

5. Remove 8 nice florets from the soup for a garnish. Rinse florets in cold water to stop the cooking and set color. Reserve. Continue cooking rest of broccoli soup for 20 minutes or until broccoli and leeks are very tender.

6. Strain or lift vegetables from soup and puree with metal blade in 1 or 2 batches. If you have the DLC-7 or DLC-X, this can be done in 1 batch, but with the DLC-8 and DLC-10, it should be done in 2 batches.

7. Return pureed vegetables to the soup base and add cream if you are using it. If the soup is too thick and you are not using the cream, add additional stock. Heat thoroughly. Taste and reseason if necessary. Serve garnished with a broccoli floret.

Cream of Spinach Soup

Spinach is a delicious vegetable and it has certainly come a long way from the time when people avoided it. When buying fresh spinach you have a choice between the loose leaf spinach and that in the cellophane packages. The advantage of the loose leaf spinach is that you can see easily whether or not all the leaves are fresh, but this spinach is often very sandy and must be washed thoroughly — sometimes 3 or 4 times. The advantage of the packaged spinach is that it has already been washed a few times for you, but often some of the spinach in the center is bad because of improper drying. Whichever you choose, make sure the spinach is very clean before cooking — the Cuisinart® is wonderful but it does not puree sand!

2	medium-sized onions, peeled and quartered	2	1 tsp	salt (more or less depending on the stock)	5 mL
1	clove garlic, peeled	1	½ tsp	freshly ground pepper	2 mL
3 tbsp	unsalted butter	50 mL	¼ tsp	freshly ground nutmeg	1 mL
1 lb	fresh spinach, well washed and trimmed	500 g	1 cup	sour cream or unflavored yogurt	250 mL
	Handful fresh dill		**Garnish:**		
	Handful fresh parsley			Sprigs fresh dill	
2	medium-sized potatoes, peeled (approximately 12 oz/375 g)	2			
1 tbsp	Dijon mustard	15 mL			
4 cups	chicken stock, homemade (see page 46) or commercial	1 L	**Serves 8**		

1. Fit work bowl with metal blade. Add onions and garlic and chop with 4 or 5 on/off pulses until onion is finely chopped.
2. Heat butter in a heavy, large saucepan or soup pot. Add onions and garlic and cook until tender and fragrant but do not brown.
3. Add spinach and stir. Cover and cook over medium heat just a few minutes or until spinach wilts.
4. With work bowl still fitted with metal blade, add dill and parsley.

Chop using a few on/off pulses. Reserve.
5. Fit work bowl with medium slicing disc. Insert potatoes into feed tube and slice. Add to spinach along with mustard, stock, herbs, salt, pepper and nutmeg.
6. Cover soup and bring to the boil. Reduce heat and cook gently until potatoes are tender — about 20 minutes.
7. Refit the work bowl with metal blade. Strain vegetables from the

liquid and puree vegetables with a small amount of liquid in 2 or 3 batches. Do not overpuree or potatoes may become sticky.

8. Return all pureed soup to the saucepan and heat thoroughly. Taste and reseason if necessary.

9. Serve soup with a spoonful of sour cream and place a sprig of dill on the sour cream.

Note: This soup is also great cold — chill before adjusting seasoning. Stir sour cream or yogurt into soup and garnish each serving with sprigs of dill.

Cream of Asparagus Soup

Although we can get most vegetables throughout the year now, asparagus still tastes best when it is fresh in the spring. This soup is one of my favorite ways to eat it. Be sure to clean the asparagus thoroughly, however, as it can be very sandy. And if the asparagus is especially tough, it's a good idea to strain it before serving or pass it through a food mill just to be sure there are no bits of tough skin left unprocessed.

3 lb	fresh asparagus	1.5 kg	1 tsp	dried tarragon	5 mL
2	shallots, peeled	2	1 tsp	salt (more or less)	5 mL
3 tbsp	unsalted butter	50 mL	¼ tsp	freshly ground pepper	1 mL
3 tbsp	flour	50 mL			
4 cups	chicken stock, homemade (see page 46) or commercial, hot	1 L	1 cup	whipping cream	250 mL

Serves 8

1. Wash asparagus well and trim and discard 1 in/2.5 cm off the ends. Bring water to a boil in large, deep skillet and cook asparagus about 5 minutes (depending on thickness of stalks). Drain well. Cut off tips and reserve about 20 tips for garnish.

2. Cut remaining asparagus stalks into 2-in/5-cm pieces and fit work bowl with metal blade. Chop asparagus stalks and remaining tips in batches. Reserve.

3. Leave metal blade in place and, with machine running, drop shallots through feed tube and chop.

4. Melt butter in a Dutch oven or large saucepan and add shallots. Cook a few minutes until tender and fragrant and whisk in flour. Cook at least 5 minutes, stirring constantly. Do not brown.

5. Whisk in hot chicken stock, chopped asparagus, tarragon, salt and pepper. Bring to a boil, cover, reduce heat and simmer gently 15 minutes.

6. Lift or strain vegetables from soup. With work bowl fitted with metal blade, puree vegetables in 1 or 2 batches. Return pureed vegetables to stock.

7. Return soup to heat, add cream and heat thoroughly. Taste and adjust seasoning if necessary. Serve garnished with a few reserved asparagus tips.

Note: Before adding cream, if soup is still too coarse, simply strain or pass through a food mill. Return to heat, add cream and heat thoroughly.

Iced Celery and Coriander Soup

This recipe was developed by Toronto chef Terry Seed while he was working at the Church Restaurant in Stratford, Ontario. He offered it to me for my CKFM "Hour Toronto" radio spot and listeners literally ate it up. The flavor of the coriander seeds is very different from the fresh coriander in the garnish — try to obtain both. The coriander seeds are available at spice shops and Indian supply shops and the fresh coriander (see page 19) is available in Mexican, Indian or Chinese fresh vegetable markets.

1	onion, peeled and quartered	1		1	small bay leaf	1
2 tbsp	unsalted butter	25 mL			Salt and freshly ground white pepper to taste	
6	ribs celery	6		1 cup	whipping cream	250 mL
2	medium-sized potatoes, peeled	2		**Garnish:**		
				2 tbsp	toasted hazelnuts	25 mL
4 cups	chicken stock, homemade (see page 46) or commercial	1 L			Handful fresh coriander or Italian parsley	
1½ tbsp	coriander seeds	20 mL		½ cup	sour cream	125 mL
1 tsp	celery seeds	5 mL				
8	whole white peppercorns	8				

Serves 6 to 8

1. Fit work bowl with medium slicing disc. Slice onion. Heat butter in a Dutch oven or large saucepan and add onions. Cook a few minutes until tender and fragrant.

2. Meanwhile stand celery in small feed tube and slice with slicing disc. Add celery to onions and cook a few minutes. Do not brown. Slice potatoes using large feed tube. Add to celery and cook a few minutes.

3. Add stock and bring to a boil.

4. Meanwhile crush coriander coarsely with celery seeds. Make a bouquet garni (spice bag) by wrapping coriander, celery seeds, peppercorns and bay leaf in cheesecloth and tying securely with string. Add to soup. Add a little salt and pepper depending on saltiness of stock. Reduce heat and cook gently about 30 minutes or until potatoes are tender.

5. Remove spice bag. Lift/strain vegetables from stock. Puree vegetables with a small amount of liquid in 3 or 4 batches, depending on size of your Cuisinart®. Do not overprocess. Return vegetables to stock.

6. Chill soup and then stir in whipping cream. Taste and season as necessary.

7. Fit clean work bowl with metal blade. Add hazelnuts and chop coarsely with 2 or 3 on/off pulses. Remove hazelnuts and reserve.

8. With work bowl still fitted with metal blade, chop fresh coriander with 3 or 4 on/off pulses. Remove and reserve.

9. When ready to serve, place a spoonful of sour cream in the center of each serving and sprinkle the sour cream with hazelnuts and fresh coriander.

Chilled Cream of Sorrel Soup

Sorrel is sometimes called sour grass or schav. It has always been popular with Middle European cooks but lately, with the advent of nouvelle cuisine, sorrel has become much more widely recognized and, at the same time, more expensive.

When potatoes are used in a soup that is to be pureed, be sure not to overprocess the vegetable mixture in the Cuisinart®. Otherwise the potatoes may become sticky.

This soup can be served hot or cold.

1	medium-sized onion, peeled and quartered	1	1 tsp	salt (less if commercial stock is used)	5 mL
3 tbsp	unsalted butter	50 mL	¼ tsp	freshly ground pepper	1 mL
4 oz	fresh sorrel	125 g	¼ tsp	dried tarragon (2 tsp/10 mL fresh tarragon)	1 mL
3	medium-sized potatoes, peeled (approximately 1 lb/500 g)	3	½ cup	whipping cream	125 mL
4 cups	chicken stock, homemade (see page 46) or commercial	1 L		Serves 6 to 8	

1. Fit work bowl with metal blade. Add onion and chop coarsely using on/off technique. Melt butter in a large saucepan and cook onion gently until fragrant.

2. Meanwhile, add sorrel to work bowl still fitted with metal blade and chop coarsely. Add to onions. Cook until wilted.

3. Refit work bowl with medium slicing disc. Cut potatoes to fit large feed tube and slice potatoes using medium pressure. Add potatoes to onion mixture.

4. Add stock, salt, pepper and tarragon. Bring to a boil. Reduce heat, cover and simmer gently until potatoes are tender, about 25 minutes.

5. Lift or strain vegetables out of stock. Puree vegetable mixture in 3 batches and be careful not to overprocess. Use about ½ cup/125 mL chicken stock with each batch to help prevent overprocessing. Return all of mixture to the stock.

6. Chill overnight or until thoroughly cold. Stir in cream just before serving. Taste and reseason if necessary.

Sweet Onion Soup

This soup will remind you how sweet onions can be. The combination of big Bermuda onions and chicken stock will show you why they once talked about — to many people's disbelief — using onions as a sugar substitute. If the soup is too sweet for you, the next time you make it use regular cooking onions and beef stock. The red onions add a nice color and a special flavor. As for using a food processor for this recipe — when the processor was first introduced, a few students told me if they only used it to make onion soup it was worth the price of the machine.

3	cloves garlic, peeled	3
3	large Bermuda onions, peeled (approximately 2 lb/1 kg)	3
2	red onions (approximately ½ lb/250 g peeled)	2
¼ cup	unsalted butter	50 mL
2 tbsp	all-purpose flour	25 mL
1 qt	chicken stock, homemade (see page 46) or commercial	1 L
1 cup	dry white wine	250 mL
	Salt and freshly ground black pepper to taste	
½ tsp	dried thyme	2 mL
1	bay leaf	1

Croutons:

½ cup	unsalted butter	125 mL
8	slices French bread	8
2 tbsp	Dijon mustard	25 mL
1 lb	Swiss cheese (preferably Gruyère)	500 g
¾ cup	grated Parmesan cheese (if using freshly grated Parmesan, grate cheese before proceeding with rest of recipe — see page 14)	175 mL

Serves 8

1. Fit work bowl with metal blade and, with machine running, drop garlic through opening in feed tube. Process continuously until garlic is minced.

2. Without removing garlic from the work bowl, refit bowl with medium slicing disc. Cut both kinds of onions into quarters or eighths, pack into large feed tube, and process until all onions are sliced.

3. Heat butter in a Dutch oven or large saucepan and add onion-garlic mixture. Cook, until onions are tender and fragrant — approximately 20 minutes. Stir in flour and cook without browning — about 5 minutes.

4. Stir in chicken stock and white wine and bring to a boil. Add salt and pepper, thyme and bay leaf. Cover, reduce heat and simmer gently for 30 minutes. Taste soup and adjust seasoning if necessary.

5. Heat ¼ cup/50 mL butter in a large skillet and cook 4 slices of bread until golden on each side. Remove and cook second batch in remaining butter. Spread a little mustard on each crouton.

6. Rinse work bowl and dry. Fit with shredding disc and grate Gruyère cheese using gentle pressure. Remove from work bowl and reserve.

7. Just before serving, preheat oven to 400°F/200°C. Fill 8 ovenproof

bowls with soup and arrange crouton, mustard side up, on each. Divide grated Swiss cheese among the bowls and sprinkle over crouton. Sprinkle with grated Parmesan. Bake 15 minutes until cheese melts

and bubbles. If it is not brown enough for you, turn on broiler but watch closely. It should only need 1 or 2 minutes.

Note: If you do not want to use wine, simply use more chicken stock.

Celery Soup

The flavor of celery is light and refreshing and this soup is good served hot or cold. This is a recipe we teach in our "Eat and Run" course at the cooking school as it is low in calories and easy to prepare. (If you do want to enrich it, you can add 1 cup/ 250 mL cream just before serving.)

2	onions, peeled and cut in half	2	4 cups	chicken stock, homemade (see page 46) or commercial	1 L
1	bunch celery (approximately 12 ribs)	1	1	bay leaf	1
1	potato, peeled	1	1 tsp	dried thyme	5 mL
	Handful fresh parsley			Salt and freshly ground black pepper to taste	
3 tbsp	unsalted butter	50 mL			

Serves 6 to 8

1. Fit work bowl with medium slicing disc. Fit onions into small feed tube and slice using firm pressure. Reserve.
2. Separate celery ribs. Insert a few ribs at a time into small feed tube. Exert gentle pressure and slice. Reserve separately.
3. Cut potato into quarters and fit into large feed tube. Slice using firm pressure. Reserve in cold water to prevent discoloration.
4. Refit work bowl with metal blade. Add parsley and process using on/off pulses until finely chopped. Remove and reserve.
5. In a Dutch oven or large saucepan heat butter and cook onions until they are tender and fragrant but do not brown — this should take about 5 minutes. Add celery and cook

about 5 minutes longer until it is slightly wilted. Drain potatoes and add to vegetable mixture along with most of the parsley (reserve about 1 tbsp/15 mL for the garnish) and the chicken stock. Add bay leaf, thyme and just a little salt and pepper (be very cautious with salt if you are using commercial stock). Bring to a boil and simmer gently 20 to 25 minutes or until potatoes are tender. Remove bay leaf.
6. Strain vegetables from broth and add to work bowl fitted with metal blade (do this in 1 or 2 batches depending on the size of your machine). Add about ½ cup/125 mL stock to vegetables and puree until smooth. Pour vegetable mixture back into stock and heat thoroughly. Taste and adjust seasoning if necessary.

Chinese Fish Ball Soup

On a recent trip to Taiwan, the chef who taught us Eastern regional cuisine showed us this recipe for soup. (The fish balls could also be deep fried and served as an appetizer for a pleasant variation.) This soup is very delicate and serves as a great first course even in a Western menu. In a Chinese menu, the soup would be served towards the end of the meal rather than at the beginning.

1 lb	white-fleshed fish fillets (or raw shrimp)	500 g
1	piece ginger root, size of a quarter and 1 in/2.5 cm thick, sliced and smashed	1
4	green onions, smashed	4
¾ cup	cold water	175 mL
1 tbsp	rice wine or vodka	15 mL
1	egg white	1
1 tsp	salt	5 mL
3 cups	cold water	750 mL
Soup:		
	Poaching liquid from above	
1 tsp	salt	5 mL
1 tsp	rice wine or vodka	5 mL
1 tbsp	cornstarch	15 mL
1 tbsp	cold water	15 mL
Vegetables:		
3	green onions	3
3 tbsp	vegetable or peanut oil	50 mL
8 oz	fresh spinach or other leafy, green vegetable, coarsely chopped	250 g
1 tbsp	rice wine or vodka	15 mL
½ tsp	salt	2 mL
½ tsp	oriental sesame oil	2 mL

Serves 6 to 8

1. Remove any bones from the fish and cut into 1-in/2.5-cm pieces. Pat dry. Fit work bowl with metal blade and add fish pieces.
2. Squeeze ginger and green onions in ¾ cup/175 mL cold water so that they release their flavor into the water. Remove ginger and onions and discard. Add rice wine to water.
3. Chop fish using on/off pulses and when fish is in tiny bits, slowly add flavored water through feed tube while machine is running. Add egg white and blend. Add salt and blend.
4. Place 3 cups/750 mL cold water in a large, flat pot and shape fish mixture into 1 ½-in/4-cm balls. As you make the balls, place them in the cold water. Bring water to a boil and cook until balls rise to the surface – about 5 minutes. Remove the fish balls and reserve. Strain the poaching liquid and reserve.
5. When ready to serve, place poaching liquid with other soup ingredients in a pot and bring to a boil. Add fish balls and simmer gently a few minutes until heated through.

6. Meanwhile rinse work bowl and fit with metal blade. Cut green onions into 2-in/5-cm lengths and add to bowl. Chop using on/off pulses until finely minced. Heat wok. Add oil and heat. Add chopped spinach and onions and stir-fry until vegetables are wilted. Add rice wine, salt and sesame oil and combine.

7. Place vegetables in large bowl or soup tureen. Pour fishballs and broth over top. Serve immediately.

Seafood Soup with Garlic and Ginger

This is a light, low-calorie soup that has an exceptionally delicious oriental flavor.

2	onions, peeled and quartered	2
2	cloves garlic, peeled	2
1	piece ginger root, size of a quarter and ½ in/1 cm thick, peeled	1
2	leeks, white part only, well washed	2
3 tbsp	unsalted butter	50 mL
8 oz	raw shrimps, shelled	250 g
8 oz	scallops	250 g
3 cups	chicken or fish stock, homemade (see pages 46 and 47) or commercial	750 mL
¼ tsp	saffron threads	1 mL
	Salt and freshly ground black pepper to taste	
5	green onions	5

Serves 6

1. Fit work bowl with metal blade. Add onions, garlic and ginger and chop with 4 or 5 quick on/off pulses. Remove from work bowl.

2. Refit bowl with thin or medium slicing disc. Slice leeks through the small feed tube. Remove from work bowl.

3. Heat butter in a saucepan and add onions, garlic, ginger and leeks. Cook approximately 10 minutes on gentle heat until vegetables are very tender and fragrant.

4. Meanwhile cut shrimps and scallops into approximately ½-in/1-cm pieces. Add to vegetables and cook 1 minute or until well coated with butter and vegetables.

5. Add stock and bring to a boil.

6. With the back of a spoon crush the saffron threads as much as possible and mix in a little bit of the hot stock. Add to the soup. Cook 5 minutes. Taste and season with salt and pepper.

7. Meanwhile with work bowl fitted with the slicing disc, slice the green onions through small feed tube. Add to soup. Cook 1 minute and then serve.

Soupe au Pistou

This is a very flavorful vegetable soup served with a potent sauce called pistou. It is best made when fresh basil is available but you can substitute fresh parsley. Or you can make some of the paste mixture when basil is available and then freeze it. Dried basil is not a satisfactory substitute at all.

Pistou can also be stirred into rice, served on pasta or boiled potatoes, or served as a sauce with lamb.

2	cloves garlic, peeled	2
2	onions, peeled	2
	Handful fresh parsley (without stems)	
1	28-oz/796-mL can plum tomatoes	1
2	ribs celery	2
2	carrots, peeled	2
1	zucchini	1
2	potatoes, peeled	2
¼ cup	olive oil (see page 18) or vegetable oil	50 mL
3 cups	beef stock, homemade (see page 45) or commercial	750 mL
3 cups	water	750 mL
¼ tsp	hot, red pepper flakes	1 mL
	Salt and freshly ground black pepper to taste	

1	19-oz/540-mL can cannellini beans (white kidney beans)	1
4 oz	pasta (macaroni, shells, etc.)	125 g

Pistou:

4	cloves garlic, peeled	4
3 oz	grated Parmesan cheese (if using freshly grated Parmesan, grate cheese before proceeding with rest of recipe – see page 14)	100 g
2	large handfuls fresh basil or fresh parsley leaves	2
½ cup	olive oil (see page 18)	125 mL

Serves 8 to 10

1. Fit work bowl with metal blade. With machine running, drop garlic through feed tube and process continuously until minced. Cut onions into quarters and add to work bowl. Process using on/off pulses until diced. Be careful not to overprocess. Remove onion-garlic mixture and reserve. Add parsley and process using on/off pulses until finely chopped. Remove and reserve.

2. Drain tomatoes and reserve the juice. Place tomatoes in work bowl (still fitted with metal blade) and process using on/off pulses until chopped. Reserve with the tomato juices.

3. Refit work bowl with medium slicing disc. Cut celery ribs in half lengthwise and fit into small feed tube, standing up. Slice. Without removing celery, cut carrots into quarters lengthwise and fit into small feed tube and slice. Cut zucchini into quarters lengthwise and fit into small feed tube and slice. Do the same with the potatoes, although you may have to cut them into eighths to fit the tube. The result should be that the vegetables are diced.

4. Heat oil in a Dutch oven and add onion-garlic mixture. Cook 5 minutes until mixture is fragrant and then add remaining diced vegetables. Cook, stirring, about 5 minutes, until vegetables wilt but do not brown. Add chopped tomatoes and their juices, beef stock and water. Add parsley, red pepper flakes and a little salt and pepper. Bring to a boil. Cover, reduce heat and simmer gently 35 minutes or until potatoes are tender.

5. Drain tin of beans and rinse under cold water. Add to soup and cook 15 minutes. Add pasta and cook 15 minutes longer or until pasta is tender.

6. Prepare pistou (below).

7. To serve soup, place spoonful of pistou on each serving as garnish. Pass remaining pistou at table.

Pistou:

1. Rinse and dry work bowl and fit with metal blade. With machine running, drop garlic through feed tube and process until minced.

2. Cut any rind off cheese, cut cheese into chunks and add to work bowl. Process using on/off pulses until grated.

3. Add basil or parsley and process using on/off pulses until chopped. Add oil through feed tube and process until well combined.

Cold Carrot Soup with Ginger

Although fresh ginger root used to be hard to find in our markets, it is now fairly common. Store it at room temperature or, if you are not using it within a few weeks, peel it and store it in a jar of sherry or brandy.

1	medium-sized onion, peeled and quartered	1	3 tbsp	raw rice	50 mL
1	clove garlic, peeled	1	4 cups	chicken stock, homemade (see page 46) or commercial	1 L
1	piece fresh ginger root, size of a quarter and ½ in/1 cm thick, peeled	1	1 tsp	salt (more or less to taste)	5 mL
3 tbsp	unsalted butter	50 mL	¼ tsp	freshly ground pepper	1 mL
2 lb	carrots, peeled (approximately 10 medium-sized)	1 kg	1 cup	unflavored yogurt	250 mL
			4	green onions	4

Serves 8

1. Fit work bowl with metal blade. Add onions, garlic and ginger and process with 3 or 4 on/off pulses until vegetables are finely chopped.
2. Melt butter in Dutch oven or large saucepan and add chopped vegetables. Cook until tender and fragrant but do not brown.
3. Meanwhile refit work bowl with medium slicing disc. Slice carrots through small feed tube and add to pot. Add rice and chicken stock. Add salt (depending on saltiness of stock) and pepper. Cover and bring to a boil. Reduce heat and simmer gently until carrots are very tender – about 30 minutes.
4. Refit work bowl with metal blade. Strain or lift vegetables from broth and puree vegetables in 2 to 4 batches depending on size of machine.
5. Return puree to broth and combine well. Refrigerate until well chilled or overnight.
6. Stir in yogurt, taste and adjust seasoning if necessary.
7. Fit clean work bowl with thin or medium slicing disc. Cut green onions into thirds of equal lengths. Fit tightly into small feed tube. Slice. Garnish each serving of soup with some green onions.

Main Courses

The main course should always be the feature attraction of the meal, so when you plan a menu you should choose your main course first and design the other courses around it.

It is actually very hard to plan good menus. When I was doing my chef training our instructors would give us exercises in menu planning that included planning twelve-course dinners. But no matter how perfect I thought my menus were, if I looked at them a few days later I could always find a flaw. It was very frustrating, although I have to admit that after those exercises, three- and four-course dinners were a breeze!

Basically you should aim for variety and balance in your menus. If your main course has a sauce, for example, the vegetables should be relatively plain, but if the main course is plain, then you can go all out with the vegetables. If your main course is white (sole with a cream sauce, for example), add color to the meal with the vegetables and try not to serve a bland-colored appetizer or dessert. If the main course is rich and contains cream, do not serve a heavily cream-laden dish elsewhere in the meal. And if the main course is "wrapped," i.e. served in a crepe or a crust, then nothing else in the menu should be.

One exception to this "no repetition" rule is the theme dinner. I have heard of dinners on St. Patrick's Day where everything served is green; dinners where every course contains potatoes, or dinners where every course is wrapped. But these are unusual exceptions.

Good menu planning requires skill, time and experience, but the result will be a special and memorable meal that your guests will truly appreciate.

Salmon Steaks with Butter Provençale

Salmon or halibut steaks can be barbecued as well as broiled or pan-fried. Because they are small enough to flip with a spatula, they do not fall apart too badly when cooked directly on a grill. If you want to barbecue large pieces, invest in a fish grill to make turning easier. I love barbecued fish, but this also tastes good broiled or pan-fried.

The butter can be prepared ahead and frozen or refrigerated until ready to serve. It is also great with steak or lamb.

Butter Provençale:		
1	clove garlic, peeled	1
1	green onion, cut into 1-in/2.5-cm lengths	1
	Small handful fresh parsley	
½ tsp	salt	2 mL
¼ tsp	freshly ground pepper	1 mL

¾ cup	unsalted butter, left at room temperature for 30 minutes before using	175 mL
1 tbsp	lemon juice	15 mL
6	salmon steaks (6 to 8 oz/175 to 250 g each and 1 in/2.5 cm thick)	6

Serves 6

1. Prepare Butter Provençale.
2. If you are barbecuing or broiling fish, brush fish with a little vegetable oil. Preheat barbecue or grill for 3 or 4 minutes. Brush grill or broiler rack with oil. Barbecue or broil fish 5 minutes on each side. If you are pan-frying fish, add approximately ¼ cup/50 mL unsalted butter or oil to a skillet. Cook fish on medium-high heat for 5 minutes per side.
3. To serve, slice butter ¼ in/5 mm thick. Place 2 slices of butter on each hot fish steak. Serve immediately.

Butter Provençale:

1. Fit work bowl with metal blade. With machine running, drop garlic through feed tube and process until chopped. Add green onion and parsley and chop with 5 or 6 on/off pulses. Add salt and pepper.
2. Cut butter into 8 even-sized cubes and add to work bowl. Process on/off until butter is chopped and then continuously until butter and vegetables are creamed together. Add lemon juice and blend into butter.
3. Remove butter to a piece of waxed paper. Fold over paper to enclose butter and use back of French knife or heavy ruler to force butter into cylindrical shape (see diagram). Tuck in edges of waxed paper, roll up and refrigerate.

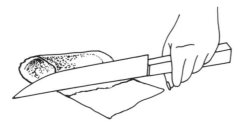

64

Poached Chicken Breasts Tonnato (see page 68).

Fish Cutlets with Dill Butter

You can use frozen fish in this dish, but I always prefer to use fresh if it is available. The dill butter serves as a delicious sauce and provides a pretty garnish for something that otherwise might be very plain. This butter freezes very well, so you could double the recipe and have some on hand. It is also very good with veal or lamb chops.

Dill Butter:		
	Large handful fresh dill	
	Handful fresh parsley	
½ tsp	salt	2 mL
pinch	freshly ground pepper	pinch
½ cup	unsalted butter, left at room temperature for 30 minutes	125 mL
2 tsp	lemon juice	10 mL
Fish Mixture:		
8	slices French or Italian bread	8

1½ lb	raw fish fillets (salmon, whitefish, sole, halibut, snapper, etc.)	750 g
¾ cup	cream, unflavored yogurt or sour cream	175 mL
1 tsp	salt	5 mL
¼ tsp	freshly ground pepper	1 mL
pinch	cayenne pepper	pinch
pinch	freshly ground nutmeg	pinch
⅓ cup	unsalted butter or vegetable oil	75 mL
Serves 6		

1. Prepare Dill Butter.
2. Fit work bowl with metal blade. Cut crusts off bread and reserve for another purpose. Cut bread into cubes and place in work bowl. Process until you have fine breadcrumbs. Reserve ¾ cup/175 mL crumbs for patties. Place remaining crumbs in a dish for breading.
3. Pat fish dry and cut into 2-in/5-cm cubes. Add to work bowl and process with 4 or 5 on/off pulses until fish is coarsely chopped. Add breadcrumbs, cream and seasonings. Process until well mixed.
4. Remove mixture from work bowl and shape into 6 even-sized patties. Dip each into reserved breadcrumbs and pat in gently. Refrigerate until ready to cook.
5. Heat butter or oil in a heavy skillet and add fish patties. Cook approximately 8 minutes on each side on medium-high heat. Place on a serving platter and slice dill butter ½ in/1 cm thick. Arrange 1 or 2 slices of dill butter on each cutlet.

Dill Butter:
1. Prepare butter ahead of time. Fit work bowl with metal blade. Add dill and parsley and chop on/off until finely chopped.
2. Cut butter into cubes. Add salt, pepper and butter cubes to work bowl. Process with 5 or 6 on/off pulses until butter is in small bits. Process continuously until butter is creamed. If necessary, scrape down sides of work bowl with a spatula a few times. Add lemon juice and blend into butter.
3. Remove butter to a piece of waxed paper and shape butter roughly into a log. Roll up tightly and refrigerate a few hours or freeze 1 hour. Butter should be firm.

Chicken Stuffed with Chicken Mousse (see page 70).

Spicy Szechuan Shrimp

You can serve this as part of a larger Chinese menu or with steamed rice for an easy, simple dinner. If you do not like hot foods, simply reduce or omit the red pepper flakes and the hot chili sauce. And remember to eat starch (rice, bread, etc.), which will absorb the heat rather than spread it through your mouth the way a liquid will.

1 lb	raw shrimp, peeled and deveined	500 g	1 tsp	sugar	5 mL
1 tbsp	cornstarch	15 mL	½ tsp	salt	2 mL
2	cloves garlic, peeled	2	3 tbsp	ketchup	50 mL
1	piece fresh ginger root, size of a quarter and ½ in/1 cm thick, peeled	1	1 tbsp	hot Chinese chili paste, optional	15 mL
			1 tsp	oriental sesame oil	5 mL
			1 cup	fresh or frozen peas	250 mL
3	green onions	3	1	10-oz/284-mL can bamboo shoots, drained	1
½ tsp	hot, red pepper flakes, optional	2 mL			
2 tbsp	rice wine or vodka	25 mL	4 cups	peanut or vegetable oil	1 L
2 tbsp	soy sauce	25 mL			

Serves 3 or 4

1. Combine shrimps in a bowl with cornstarch. Stir well to coat.

2. Fit work bowl with metal blade. With machine running, drop garlic through the feed tube and process until chopped. Drop ginger through the tube and process with garlic until chopped.

3. Cut green onions into 1-in/2.5-cm lengths and add to work bowl. Chop with 5 or 6 on/off pulses until finely chopped and mixed. Mix in red pepper flakes. Remove to a small bowl and reserve.

4. With work bowl still fitted with metal blade add rice wine, soy sauce, sugar, salt, ketchup, chili paste and sesame oil. Process until blended. Remove to a small bowl and reserve.

5. Place peas in a bowl and reserve. If the bamboo shoots are not already sliced or julienned, slice or julienne them in Cuisinart® and then reserve with peas.

6. Heat a wok. Add oil and heat to 400°F/200°C. Add shrimps carefully and cook only 2 or 3 minutes until they are almost cooked through. When you put them into the oil, stir gently to separate.

7. Remove shrimps with a lifter-strainer and reserve. Remove all but 3 tbsp/50 mL oil from wok (strain excess oil and refrigerate to be used again) and heat.

8. Add garlic-ginger-onion-chili mixture and cook 30 seconds or until very fragrant. Add peas and bamboo shoots and stir to coat. Add reserved sauce mixture and bring to a boil. Return shrimp to wok and stir well. Heat thoroughly. Serve immediately with steamed rice.

Chinese Barbecued Chicken

This dish can be baked or barbecued and can also be prepared with pork chops or ribs. Marinate the chicken for at least 1 hour at room temperature, or overnight in the refrigerator if possible.

3	cloves garlic, peeled	3	1 tbsp	rice wine or vodka	15 mL
1	piece fresh ginger root, size of a quarter and 1 in/2.5 cm thick, peeled	1	1 tsp	salt	5 mL
½ cup	ketchup	125 mL	¼ tsp	ground anise or 5-spice powder, optional	1 mL
2 tbsp	hoisin sauce	25 mL	1	4-lb/2-kg chicken cut into serving pieces or 6 legs and thighs or 6 chicken breasts	1
3 tbsp	honey	50 mL			
1 tbsp	hot Chinese chili paste	15 mL			

Serves 6

1. Fit work bowl with metal blade. With machine running, drop garlic and ginger through the feed tube. Add ketchup, hoisin sauce, honey, chili paste, rice wine, salt and anise. Process until ingredients are well blended.

2. Place marinade ingredients and chicken pieces in a large plastic bag and press out the air. Tie securely. Massage marinade into the chicken pieces. Allow to marinate at least 1 hour at room temperature or longer in the refrigerator.

3. Preheat oven to 375°F/190°C. Arrange chicken pieces skin side down in a greased baking dish. Bake 20 minutes. Turn chicken and bake 20 minutes longer or until chicken is cooked through. If you are barbecuing, be careful that the chicken does not burn, as the honey and ketchup can darken quickly. Chicken usually requires 15 to 20 minutes a side on the barbecue, but you may have to turn pieces often to prevent burning. (When barbecuing, you could also prebake chicken for 20 minutes and then finish on the barbecue.)

Poached Chicken Breasts Tonnato

The tuna dressing used here is a famous Italian sauce for cold, thinly sliced veal. Made with chicken it is faster and less expensive to prepare but just as delicious. The sauce can also be served with poached turkey breasts. This is a wonderful dish for a brunch or summer dinner. The dressing is also great on vegetable salads made with potatoes, rice, green beans or broccoli.

1	carrot, peeled and trimmed	1	1 tsp	dry mustard	5 mL
1	rib celery	1	pinch	cayenne pepper	pinch
1	onion, peeled and quartered	1	½ tsp	salt (or more to taste)	2 mL
	Few sprigs fresh parsley		1½ cups	corn oil	375 mL
½ cup	dry white wine	125 mL	1	7-oz/184-mL can flaked white tuna	1
3 cups	water	750 mL	4	anchovy fillets, drained	4
3	whole chicken breasts, split, skinned and boned (save skin and bones)	3	½ cup	sour cream or unflavored yogurt	125 mL
Tonnato Dressing:			**Garnish:**		
1	egg, at room temperature	1		Lemon slices	
	Juice of 1 lemon (approximately ¼ cup/50 mL)			Black olives, well-drained	
				Capers, well-drained	
				Chopped fresh parsley	
			Serves 6		

1. Fit work bowl with medium slicing disc. Insert carrot into small feed tube and slice. Slice celery and onion the same way.

2. Place vegetables, parsley, wine, water and chicken bones and skin in a flat, deep skillet and bring to a boil. Skim off any scum that rises to the surface and cook 30 minutes.

3. Arrange chicken breasts on top of vegetables and bones. Cover with a piece of parchment paper or waxed paper and poach gently 10 to 15 minutes. Do not overcook.

4. Remove chicken, drain on paper towels and cool. Strain broth and use as chicken stock.

5. Prepare Tonnato Dressing (below).

6. Arrange chicken breasts on serving platter. Spoon tuna dressing over chicken breasts. Surround outside edge of platter with lemon slices. Spoon black olives between chicken breasts and sprinkle top of each chicken piece with parsley and capers. Serve immediately at room temperature or refrigerate until ready to serve.

Tonnato Dressing:

1. Wipe work bowl clean and fit with metal blade. Add egg, lemon juice, mustard, cayenne, salt and ¼ cup/ 50 mL oil. Blend ingredients for 3 or 4 seconds.

2. With machine running, slowly pour remaining oil into the egg mixture through the opening in the feed tube. Mixture should thicken into mayonnaise consistency. If it does not thicken, see page 123.

3. Add tuna and anchovies and blend in until smooth. Blend in sour cream. Taste and season as necessary.

Chicken Breasts Diable

This is a flavorful, easy chicken recipe that can be prepared two ways. If I think that I want something low calorie, I bake it; if I am feeling very thin, I sauté it in butter. Liver, veal chops or veal cutlets can also be prepared this way.

10	slices French or Italian bread	10	1 tbsp	oil	15 mL
			1 tsp	salt	5 mL
1	clove garlic, peeled	1	¼ tsp	freshly ground pepper	1 mL
	Handful fresh parsley		1 tbsp	lemon juice	15 mL
½ cup	Dijon mustard	125 mL	3	chicken breasts, split, skinned and boned	3
1 tbsp	Worcestershire sauce	15 mL			
¼ tsp	Tabasco sauce	1 mL	**Serves 6**		

1. Cut crusts from bread and reserve for another purpose. Cut bread into cubes. Fit work bowl with metal blade and add bread (you may have to do this in 2 batches, depending on the size of your machine). Process bread on/off at first and then run continuously until fine crumbs are formed. Remove from work bowl and place in a large, flat dish or cookie sheet.

2. With machine running, drop garlic through the feed tube and chop until fine. Add parsley to work bowl with garlic and chop with 5 or 6 on/ off pulses until finely chopped. Add mustard, Worcestershire sauce, Tabasco, oil, salt, pepper and lemon juice. Blend ingredients together. Remove to a flat dish.

3. Brush or dip chicken breasts into mustard mixture and then dip into breadcrumbs. Pat breadcrumbs into chicken firmly. Arrange on a cookie sheet, to dry and refrigerate until ready to cook.

4. If you are going to bake the chicken, preheat oven to 400°F/200°C. Lightly oil a cookie sheet and place it in the oven for 5 minutes. Arrange chicken breasts on hot pan and bake 10 to 15 minutes per side. If you want to pan-fry the chicken, melt 3 tbsp/50 mL unsalted butter or vegetable oil in a large skillet and cook chicken 8 to 10 minutes on each side or until golden brown and cooked through.

Chicken Stuffed with Chicken Mousse

This recipe looks more difficult than it is. When a chicken is boned completely and stuffed this way it is called a ballotine when served hot and a galantine when served cold. Bone the chicken as explained below — it's a lot like undressing a chicken carcass and really is amazingly easy. The mousse mixture itself can be used as a stuffing or baked in a loaf pan or soufflé cups. Serve it hot with the lemon butter sauce or cold with mayonnaise as an appetizer.

Chicken Mousse:

	Small handful fresh parsley	
¼ cup	toasted pistachio nuts	50 mL
1	large chicken breast, split, skinned and boned	1
2	egg whites, cold	2
¾ cup	whipping cream, cold	175 mL
1½ tsp	salt	7 mL
½ tsp	dried tarragon	2 mL
¼ tsp	freshly ground pepper	1 mL
10 oz	fresh spinach, cooked, squeezed dry and coarsely chopped	284 g
4 oz	cooked ham, cut into julienne strips	125 g

Chicken:

1	large chicken (4 to 5 lb/2 to 2.5 kg)	1

	Salt and freshly ground black pepper to taste	
2 tbsp	Cognac or brandy	25 mL
¼ cup	unsalted butter, melted	50 mL

Lemon Butter Sauce:

	Peel of 1 lemon	
½ tsp	salt	2 mL
2	shallots, peeled	2
½ cup	dry white wine	125 mL
½ cup	chicken stock, homemade (see page 46) or commercial	125 mL
¾ cup	whipping cream	175 mL

Garnish:

Fresh watercress

Serves 8

1. Prepare Chicken Mousse.
2. Place chicken on cutting board with breast side up and legs away from you. Cut feet off chicken with cleaver and remove wings.
3. With a sharp boning knife cut through skin down center of breast bone. Carefully cut and scrape meat from breast bone, one side at a time, right down to the base.
4. Very gently cut carcass from bottom skin, trying not to puncture skin. Cut through joint connecting thigh to carcass to free carcass completely. Remove carcass.
5. Remove thigh bone by scraping meat from bone. Do this on the inside, so that once again you leave the skin intact. Continue down past the knee joint into the leg, scraping

70

the meat away from the bone until the bone comes free. There will be a few holes where the wings were, but don't worry. Everything will bake together. Save carcass and all bones for stock.

6. Sprinkle chicken with salt and pepper and 1 tbsp/15 mL Cognac. Spread cold spinach mousse evenly over the chicken and into the legs. Then top with plain mousse. Arrange julienne slices of ham lengthwise over mousse and sprinkle with parsley and pistachios.

7. Reshape chicken as best you can. With a trussing needle and kitchen thread, sew chicken where you cut it. Tie at 2-in/5-cm intervals to create a roll. I usually tuck the legs in against the body of the chicken and tie in place.

8. Preheat oven to 375°F/190°C. Place chicken on a buttered roasting rack in a roasting pan. Combine remaining Cognac (1 tbsp/15 mL) with melted butter and brush all over chicken. Roast chicken 1¼ to 1½ hours, basting every 20 minutes.

9. While the chicken is roasting, fit clean work bowl with metal blade. Pat lemon peel dry. Cut into 1-in/2.5-cm pieces. With machine running, add peel and salt through the tube. Process until chopped (don't worry if it isn't too fine, as you will strain sauce before serving).

10. Add shallots and process until chopped.

11. When chicken is ready, remove to a carving board and allow to rest 10 minutes before carving. Discard any excess fat from roasting pan and place pan on heat. Add lemon peel and shallot mixture.

12. Add wine and chicken stock and deglaze pan by scraping any bits of chicken off the bottom into the liq-uid. Cook over high heat, and reduce liquid to about ¼ cup/50 mL.

13. Add whipping cream and cook until sauce thickens slightly. Strain.

14. Slice chicken and serve with sauce.

Chicken Mousse:

1. Fit work bowl with metal blade. Add parsley to work bowl and process with 5 or 6 on/off pulses until chopped. Remove and reserve.

2. Add pistachio nuts to work bowl still fitted with metal blade. Process with 3 or 4 on/off pulses until coarsely chopped. Remove and reserve.

3. Cut chicken breast meat into 2-in/5-cm cubes. Pat dry with paper towels. Add to work bowl still fitted with metal blade. Chop with 9 or 10 on/off pulses until coarsely chopped.

4. Add egg whites and process with chicken until pureed. Scrape down sides of bowl.

5. Add whipping cream through the feed tube while the machine is running. Process until blended, but do not overprocess. Add salt, tarragon and pepper. Blend.

6. Remove half of mousse, taste and adjust seasoning if necessary. Refrigerate.

7. To other half of mousse in work bowl add cooked spinach and process until well mixed. Taste and adjust seasoning if necessary. Refrigerate.

8. Reserve ham, nuts and parsley, and refrigerate chicken mousse until ready to assemble.

Note: If you want to bring a platter to the table, surround the chicken slices with fresh watercress for a beautiful presentation.

Chicken Curry

This is a dish I teach in the "Eat and Run" course at the school because it is fast and low in calories, but has a wonderful flavor. Serve with a rice pilaf and raita, a yogurt salad (see page 122).

1 tsp	ground cumin	5 mL		6	onions, peeled and quartered	6
2 tbsp	ground coriander	25 mL		2 tbsp	vegetable oil or clarified butter	25 mL
1 tsp	turmeric	5 mL				
1½ tsp	salt	7 mL		3	whole chicken breasts, skinned, boned and cut into 2-in/5-cm cubes	3
½ tsp	ground cinnamon	2 mL				
¼ tsp	ground cloves	1 mL				
1 tsp	ground cardamom	5 mL		½ cup	tomato juice	125 mL
1 tsp	cayenne pepper (more or less to taste)	5 mL		**Garnish:**	Sprigs fresh coriander, if available, or parsley	
2	cloves garlic, peeled	2				
1	piece fresh ginger root, size of a quarter and 1 in/2.5 cm thick, peeled	1		**Serves 6**		

1. Fit work bowl with metal blade. Add cumin, coriander, turmeric, salt, cinnamon, cloves, cardamom and cayenne. Process 3 seconds until blended. Remove and reserve.

2. With machine running, drop garlic and ginger through feed tube and process until finely chopped. Remove and reserve.

3. With work bowl still fitted with metal blade, chop onions in 2 batches using 5 or 6 on/off pulses. Remove and reserve.

4. Heat oil in a large, deep skillet that has a cover. Add garlic-ginger mixture to oil. Cook 30 seconds or until just fragrant. Add dry spice mixture and cook 30 seconds, but stir constantly and make sure it does not start to burn.

5. Add onions, reduce heat and cook 7 to 8 minutes or until onions begin to soften. Do not brown. If onions get very dry add ¼ cup/50 mL water and continue cooking.

6. Add cubes of chicken and stir until they are well coated with the onion-spice mixture. Add tomato juice and bring to the boil. Reduce heat, cover and cook at medium heat for 10 minutes or until chicken pieces are cooked through. Garnish with fresh coriander. Serve with steamed rice or rice pilaf.

Spicy Barbecued Ribs

This is my version of a "secret" barbecue sauce I once tasted in a Boston restaurant. It is probably not nearly the same, but it tastes terrific anyway. I think the secret of tender barbecued ribs is precooking the ribs so that they don't have to be barbecued too long, where they tend to dry out a little. If you are buying side ribs buy a little extra, as they are not quite as meaty.

4 lb	back ribs, cut into 6 strips	2 kg	1 tsp	ground cumin	5 mL
1	medium-sized onion, peeled	1	2 tbsp	Dijon mustard	25 mL
1	bay leaf	1	½ tsp	cayenne pepper	2 mL
3	whole cloves	3	½ tsp	freshly ground pepper	2 mL
1	lemon	1	pinch	ground cloves	pinch
2 tbsp	brown sugar	25 mL	¼ cup	cider vinegar	50 mL
2	onions, peeled and quartered	2	2 tbsp	Worcestershire sauce	25 mL
2	cloves garlic, peeled	2	1 tsp	Tabasco sauce	5 mL
	Handful fresh parsley or fresh cilantro		2 cups	ketchup	500 mL
2 tbsp	molasses	25 mL	1 cup	beef stock, homemade (see page 45) or commercial	250 mL

Serves 4 to 6

1. Place ribs in a large pot and cover with cold water. Bring to a boil, skim off any scum that rises to the surface and reduce heat to a simmer.
2. Prepare an "onion clouté" by sticking a bay leaf to the onion with the 3 whole cloves. Add to pot.
3. Cook ribs 45 minutes. Drain well. Cool.
4. Fit work bowl with metal blade. Cut rind off lemon, pat dry, and add to work bowl with sugar. Process continuously until rind is chopped. Place in a saucepan.
5. Juice lemon and add juice to peel and sugar.
6. Add onions, garlic and parsley to work bowl still fitted with metal blade. Chop using on/off technique. Add to peel and sugar.
7. Add remaining ingredients to saucepan and bring to the boil. Cook for 10 minutes. Cool.
8. When ribs and sauce have cooled, place in a plastic bag. Marinate in the refrigerator for a few hours or up to 2 days.
9. When ready to cook, preheat the barbecue. Brush grill with oil and heat to prevent sticking. Arrange ribs on grill and barbecue 10 to 15 minutes per side. Brush with sauce as ribs cook.
10. Boil any excess sauce to serve with ribs, for 5 minutes. Serve immediately.

Note: You can also bake these ribs after precooking in a 375°F/190°C oven for 30 minutes. Baste every 10 minutes.

Tex-Mex Chicken Crepes

These crepes are a cross between French crepes and tortillas, but they are much easier to prepare than tortillas. They also taste great spread with jam and cream cheese.

Crepes:		
4	eggs	4
¾ cup	yellow cornmeal	175 mL
¾ cup	all-purpose flour	175 mL
1 tsp	salt	5 mL
1 tbsp	sugar	15 mL
1¼ cups	beer	300 mL
3 tbsp	unsalted butter, melted	50 mL

Filling and Topping:		
8 oz	medium Cheddar cheese, cold	250 g
8 oz	Farmer's or Brick cheese, cold	250 g
	Handful fresh cilantro or fresh parsley	
1 cup	black pitted olives, well-drained	250 mL
1	4-oz/can chopped green chili peppers (medium hot)	113 g

3 cups	shredded cooked chicken (or turkey or ham)	750 mL

Sauce:		
2	cloves garlic, peeled	2
2	onions, peeled and quartered	2
1	red pepper	1
1	green pepper	1
3 tbsp	vegetable oil	50 mL
2	28-oz/796-mL cans tomatoes (not plum tomatoes), partially drained	2
¼ tsp	hot, red pepper flakes	1 mL
1 tsp	chili powder	5 mL

Serves 8

1. Fit work bowl with metal blade. Add eggs, cornmeal, flour, salt and sugar and blend until smooth. Scrape down sides of work bowl if necessary.
2. Add beer and blend well.
3. Add melted butter and process until blended. Transfer to a bowl. Cover with plastic wrap and allow to rest at room temperature for 1 hour (or longer in the refrigerator). Prepare filling and sauce while crepe batter is resting.
4. Fit clean work bowl with shredding disc. Cut cheese to fit large or small feed tube and grate Cheddar and Farmer's cheese. Remove from work bowl, mix cheeses together and reserve 2 cups/500 mL for the topping and the remaining for the filling.
5. Refit work bowl with metal blade. Add cilantro or parsley and chop with 5 or 6 on/off pulses. Combine with cheese for the filling.

6. Add olives to work bowl. Chop with 3 or 4 on/off pulses. Add to cheese mixture for the filling.

7. Add green chilies and shredded chicken to cheese mixture.

8. To prepare sauce, wipe work bowl dry and fit with metal blade. Drop garlic through feed tube and process until chopped. Add onions and process with 5 or 6 on/off pulses until coarsely chopped. Remove and reserve.

9. Cut peppers in half and remove ribs and seeds. Cut into 2-in/5-cm cubes. Add to work bowl and chop with 3 or 4 on/off pulses until coarsely chopped. Reserve.

10. Heat oil in a saucepan and add onion mixture. Cook, without browning, until tender and fragrant. Add peppers and cook a few minutes longer.

11. Add tomatoes to work bowl and process just until chopped. Add to saucepan. Add red pepper flakes and chili powder. Cook 30 minutes or until sauce begins to thicken. Taste and adjust seasoning. Stir ½ cup/125 mL sauce into filling mixture.

12. To prepare crepes, heat 1 tbsp/ 15 mL butter in a 8-in/20-cm crepe or omelet pan. Add ¼ cup/50 mL batter and cook until browned. Turn and cook on second side. This is a test crepe. If crepe sticks, rub sticking spot with oil and salt.

13. When pan is ready, pour ¼ cup/ 50 mL batter into pan and swirl to cover the bottom. Pour any excess batter back into batter bowl. Cook until crepe is browned on bottom. Flip and cook second side for 30 seconds (second side never browns as well).

14. Repeat until all batter is used. Stack crepes as they are cooked. You should have at least 16 crepes.

15. To assemble, divide filling among crepes and fill the less attractive side. Roll up. Place crepes into a large buttered baking dish in 1 layer. Pour tomato sauce over the top and spread evenly. Sprinkle with reserved 2 cups/500 mL cheese.

16. Before serving preheat oven to 350°F/180°C. Bake 35 to 45 minutes or until heated through and bubbling.

Lamb Chops with Rosemary Butter

Flavored butters (or compound butters) make delicious sauces and beautiful garnishes for plain grilled, broiled or barbecued foods. This rosemary butter is especially good with lamb, but could also be used with halibut steaks.

Rosemary Butter:		
	Small handful fresh parsley	
2	green onions, cut into 2-in/5-cm pieces	2
2 tsp	dried rosemary (2 tbsp/25 mL fresh)	10 mL
1 tsp	salt	5 mL
¼ tsp	freshly ground pepper	1 mL

¾ cup	unsalted butter, left at room temperature for 30 minutes	175 mL
1 tbsp	lemon juice	15 mL
12	lamb chops, preferably rib, 3 oz/100 g each	12
2 tbsp	vegetable oil	25 mL

Serves 6

1. Prepare Rosemary Butter at least a few hours ahead of time.
2. Cook lamb chops on top of the stove, under broiler or on barbecue. If using a skillet, heat pan with the oil and cook chops on medium-high heat about 5 minutes per side if chops are 1 in/2.5 cm thick and you like them medium rare. If you are broiling the chops, preheat broiler and heat broiler pan brushed with the oil. Place chops on broiler pan and broil about 4 in/10 cm from heat 5 minutes or longer on each side. If you are barbecuing chops, brush grill with oil and heat thoroughly. Arrange chops on grill and barbecue 5 or 6 minutes on each side.
3. Just before chops are ready, remove butter from refrigerator and unwrap. Slice into ¼-in/5-mm slices. Place 2 slices on each chop just before serving. The butter will melt into a moist, delicious sauce.

Rosemary Butter:
1. Fit work bowl with metal blade. Add parsley, green onions and rosemary to work bowl. Chop with 5 or 6 on/off pulses. Add salt and pepper.
2. Cut butter into cubes and add. Chop butter into tiny pieces with a few on/off pulses. Then blend continuously until smooth. If necessary, scrape down sides of work bowl with spatula a few times. Blend in lemon juice.
3. Remove butter to a piece of waxed paper. Roll up butter in a cylinder as for refrigerator cookies. Refrigerate a few hours or freeze 1 hour.

Note: Flavored butters can be frozen for a few months, so you can make extra to have on hand.

Lamb Chops with Salsa Verde

This traditional Italian "green sauce" is usually served with plain boiled meats or plain cooked fish, but I think it tastes great with lamb. The sauce should be served at room temperature but can be prepared well ahead of time. The lamb can be pan-fried, broiled or barbecued.

Salsa Verde:

2	slices French or Italian bread	2
3 tbsp	red wine vinegar	50 mL
3	cloves garlic, peeled	3
1 tbsp	capers, well-drained	15 mL
6	anchovy fillets	6
2	large handfuls fresh parsley	2
2	green onions, cut into 1-in/2.5-cm lengths	2
¼ tsp	freshly ground pepper	1 mL
½ cup	olive oil (see page 18)	125 mL
6	leg or shoulder lamb chops (approximately 8 oz/250 g each) or 12 smaller rib chops (approximately 4 oz/125 g each)	6
1 tbsp	vegetable oil	15 mL

Serves 6

1. Prepare Salsa Verde.
2. To cook the lamb chops, brush a large skillet with oil. Heat. Cook chops about 6 minutes per side (rare).
3. Before serving, bring sauce to room temperature. Place a spoonful of sauce on each chop and serve the rest at the table.

Salsa Verde:

1. Break bread into small pieces and place in a bowl. Add vinegar to bread and allow to rest a few minutes to moisten.
2. Fit work bowl with metal blade. With machine running, add garlic through the feed tube and process until chopped.
3. Add capers and anchovies and process until finely chopped. Add parsley and green onions and process on/off until finely chopped.
4. Add pepper and bread. Process until blended.
5. With machine running, slowly add oil through the feed tube. Refrigerate sauce if prepared ahead of time.

Butterflied Leg of Lamb

For this recipe you can use New Zealand lamb or domestic spring lamb. You can bake it, broil it or barbecue it. Marinades are usually used to tenderize, preserve and flavor meats, and generally you should marinate foods for at least 24 hours in order for the marinade to have any real effect on the meat. But because a leg of lamb is usually a tender cut, in this case you do not have to worry. Even if you have only a few hours, this mixture will flavor the meat delicately and form a great crust on the outside.

4	cloves garlic, peeled	4	½ tsp	ground cumin	2 mL	
1	large onion, peeled and quartered	1	1 tsp	ground coriander	5 mL	
1	hot banana pepper, fresh or preserved	1	½ tsp	freshly ground pepper	2 mL	
¼ cup	Dijon mustard	50 mL	1	leg of lamb, boned (approximately 4 to 6 lb/2 to 3 kg after boning)	1	
2 tbsp	lemon juice	25 mL				
2 tbsp	balsamic or red wine vinegar	25 mL				
¼ cup	vegetable oil	50 mL				
1 tbsp	Worcestershire sauce	15 mL				

Serves 8 to 10

1. Fit work bowl with metal blade. Drop garlic through feed tube while the machine is running and process until finely chopped. Add onion and chop with 4 or 5 on/off pulses.

2. Carefully halve and seed the hot banana pepper (if you have sensitive skin, wear plastic gloves when handling hot pepper). Cut into pieces and add to garlic and onions. Process until finely chopped and well mixed.

3. Add mustard, lemon juice, vinegar, oil, Worcestershire, cumin, coriander and pepper. Process until blended.

4. Trim excess fat from lamb and place in a plastic bag (I use the white kitchen garbage bags). Add marinade and massage mixture into lamb. Press air out of bag and tie securely. Marinate at room temperature for 1 hour, or up to 2 days in the refrigerator.

5. If you are cooking this on the barbecue, have the heat medium-high. Brush the grill with vegetable oil and preheat grill so lamb will not stick. Barbecue 15 to 20 minutes on each side (for rare). The lamb will cook quickly because it is relatively thin. You can also broil the lamb the same length of time, about 6 in/15 cm from the broiler. Or you can roast the lamb, without turning, 40 minutes at 375°F/ 190°C.

6. Allow meat to rest about 5 minutes before carving and then carve meat on the diagonal.

Veal Scallops with Lime-Ginger Butter

The lime and ginger in the butter go perfectly with the delicate flavor of the veal. As with all compound butters, it can be made ahead and frozen. This butter is also great with veal or calf liver, cooked quickly on the barbecue or pan-fried. You could also prepare this with chicken or turkey breasts (cut into scallops).

	Lime-Ginger Butter:	
2	pieces fresh ginger root, size of a quarter and 1 in/2.5 cm thick, peeled	2
3	green onions, cut into 1-in/2.5-cm lengths	3
½ tsp	salt	2 mL
¼ tsp	freshly ground pepper	1 mL

¾ cup	unsalted butter	175 mL
6 tbsp	lime juice	100 mL
6 tbsp	olive oil (see page 18)	100 mL
1½ lb	veal scallops, very thinly sliced or pounded	750 g
⅓ cup	unsalted butter	75 mL

Serves 6

1. Prepare Lime-Ginger Butter by fitting work bowl with metal blade. Cut piece of ginger in half and drop through feed tube with machine running. Process until chopped. Remove half the chopped ginger and reserve.

2. Add green onions to work bowl and process with 5 or 6 on/off pulses. Add salt and pepper.

3. Cut butter into 2-in/5-cm cubes and add to herbs. Process on/off until creamed. Add 3 tbsp/50 mL lime juice. Transfer butter to a sheet of waxed paper and form into a log (see page 64). Wrap well and refrigerate or freeze.

4. Place reserved chopped ginger in a flat dish with remaining lime juice and olive oil. Add veal scallops and marinate for 1 hour or until ready to cook.

5. Just before serving, heat butter in a large skillet and pat veal dry. Cook veal 1 to 2 minutes per side, depending on thickness of scallops. Cook in 2 or 3 batches if necessary and keep cooked veal warm in a 200°F/100°C oven.

6. Slice butter ¼ in/5 mm thick and place a few slices on each serving. Serve immediately.

Veal Prince Orloff

This is one of the most practical and popular of all the party dishes that we teach at the school. Although the recipe is long, it is not difficult and the results are elegant and delicious. It also makes a perfect buffet main course as the meat is presliced and guests can help themselves. And it can be made ahead and frozen.

Although I usually chop all the onions for the entire recipe at one time, I am organizing this recipe in separate steps so it will be easier to visualize the entire dish. The veal is cooked ahead of time and cooled so that it can be sliced thinly. It is then spread with a thick onion puree (soubise), covered in a silky velouté sauce and sprinkled with buttered breadcrumbs. The soubise filling and velouté sauce can both be made ahead of time.

Any cut of veal will turn out well in this recipe so you do not have to buy the most expensive roast. As long as it is boned, rolled and tied you could use a shoulder, leg or loin roast. This dish can also be made with sliced turkey breast or pork roast.

Roast:

3 tbsp	vegetable oil	50 mL
4 lb	veal roast, boned, rolled and tied	2 kg
2	cloves garlic, peeled	2
2	onions, peeled and quartered	2
1	carrot, peeled and trimmed	1
1	rib celery	1
¾ cup	dry white wine	175 mL
1 tsp	salt	5 mL
¼ tsp	freshly ground pepper	1 mL
1	bay leaf	1
1 tsp	dried thyme	5 mL
	Handful fresh parsley	

Soubise Filling:

12	medium-sized onions, peeled and quartered	12
¼ cup	unsalted butter	50 mL
¾ cup	long-grain white rice	175 mL
1¼ cups	chicken stock, homemade (see page 46) or commercial	300 mL

2	egg yolks	2
⅓ cup	whipping cream	75 mL
	Salt and freshly ground black pepper to taste	

Velouté Sauce:

¼ cup	unsalted butter	50 mL
⅓ cup	all-purpose flour	75 mL
3½ cups	stock (combination of cooking juices from roast and enough extra chicken or veal stock to measure), hot	875 mL
½ cup	whipping cream	125 mL
2 tbsp	Cognac or brandy	25 mL
	Salt, pepper and nutmeg to taste	
3 oz	Swiss cheese, cold	100 g

Topping:

3	slices French or Italian bread	3
¼ cup	unsalted butter, melted	50 mL

Serves 8 to 12

MAIN COURSES

Roast:

1. Heat oil in a Dutch oven and brown roast well on all sides.

2. Fit work bowl with metal blade and add garlic through the feed tube while the machine is running. Add onions and chop with 5 or 6 on/off pulses. Remove to a bowl. Cut carrot into 2-in/5-cm chunks and add to work bowl. Chop with a few on/off pulses. Transfer to bowl with onions. Repeat with celery and add to onions and carrots.

3. Remove roast from pan and discard excess fat if there is more than about ¼ cup/50 mL. Add vegetables to pan and cook about 5 minutes.

4. Place veal on top of vegetables. Add wine. Sprinkle seasonings and parsley on top. Cover and cook on medium-low heat on top of stove or in 350°F/180°C oven for 2 hours (or until meat thermometer registers 160°F/80°C).

5. Remove roast from pan and cool completely for easy slicing. Strain cooking juices into a measuring cup and remove fat from surface. Add enough stock to measure 3½ cups/875 mL.

Soubise Filling:

1. Fit work bowl with medium slicing disc. Place onions in large feed tube until they are well packed. Slice. Repeat until all onions are sliced. If necessary transfer batches of sliced onions to another bowl.

2. Melt butter in 3-qt/3-L saucepan and add sliced onions. Cook over medium-low heat until they are very fragrant and tender, about 20 minutes.

3. Stir in rice and coat well with butter and onions.

4. Add stock and bring to a boil. Lower heat and cook gently, covered, for 45 minutes.

5. Fit clean work bowl with metal blade and transfer rice-onion mixture to it. If you have the DLC-10 or DLC-8, do this in 2 batches. Puree mixture. Do not overprocess.

6. Return puree to saucepan. Beat egg yolks with cream and stir into rice puree. Heat gently but do not boil. Season to taste. Cool.

Velouté Sauce:

1. Melt butter in a saucepan and whisk in flour. Cook gently, without browning, for 5 minutes.

2. Whisk in hot stock and bring to a boil. Reduce heat and cook 10 minutes, stirring occasionally.

3. Add cream, Cognac and a little salt, pepper and nutmeg. Cook a few minutes.

4. Fit work bowl with shredding disc. Grate Swiss cheese and stir into sauce. Taste sauce and adjust seasoning if necessary. Cool.

Topping:

1. Fit work bowl with metal blade. Cut bread into cubes and add to work bowl. Process continuously until coarse crumbs are formed.

2. Add melted butter and blend into crumbs.

To assemble:

1. Slice veal into ¼-in/5-mm slices. Spread about 1 cup/250 mL velouté sauce over the bottom of a large, flat casserole dish. Spread each slice of veal with some soubise filling and arrange slices overlapping in casserole dish. Spread any extra soubise on top. Spread remaining velouté sauce over all. Sprinkle with crumbs.

2. Preheat oven to 400°F/200°C. Cook until sauces begin to bubble and top is golden brown — 35 to 45 minutes (if the dish has been frozen it may take 1¼ hours or slightly longer to reheat).

Breaded Veal Cutlets with Florentine Sauce

Breaded veal cutlets are always delicious, but this spinach sauce makes them very special. The sauce can be made ahead and reheated and the cutlets can be breaded ahead, but the veal does taste best when cooked at the last minute. When the cutlets are thin, they really do not take more than 5 to 7 minutes to cook. The sauce is also good served with breaded sole or fettucine.

10	slices French or Italian bread	10	1	clove garlic, peeled	1
2	eggs	2	1	onion, peeled and quartered	1
1 tsp	vegetable oil	5 mL	3 tbsp	unsalted butter	50 mL
1 cup	all-purpose flour	250 mL	1½ cups	whipping cream	375 mL
6	veal scallops (approximately 4-6 oz/125-175 g each)	6	1 tsp	salt	5 mL
			¼ tsp	freshly ground pepper	1 mL
⅓ cup	unsalted or clarified butter	75 mL	¼ tsp	freshly ground nutmeg	1 mL

Florentine Sauce:

10 oz	fresh spinach, well washed and trimmed	284 g

Serves 6

1. Fit work bowl with metal blade. Cut crusts off bread and reserve for another purpose (see page 13). Cut trimmed bread into cubes and add to work bowl in 1 or 2 batches, depending on the size of your machine. Process using 10 to 15 on/off pulses until crumbs are fine. Remove to a flat dish and reserve.
2. Beat eggs with oil in another flat dish.
3. Place flour in third flat dish.
4. Pat veal dry with paper towels. Dip into flour and shake off excess. Dip into egg and allow excess egg to drip off. Dip into crumbs and press them firmly into both sides. Place veal on a rack over a cookie sheet and refrigerate until ready to cook.
5. Prepare Florentine Sauce.

6. To cook veal, heat butter in large skillet. Add breaded veal and cook 3 to 5 minutes per side. Scallops should be golden brown. Serve immediately with Florentine sauce.

Florentine Sauce:

1. Place washed spinach in a large saucepan or Dutch oven. Cover and cook 2 minutes or until wilted. Cool and wring out in a tea towel until dry.
2. Place spinach in work bowl still fitted with metal blade. Process with 4 or 5 on/off pulses until finely chopped. Remove and reserve.
3. Add garlic and onion to work bowl. Chop finely with 6 to 10 on/off pulses.

4. Melt butter in a skillet and add onion-garlic mixture. Cook until very fragrant and tender but do not brown. Add spinach and combine well. Cook until completely dry. Return mixture to work bowl still fitted with metal blade and puree.

5. Return spinach mixture to skillet with cream. Add salt, pepper and nutmeg. Bring to a boil and, stirring constantly, cook until sauce thickens and cream has reduced. Either keep warm on gentle heat while cooking the veal or remove from heat and reheat just before serving. Taste and adjust seasoning if necessary.

Brisket

Although I rarely use packaged products, I have to admit that the way my mother prepares a brisket (a roast from the breast of beef) with a package of dry onion soup mix is really delicious.

4	onions, peeled and quartered	4	2 tbsp	ketchup	25 mL
4	carrots, peeled and trimmed	4	2 tbsp	Dijon mustard	25 mL
4	ribs celery	4	1	1½-oz/40-g package onion soup mix	1
1	brisket roast (approximately 4 to 5 lb/2 to 2.5 kg)	1	1 cup	water	250 mL
			1 tbsp	sweet paprika	15 mL
4	cloves garlic, peeled	4			

Serves 6 to 8

1. Fit work bowl with medium slicing disc. Pack large feed tube with onions and slice. Repeat until all onions are sliced. Slice carrots and celery through small feed tube.
2. Spread vegetables on the bottom of a large roasting pan or Dutch oven. Arrange brisket on top of vegetables.
3. Refit work bowl with metal blade. While machine is running, add garlic through feed tube and chop.
4. Add ketchup, mustard, onion soup mix and water and blend thoroughly.

5. Pour liquid over the roast and sprinkle with paprika. Cover and bake in a preheated 325°F/160°C oven for 3½ to 4 hours or until meat is very tender. Check roast every 30 minutes and if water evaporates add more. Leave roast uncovered for the last 30 minutes of cooking.

Note: If you like, 1 hour before the roast is finished, surround it with peeled, quartered potatoes and spoon juices over them. Cover and continue baking until potatoes and roast are tender.

Osso Bucco (Braised Veal Shanks)

When Edward Weil, President of Weil Company Ltd., the exclusive distributor of Cuisinart® food processors in Canada, went to Italy last year, he brought me back a set of special spoons that are used to extract the bone marrow from braised veal shanks. Now my silverware is truly complete. Osso bucco is traditionally served with risotto (see page 110).

8	large pieces veal shank, 1½ in/4 cm thick	8	1 tsp	finely grated lemon peel (see page 19)	5 mL
¼ cup	vegetable oil	50 mL	1	28-oz/796-mL can plum tomatoes	1
	Flour for dredging veal		1 cup	dry white wine	250 mL
3	onions, peeled and quartered	3	1 tsp	salt	5 mL
2	cloves garlic, peeled	2	¼ tsp	freshly ground pepper	1 mL
3	carrots, peeled and trimmed	3	½ tsp	dried thyme	2 mL
2	ribs celery	2	1	bay leaf	1
	Handful fresh parsley				

Serves 8

1. Tie string securely around the outside middle of the shanks so that they do not come apart while being cooked. Sometimes I crisscross the string across the marrow bone as well to ensure that the delicate marrow does not fall out when cooked.

2. Heat oil in a Dutch oven or large, heavy, deep skillet. Dredge veal in flour, shake off excess and brown well on both sides.

3. Fit work bowl with metal blade. Add onion quarters and garlic and chop with 5 or 6 on/off pulses. Remove to a bowl.

4. Cut carrots into 2-in/5-cm lengths and add to work bowl. Chop coarsely with 4 or 5 on/off pulses. Reserve with onions. Repeat with celery.

5. Place parsley in work bowl and chop with 6 or 7 on/off pulses. Add parsley and lemon peel to vegetables.

6. When veal is nicely browned, remove from pan. Discard any excess fat remaining in pan – you should have about 3 tbsp/50 mL left. Add onion mixture and cook 5 to 10 minutes or until vegetables are tender, fragrant and wilted.

7. Drain tomatoes, adding juice to vegetables in pan. Add tomatoes to work bowl still fitted with metal blade. Chop with 4 or 5 on/off pulses. Add to pan along with wine. Bring to a boil.

8. Return veal pieces and mix in with vegetables to coat meat. Add salt, pepper, thyme and bay leaf. Cover pan with a piece of foil and then the lid. Bake in 350°F/180°C oven for 2 hours or until veal is very tender.

9. Transfer veal to a serving platter and remove strings. If sauce is not thick enough, reduce over high heat, stirring constantly for few minutes. Pour over veal.

Steaks with Wild Mushroom Sauce

Any tender cut of beef will be delicious with this sauce — the sauce can also be served with a roast of beef, veal or fettucine. The sauce can be prepared ahead and reheated just before serving.

Wild Mushroom Sauce:

1	½-oz/15-g package dried wild mushrooms (preferably Italian porcini)	1
1 cup	warm water	250 mL
2	shallots, peeled	2
3 tbsp	unsalted butter	50 mL
1 lb	fresh mushrooms, cleaned	500 g
1½ cups	whipping cream	375 mL
1 tsp	salt	5 mL
½ tsp	freshly ground pepper	2 mL
6	steaks, approximately 8 oz/250 g each, depending on cut	6
2 tbsp	vegetable oil	25 mL
¼ cup	dry white wine	50 mL

Serves 6

1. Place dried mushrooms in a bowl and cover with warm water. Allow to soak 30 minutes or until softened. Strain soaking liquid through a sieve lined with cheesecloth and reserve liquid. Wash mushrooms well. Reserve.
2. Fit work bowl with metal blade. With machine running, drop shallots through feed tube and process until chopped.
3. Melt butter in a heavy skillet and add shallots. Cook until fragrant and tender but not brown.
4. Refit work bowl with medium slicing disc. Fit fresh mushrooms in small feed tube and process until all are sliced. Add to shallots along with softened dried mushrooms (if dried mushrooms are large, chop coarsely). Cook until any liquid in pan evaporates.
5. Add soaking liquid from mushrooms and cook until mushrooms absorb the liquid. Add cream, salt and pepper and continue to cook until cream reduces and sauce thickens slightly. Either keep warm or remove from heat and reheat before serving.
6. Pat steaks dry with paper towels. Heat oil for cooking steaks in a large, heavy skillet. Add steaks and if they are about 1½ in/4 cm thick and you want them rare, cook about 5 minutes on each side.
7. Remove steaks to a serving platter and keep warm. Discard any fat in pan from steaks and add wine. Deglaze pan by scraping bits of steak into liquid and reduce to about ¼ cup/50 mL. Add this mixture to the mushroom sauce. Taste sauce and adjust seasoning if necessary.
8. Serve steaks with sauce immediately (steaks can also be broiled or barbecued — just omit deglazing).

Spaghetti and Meat Sauce

This is a great all-purpose meat sauce that freezes beautifully. It can be used on spaghetti, or in lasagna or other pasta dishes.

2	cloves garlic, peeled	2	¾ cup	dry white wine	175 mL
1	onion, peeled and quartered	1	1 tsp	salt	5 mL
1	carrot, peeled and trimmed	1	¼ tsp	freshly ground pepper	1 mL
1	rib celery	1	1½ lb	spaghetti	750 g
1 lb	lean cold beef, cut into 1-in/2.5-cm cubes	500 g	⅓ cup	unsalted butter, cut into bits	75 mL
4 oz	pancetta (unsmoked bacon), optional	125 g	½ cup	grated Parmesan cheese (if using freshly grated Parmesan, grate cheese before proceeding with rest of recipe — see page 14)	125 mL
1	28-oz/796-mL can plum tomatoes	1			
3 tbsp	olive oil (see page 18)	50 mL			
¼ tsp	hot, red pepper flakes	1 mL	**Serves 6 to 8**		

1. Fit work bowl with metal blade. With machine running, add garlic through the feed tube and chop. Add onion to work bowl and chop using 5 or 6 on/off pulses. Remove and reserve.

2. Cut carrot into 1-in/2.5-cm pieces and add to work bowl. Chop finely with 6 to 10 on/off pulses. Add to onions. Repeat with celery.

3. Wipe work bowl dry. Pat beef dry. Add beef to bowl and process using on/off technique until beef is finely chopped. Remove and reserve. Add pancetta and chop finely using on/off pulses. Reserve.

4. Puree drained tomatoes in work bowl. Reserve with tomato liquid.

5. Heat oil in Dutch oven. Add pancetta and red pepper flakes and cook a few minutes until fat begins to render out. Add vegetables and cook, without browning, until very fragrant. Add chopped beef and cook until browned.

6. Add tomatoes and wine, salt and pepper. Bring to a boil, reduce heat and simmer very gently 2 to 3 hours until everything is very tender and sauce is thick. Keep warm or reheat when ready to serve. Taste and adjust seasoning.

7. Bring a large pot of water (8 qt/8 L) to a boil. Add 1 tbsp/15 mL salt. Add spaghetti and bring back to a boil. Stir to make sure it does not stick. Cook at a low boil for 10 to 12 minutes.

8. Warm serving bowl and place butter bits in bottom.

9. When spaghetti is ready, drain well in a colander and shake out excess liquid. Place in serving bowl with butter. Pour sauce over the top, sprinkle with cheese. Toss well before serving. Serve immediately.

Pasta Shells with Zucchini and Fresh Herbs

This is a light, quick meal. If you are watching calories, substitute solid curd cottage cheese for the cream cheese and omit the butter at the end.

2 lb	zucchini	1 kg	1 lb	shell-shaped dried pasta (plain, three-colored or whole-wheat)	500 g
2 tsp	salt	10 mL			
3	cloves garlic, peeled	3			
¼ cup	unsalted butter	50 mL	8 oz	cream cheese	250 g
	Handful fresh parsley		¼ cup	unsalted butter	50 mL
	Handful fresh dill or basil		½ cup	grated Parmesan cheese (if using freshly grated Parmesan, grate cheese before proceeding with rest of recipe – see page 14)	125 mL
4	green onions, cut into 1-in/2.5-cm lengths	4			
	Salt and freshly ground black pepper to taste			Serves 4 to 6	

1. Fit work bowl with shredding disc, julienne disc or French-fry disc. Scrub each zucchini very clean and taste. If they are especially gritty or bitter, peel them. Otherwise leave on peel. Fit into small feed tube and process. Place zucchini in a colander over a bowl and toss with salt. Allow to rest at least 30 minutes to drain out excess liquid.

2. Meanwhile fit work bowl with metal blade. With machine running, add garlic through the feed tube and process until chopped.

3. Heat butter in a large skillet and add garlic. Cook very gently without browning until fragrant. Rinse zucchini and pat dry. Add to garlic. Cook 5 minutes, stirring occasionally, until there is no liquid in pan.

4. Add parsley, dill and green onions to work bowl still fitted with metal blade. Chop with 8 or 9 on/off pulses until finely chopped. Add to zucchini. Cook 5 minutes. Taste and add salt and pepper as needed. Remove from heat.

5. Bring a large pot of water to the boil. Add about 1 tbsp/15 mL salt. Add pasta and bring to a boil, reduce heat slightly (water should boil but not boil over) and cook 8 to 12 minutes or until shells are tender. Drain well and shake out excess water.

6. While pasta is cooking, cut cream cheese and ¼ cup/50 mL butter into small cubes and place in large serving bowl. Just before pasta is ready reheat zucchini.

7. To assemble, place the drained hot pasta in bowl over the cheese and butter. Pour zucchini over the pasta and sprinkle with the grated cheese. Toss until all cheese and butter has melted. Taste and add salt and pepper if necessary. Serve immediately.

Cheese Blintzes with Strawberry Sauce

Blintzes are very similar to crepes. The only difference is that blintzes are usually cooked on one side only, as the uncooked side is later sautéed. When I first started to cook professionally my two greatest problems were learning to make pastry and learning to make crepes. Without knowing it, my mother instilled fears into me about these two foods when she jokingly would say that making pastry was a bother and that you had to be a good person to make good blintzes. After a lot of practice I can tell you that pastry really isn't hard at all and anybody, good or evil, can make crepes. Blintzes can be cooked ahead and reheated in the oven or they can be frozen and reheated, but they really taste best if cooked just before serving.

Batter:

6	eggs	6
1½ cups	all-purpose flour	375 mL
½ tsp	salt	2 mL
1 tbsp	sugar	15 mL
1 cup	milk	250 mL
½ cup	water	125 mL
3 tbsp	unsalted butter, melted	50 mL

Cheese Filling:

1½ lb	creamed cottage cheese (solid curd, pressed)	750 g
3 tbsp	sugar	50 mL
pinch	salt	pinch
2	eggs	2
½ cup	unsalted butter	125 mL

Strawberry Sauce:

2 cups	strawberries	500 mL
⅓ cup	sugar	75 mL
⅓ cup	lemon juice	75 mL
1 cup	sour cream	250 mL

Makes 16 to 20 blintzes

1. Fit work bowl with metal blade. Place eggs, flour, salt and sugar in work bowl. Process until blended.

2. Add milk and water and process until well mixed. Scrape down sides of bowl if necessary.

3. Add melted butter and process to blend. Cover batter with plastic wrap and allow to rest 1 hour or longer in the refrigerator.

4. Prepare Cheese Filling and Strawberry Sauce.

5. To prepare crepes heat an 8-in/20-cm crepe or omelet pan. Add about 1 tbsp/15 mL butter to the pan at medium-high heat. Add about ¼ cup/50 mL batter to pan. This is a test crepe so do not worry if it isn't thin or perfect. Flip and cook second side. If pan sticks anywhere rub the spot with salt and oil and try again. Discard or eat this test crepe.

6. When pan is ready add ¼ cup/50 mL batter and swirl to coat the bottom of pan. Pour excess batter back into the bowl. Cook crepe until browned – it should be thin enough that you can see the color of the pan through the pancake. Turn out of pan (second side does not have to be cooked). Continue until all are cooked. If they start to stick just brush the pan with more butter. You can stack cooked crepes on top of one another.

7. Place crepes on counter with the cooked side up. Place a large spoonful of filling in the bottom center of each. Fold up the bottom, fold in the sides and roll up (see diagram below). Prepare all crepes in this manner. Refrigerate or freeze until ready to cook.

8. To cook, add about 3 tbsp/50 mL butter to a large skillet and place 6 or 7 blintzes in pan, folded side down. Cook until nicely browned, then turn and cook other side. This should take 5 or 6 minutes.

9. Serve blintzes with Strawberry Sauce and sour cream.

Cheese Filling:

1. Fit clean work bowl with metal blade. Add creamed cottage cheese in chunks and process a few seconds until smooth.

2. Add sugar, salt and eggs and process with 5 or 6 on/off pulses or just until ingredients are blended. Filling should be thick. Reserve.

Strawberry Sauce:

1. Wash and hull berries. Fit work bowl with medium slicing disc. Fit strawberries into small feed tube and slice using gentle pressure. Repeat until all berries are sliced.

2. Transfer berries to a bowl and toss with sugar and lemon juice. Cover and allow to marinate while cooking blintzes.

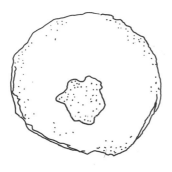

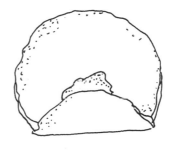

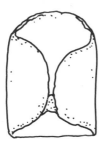

Leek Tart

Tarts like this can be served in small pieces as appetizers or as the main course for lunches, brunches and light suppers. You can also add cooked, crisp bacon, diced ham or any diced, leftover meat to the filling.

Pastry:		
8 oz	Swiss or old Cheddar cheese, cold (divided)	250 g
1½ cups	all-purpose flour	375 mL
½ tsp	salt	2 mL
3 tbsp	unsalted butter, cold	50 mL
5 tbsp	lard or shortening, cold	75 mL
3 tbsp	ice water	50 mL
1 tbsp	Dijon mustard	15 mL
Filling:		
	Handful fresh parsley	

2	cloves garlic, peeled	2
4	leeks, white part only, well washed	4
3 tbsp	unsalted butter	50 mL
4	eggs	4
1½ cups	whipping cream	375 mL
1 tsp	salt	5 mL
¼ tsp	freshly ground pepper	1 mL
pinch	nutmeg	pinch
pinch	cayenne pepper	pinch

Makes 1 tart (10 in/25 cm)

1. Fit work bowl with shredding disc and process Swiss cheese until it is all grated. Remove from work bowl and refit bowl with metal blade. Place ⅓ cup/75 mL cheese back in work bowl.
2. Add flour and salt and process until combined.
3. Cut butter and lard into small cubes and add. Process with 3 or 4 on/off pulses until fat is in tiny bits.
4. With machine running, add water slowly through feed tube and process until dough is moistened but has not yet formed a ball. Remove from work bowl and gather dough together into a ball. Wrap in plastic and refrigerate about 30 minutes.
5. Roll dough out to fit 10-in/1.5-L pie or quiche pan. Fit dough into pan and cut off edges to fit (sometimes I double over the edge so that the outside edge of the tart is especially firm). Line the pastry with parchment paper, waxed paper or foil. Add dried beans or other legumes or special pie weights to hold pastry in place. Bake in a preheated 425°F/220°C oven for 15 minutes. Remove weights and paper carefully.
6. Spread bottom of crust with Dijon mustard. Reduce oven temperature to 350°F/180°C.
7. Wipe work bowl clean and fit with metal blade. Add parsley and chop with 3 or 4 on/off pulses. Remove and reserve.
8. With machine running, add garlic through feed tube and process until chopped.
9. Refit work bowl with slicing disc. Place leeks upright in small feed tube and process until all leeks are sliced.

10. Heat butter in skillet and add leeks and garlic. Cook 10 minutes, without browning, until vegetables are very tender and fragrant.

11. Cool leeks slightly and then spread over the bottom crust. Sprinkle with remaining grated cheese.

12. Refit work bowl with metal blade. Add eggs, cream and seasonings. Blend quickly and pour into crust. Sprinkle with chopped parsley.

13. Bake 35 to 45 minutes or just until top is golden brown and slightly puffed. Allow to rest 10 minutes before serving.

Silver Dollar Buttermilk Pancakes

I originally got this recipe when I was traveling through the Maritimes for Canadian Living *magazine. It is from John Corey of Havelock, New Brunswick, and even after five years I still have not found a pancake I like better. The batter is quite loose but these pancakes cook up beautifully and are very delicate and light.*

Maureen Lollar, my chief assistant at the cooking school, taught me a trick she learned while working at the Canadian Egg Marketing Agency. When a pancake is ready to be turned over, the top will have lost its sheen.

1 cup	all-purpose flour	250 mL		2 cups	buttermilk or unflavored yogurt	500 mL
1 tsp	baking soda	5 mL		⅓ cup	unsalted butter	75 mL
¼ tsp	salt	1 mL				
3	eggs	3				

Makes approximately 36 pancakes

1. Fit work bowl with metal blade. Place flour, baking soda and salt in work bowl and blend ingredients for 4 or 5 seconds. Remove to another bowl.

2. Add eggs to work bowl still fitted with metal blade. Blend 2 seconds. Add buttermilk and blend to combine. Add flour mixture and blend a few seconds just until flour is thoroughly mixed in.

3. Melt butter in a large 12-in/30-cm skillet. Pour butter into batter and blend just to combine. Return skillet to heat with just the butter left in the bottom. This should be enough to cook pancakes as the butter in the batter prevents them from sticking.

4. When the pan is hot, spoon batter into pan in large spoonfuls. You should be able to cook 6 or 7 pancakes at one time. Cook until tops of pancakes lose their sheen, then flip and cook second side. Repeat until all batter is used.

5. Serve with maple syrup or jam.

Note: If you do this in the DLC-10, the batter just fits, so work quickly and after butter is blended in, transfer to a mixing bowl before spooning into the frying pan. If you have the DLC-8, DLC-7 or DLC-X the batter can be spooned directly from the work bowl.

Pesto Pizza

Pizza has become increasingly popular over the past few years and now people are making pizza with every imaginable topping. This pizza is sensational. It is made with the famous Italian pesto sauce that is usually served over pasta. The sauce is based on fresh basil, pine nuts, olive oil, garlic and Parmesan cheese. If fresh basil is not available, do not substitute dried — just use fresh parsley instead. The pesto sauce can be used on fettucine noodles (this is enough for 1½ lb / 750 g), potatoes, cooked rice or even as a sauce for lamb chops!

Crust:

1 tsp	sugar	5 mL
¼ cup	warm water	50 mL
1	envelope dry yeast	1
3 cups	hard white unbleached flour or all-purpose flour	750 mL
1 tsp	salt	5 mL
¾ cup	water	175 mL
2 tbsp	olive oil (see page 18) or vegetable oil	25 mL
8 oz	Mozzarella cheese, cold	250 g
4	medium-sized firm tomatoes	4

Pesto Sauce:

4	cloves garlic, peeled	4
½ cup	pine nuts	125 mL
	Handful fresh parsley	
2	large handfuls fresh basil (2 cups/500 mL, packed)	2
1 cup	grated Parmesan cheese (if using freshly grated Parmesan, grate cheese before proceeding with rest of recipe — see page 14)	250 mL
⅓ cup	olive oil (see page 18)	75 mL
1 tsp	salt	5 mL

Makes 2 medium pizzas

1. Dissolve sugar in warm water and sprinkle with yeast. Allow mixture to rest 10 minutes or until it bubbles up and doubles in volume.

2. Fit work bowl with plastic or metal blade. Place 2½ cups/625 mL flour and salt in work bowl. Combine ¾ cup/175 mL water with oil in a measuring cup. Stir down yeast and combine with water and oil. With machine running, slowly add the liquid through the feed tube. The flour should be well moistened. If the dough is sticky, add extra flour a few spoonfuls at a time until dough comes away from the sides of the bowl. Dough should be moist but not too sticky. Process 30 seconds to knead. Do not worry about how much extra flour you have to add to make a dough that is easy to handle. Remove from work bowl and place in a well-oiled bowl. Turn dough to grease completely and then cover with plastic wrap. Allow to rise in a warm place, until doubled, 1 to 1½ hours.

3. Prepare Pesto Sauce.

4. Refit work bowl with shredding disc (you do not have to clean bowl). Grate Mozzarella cheese, using gentle pressure. Reserve.

5. If tomatoes are not firm slice by hand, but if they are firm and fit into large tube they can be done in the machine. Refit work bowl with medium or thick slicing disc. Cut the top and bottom slice off each tomato so it can rest evenly on the slicing disc. Place tomato in the large feed tube and slice. Repeat for all tomatoes. Remove and reserve.

6. Preheat oven to 425°F/220°C. Oil two jelly roll pans with olive oil.

7. To assemble pizza, punch dough down and divide in half. Roll each half out into a circle — the thinner you roll the dough, the thinner the crust will be. Place each circle on a jelly roll pan. Spread each circle with half the pesto sauce. Arrange sliced tomatoes on the pesto, then sprinkle with grated Mozzarella. If you like a crisp crust, bake immediately. If you prefer a thicker crust, wait 15 minutes before placing pizzas in the oven.

8. Bake on the bottom shelf of the oven for 5 minutes. Reduce oven to 400°F/200°C for 20 to 25 minutes longer. Serve immediately.

Pesto Sauce:
1. Wipe work bowl clean. With machine running, add garlic through the feed tube and process until chopped. Add nuts and chop with garlic.

2. Add parsley and basil and process on/off 8 to 10 times until finely chopped.

3. Add grated Parmesan cheese, oil and salt and process until well mixed. Remove and reserve.

Vegetables, Rice and Pasta

Times are changing so quickly. I remember when I first opened my cooking school, students would tell me that their children, husbands, parents, or even the students themselves, did not like vegetables. But now everyone loves vegetables. And if they didn't, they probably wouldn't admit it!

Vegetables play such an important role in our diets. Not only are they vital for nutrition and fiber, they are really the most interesting part of the menu. There is such a wide range of vegetables and vegetable cooking methods to choose from—it's quite easy to see how people can become vegetarians and not miss the meat.

Pasta and rice dishes are also included in this chapter. These are two of my favorite foods and sometimes I think I started jogging so that I wouldn't feel guilty about all the carbohydrate loading I have been doing all my life. Although these foods have the reputation of being fattening, it is usually the preparation method and/or sauce that are high in calories, not the food itself. And don't forget about the pasta recipes in the appetizer chapter. The Pasta with Lemon and Garlic Sauce (page 35), for example, is great as an appetizer, but it is also wonderful served as a side dish with chicken, lamb or salmon.

Rutabagas Glazed with Maple Syrup

Rutabagas or yellow turnips are usually overlooked, but prepared this way, they make a great winter vegetable dish.

1	rutabaga (approximately 3 lb/1.5 kg)	1	2 cups	chicken stock, homemade (see page 46) or commercial, or water	500 mL
	Small handful fresh parsley		1 tsp	salt	5 mL
1	clove garlic, peeled	1	¼ cup	maple syrup or honey	50 mL
2	small onions, peeled and quartered	2			
¼ cup	unsalted butter	50 mL	**Serves 6**		

1. Cut a slice from the top and bottom of the rutabaga. Place on counter and, holding securely, slice off waxed peel from top to bottom. Cut into quarters.

2. If you have a French-fry disc, use it to cut rutabaga. If not, fit work bowl with medium or thick slicing disc. Cut rutabaga into sticks to fit into small feed tube. Slice. Remove from work bowl and reserve.

3. Fit work bowl with metal blade. Add parsley and chop with 5 or 6 on/off pulses until finely chopped. Remove parsley and reserve.

4. With machine running, drop garlic through feed tube and process until chopped. Add onions to work bowl and process with 4 or 5 on/off pulses until coarsely chopped.

5. Melt butter in a large, deep skillet and add onions and garlic. Cook a few minutes, without browning, until tender and fragrant.

6. Add rutabaga sticks or slices and turn over in butter mixture. Add chicken stock or water, salt and syrup. Add water if necessary so that liquid barely covers rutabaga. Bring to a boil.

7. Reduce heat and cook gently but steadily, uncovered, until liquid evaporates and rutabagas are tender and glazed. This should take about 20 minutes. (If liquid evaporates too soon, add more water. If it has not evaporated in 20 minutes, turn up heat and cook a little longer.)

Note: This dish can be garnished with chopped parsley or with 2 tbsp/25 mL toasted, sliced almonds.

Rainbow Vegetable Terrine

This is a colorful, delicious vegetable dish. It can be served with a roast or any plain main course, or it could also be served with a sauce (such as tomato or hollandaise) as an appetizer.

1 lb	cauliflower (weight after trimming)	500 g		Salt and freshly ground black pepper to taste		
1 lb	carrots (weight after trimming)	500 g	¼ tsp	freshly ground nutmeg	1 mL
1 lb	broccoli (weight after trimming)	500 g	6 tbsp	unsalted butter, at room temperature	75 mL
3	eggs	3	¼ tsp	ground ginger	1 mL
3	egg yolks	3	1 tsp	dried tarragon	5 mL
¾ cup	grated Parmesan cheese (if using freshly grated Parmesan, grate cheese before proceeding with rest of recipe — see page 14)	175 mL		**Serves 8**	

1. Separate cauliflower florets and steam or simmer cauliflower until tender. Drain and cool, but do not refrigerate, as vegetables will become too watery.

2. With machine fitted with slicing disc, slice carrots through small feed tube. Steam or simmer until tender. Drain and cool. Do not refrigerate.

3. Separate the florets from the broccoli stems. Peel the bottom parts of the stems if tough. Pack stems into small feed tube and slice broccoli stems. Steam or simmer florets and stems until tender. Drain and cool. Do not refrigerate.

4. Butter a 9-in x 5-in/2 L loaf pan and line with a strip of parchment paper or waxed paper (see page 27). Preheat oven to 350°F/180°C.

5. Wipe work bowl dry and refit with metal blade. Add cooked, well-drained cauliflower and process with 6 or 7 on/off pulses until cauliflower is very finely chopped. Add 1 egg, 1 yolk, ¼ cup/50 mL cheese, salt and pepper to taste, nutmeg and 2 tbsp/25 mL unsalted butter. Blend until smooth. Spread evenly into bottom of prepared pan.

6. To work bowl still fitted with metal blade, add carrots. Process with 6 or 7 on/off pulses or until carrots are finely chopped. Add 1 egg, 1 yolk, ¼ cup/50 mL cheese, salt and pepper to taste, ground ginger and 2 tbsp/25 mL unsalted butter and process continuously until smooth. Spread over cauliflower mixture.

7. To work bowl still fitted with metal blade, add broccoli. Chop on/off with 6 or 7 pulses until broccoli is

Pesto Pizza (see page 92).

finely chopped. Add remaining egg, yolk, cheese, salt and pepper to taste, remaining butter and tarragon and process until smooth. Spread over carrot mixture.

8. Cover terrine with a strip of buttered parchment paper or waxed paper and place in a large pan. Add enough boiling water to come half-way up the sides of the terrine. Bake 1¼ to 1½ hours. Cool in pan 20 minutes and then run a knife around edges of terrine. Invert onto a serving platter and remove paper. Slice and serve.

Note: Weight of each vegetable before trimming should be approximately 1½ pounds/750 g.

Baked Fennel with Parmesan Cheese

Fennel is an unusual vegetable with a slightly anise or licorice flavor. It can be prepared in many different ways but this is one of my favorites. You can do other vegetables in this manner — asparagus, leeks, etc. — but adjust the initial cooking times accordingly.

3 or 4	bulbs fennel (approximately 2½ lb/1.25 kg in total weight)	3 or 4	¼ cup	unsalted butter, cut into bits	50 mL
			1 tsp	salt	5 mL
1 cup	grated Parmesan cheese (if using freshly grated Parmesan, grate cheese before proceeding with rest of recipe — see page 14)	250 mL	¼ tsp	freshly ground pepper	1 mL
			Serves 6 to 8		

1. Trim any ribs from the fennel bulbs. Trim off root end. Fit work bowl with medium or thick slicing disc. Place fennel bulbs in large feed tube on their sides (you may have to cut a thin slice off the rounded edge to make them fit). Slice.

2. Steam fennel or cook in boiling water until slices are tender — about 15 minutes. Do not worry if they fall apart. Drain well.

3. When fennel is cooked, layer it in a 1½-qt/1.5-L baking dish with the cheese, butter bits, salt and pepper. End with a layer of cheese. Bake at 375°F/190°C for 20 to 30 minutes or until very hot.

Zucchini with Fresh Herbs and Yogurt

Here's a great recipe for zucchini — when it takes over your garden you'll need lots of ways to use it up!

2	cloves garlic, peeled	2	3 tbsp	unsalted butter	50 mL
3	green onions, cut into 1-in/2.5-cm lengths	3	¾ cup	unflavored yogurt	175 mL
			1 tbsp	Dijon mustard	15 mL
	Handful fresh parsley		1 tsp	salt	5 mL
	Handful fresh dill		¼ tsp	freshly ground pepper	1 mL
2½ lb	zucchini	1.25 kg			

Serves 6 to 8

1. Fit work bowl with metal blade. With machine running, add garlic through the feed tube. Process until chopped. Add green onions and process on/off 6 to 8 times or until onions are coarsely chopped. Remove mixture from work bowl and reserve.

2. Add parsley and dill to work bowl still fitted with metal blade. Chop with 6 to 8 on/off pulses or until finely chopped. Remove and reserve.

3. Refit work bowl with medium or thin slicing disc. Trim zucchini and scrub well. Taste a bit of each and peel if bitter. Add zucchini through small feed tube and slice one at a time. Process until all are sliced.

4. Melt butter in a large skillet and add garlic-onion mixture. Cook until very fragrant but do not brown. Add sliced zucchini and cook 5 to 7 minutes or until wilted. Do not overcook. Stir in parsley-dill mixture and combine well. Drain off excess liquid if there is any.

5. Combine yogurt with mustard, salt and pepper. Stir into zucchini and heat very briefly. Do not boil.

Carrot and Parsnip Ring

Storage vegetables such as parsnips enable you to use fresh, local produce all year round. This is a different and delicious way to use carrots and parsnips.

2 lb	carrots, peeled and trimmed	1 kg	3 tbsp	brown sugar	50 mL
2 lb	parsnips, peeled and trimmed	1 kg	1 tsp	ground ginger	5 mL
3	slices French or Italian bread	3	1 tsp	salt	5 mL
	Handful fresh parsley		5	eggs	5
3 tbsp	unsalted butter	50 mL	1 cup	whipping cream	250 mL

Serves 6 to 8

1. Fit work bowl with medium slicing disc. Cut carrots and parsnips into even lengths and pack large feed tube tightly with vegetables standing up. Slice. Repeat until all vegetables are sliced. Steam vegetables 15 to 20 minutes or until very tender.

2. While vegetables are steaming, wipe out work bowl and refit with metal blade. Cut bread into cubes and process until fine crumbs are formed. Remove from bowl and reserve.

3. Add parsley to work bowl and chop using 3 or 4 on/off pulses. Remove and reserve with crumbs.

4. Add cooked vegetables to work bowl still fitted with metal blade. If you have the DLC-7 or DLC-X, all the vegetables can be done at once. If you have the DLC-8 or DLC-10, divide vegetables and other ingredients into 2 separate batches. Puree vegetables and transfer to a large bowl.

5. Add butter, sugar, ginger, salt and eggs to work bowl and blend. Scrape down sides. Add cream, blend and scrape down sides. Add breadcrumbs and parsley mixture and blend in quickly. Stir into pureed vegetables thoroughly.

6. Butter a 6-cup/1.5-L ovenproof ring mold well and pour in vegetable mixture. Cover with a round of buttered parchment paper, waxed paper or foil. Place mold in a larger pan, adding enough boiling water to come halfway up the sides of ring mold. Bake at 350°F/180°C for 45 minutes or until a knife inserted into custard comes out clean. Allow mold to rest 10 minutes. Run a thin, flexible knife around the inside edges of mold and invert carefully onto a serving platter.

Puree of Squash au Gratin

Winter squash is harvested in the fall and can be stored all winter. Butternut squash is my favorite (shaped somewhat like a large, beige pear) but acorn or hubbard could also be used. This recipe would also work well with carrots, turnips, parsnips or a combination of these. You will need approximately 3 cups/750 mL of cooked vegetables.

3 lb	squash (weight with skin, seeds, etc.)	1.5 kg		1 tsp	ground ginger	5 mL
				½ tsp	ground cinnamon	2 mL
4	slices French or Italian bread	4		pinch	freshly ground nutmeg	pinch
2 tbsp	unsalted butter, melted	25 mL		2 tbsp	maple syrup or brown sugar	25 mL
¼ cup	unsalted butter	50 mL				
1 tsp	salt	5 mL				
¼ tsp	freshly ground pepper	1 mL				

Serves 6 to 8

1. Preheat oven to 350°F/180°C and butter a 2-qt/2-L casserole. Line a cookie sheet with foil and butter well. Cut squash in half and scoop out seeds. Place squash cut side down on buttered foil and bake 1 hour or until tender.

2. Meanwhile cut bread into cubes. Fit work bowl with metal blade and add bread. Process bread into crumbs using a continuous action. Add 2 tbsp/25 mL melted butter and blend with crumbs using a few on/off pulses. Remove from work bowl and reserve.

3. When squash has cooked, scoop out pulp. Drain well if squash is wet and place in work bowl still fitted with metal blade. Add remaining ingredients and blend together with 5 or 6 on/off pulses. Do not overblend or squash may become too moist.

4. Spread squash mixture evenly in casserole and top with breadcrumb mixture. Bake in a preheated 350°F/180°C oven for 30 minutes or until heated thoroughly.

Carrot Timbales

Pureed vegetables baked this way look and taste great. These custards can be made ahead and reheated and are even delicious cold. This same recipe can also be made with parsnips, turnips or sweet potatoes.

1½ lb	carrots, peeled and trimmed	750 g	1 tsp	grated lemon peel or orange peel	5 mL
¼ cup	unsalted butter	50 mL	¾ cup	cream, sour cream or unflavored yogurt	175 mL
4	eggs	4	**Garnish:**		
1 tsp	salt	5 mL		Sprigs fresh parsley	
¼ tsp	freshly ground pepper	1 mL			
¼ tsp	ground ginger	1 mL			
¼ tsp	freshly ground nutmeg	1 mL	**Serves 6 to 8**		

1. Fit work bowl with medium slicing disc. Slice carrots into coins through small feed tube. Steam or simmer carrots in water until tender — 15 to 20 minutes. Reserve about 16 cooked carrots for a garnish.

2. Meanwhile butter 6 or 8 individual soufflé dishes or custard cups and line the bottoms with a small circle of parchment paper or waxed paper. Preheat oven to 350°F/180°C.

3. Fit work bowl with metal blade. Add the cooked carrots and process on/off until carrots are very finely chopped. Add remaining ingredients and process until mixture is a fine puree.

4. Spoon mixture into the prepared dishes. Place molds in a large pan filled with enough boiling water to come halfway up the sides of the carrot molds.

5. Bake 35 to 40 minutes or until mixture is firm to the touch. Remove from water bath. Run a knife around edge of custards. Allow to rest 5 minutes and invert. Garnish each with 2 carrot coins and a sprig of fresh parsley.

Note: If made ahead, reheat molds in water bath in 350°F/180°C oven for 25 minutes.

Fennel Mousse

When I started the cooking school over ten years ago, fennel was difficult to find and not very popular. Now, with North Americans traveling more and tastes becoming so sophisticated, fennel is more readily available. It can be served raw, in salads or with dips. When it is raw it has a fairly strong anise (licorice) flavor that some people enjoy and others do not. When it is cooked, however, this flavor does become milder. Use just the bulbous part of the fennel as the ribs are usually quite stringy.

If you cannot find fresh fennel, simply substitute celery. The flavor will change but the texture will be similar.

1 lb	fresh fennel bulbs (2 or 3)	500 g	2	egg yolks	2
10 oz	fresh spinach	284 g	1 cup	whipping cream	250 mL
1	onion, peeled and quartered	1	1 tsp	salt	5 mL
1	clove garlic, peeled	1	¼ tsp	freshly ground pepper	1 mL
3 tbsp	unsalted butter	50 mL	pinch	freshly ground nutmeg	pinch
4	eggs	4			

Serves 6

1. Fit work bowl with medium slicing disc. Trim ribs and ends from fennel bulbs. Cut fennel to fit large feed tube and process until all fennel is sliced. Bring a large pot of water to the boil and cook fennel 15 to 20 minutes or until tender. Drain well.

2. Wash spinach well and place in a large pot with the water from the rinsing clinging to the leaves. Cover and cook 3 or 4 minutes or until spinach wilts completely. Cool until you are able to handle it and squeeze out extra liquid. Reserve.

3. Refit work bowl with metal blade. Add onion and garlic to work bowl and chop using 3 or 4 on/off pulses. Melt butter in a large skillet and add onion mixture. Cook until tender and fragrant but do not brown.

4. Add spinach and fennel to skillet and combine with onion and garlic. Cook until vegetables are fairly dry.

5. Transfer contents of pan to work bowl still fitted with metal blade. If you are using the DLC-7 or DLC-X you can do this in 1 batch, but if you are using the DLC-8 or DLC-10 do this in 2 batches. Puree until smooth. Scrape down sides of work bowl a few times.

6. Beat in eggs, egg yolks, cream and seasonings (again in 1 or 2 batches).

7. Butter a 1½-qt/1.5-L soufflé or casserole dish or 12 timbale molds or a muffin pan. If you are using timbale molds or a muffin pan, line the bottoms with parchment paper or waxed paper so that they will turn out easily. Spoon mixture into pans.

8. Place soufflé dish or individual molds in a larger pan, adding enough boiling water to come halfway up the sides of the baking pans. Bake in 400°F/200°C oven for 25 to 35 minutes for timbales or 35 to 45 minutes for 1 large pan. When

mousse is ready it should feel firm on the top and a knife inserted should come out clean. Remove from oven and water bath and allow to rest 10 minutes before turning out. The larger mousse can be served directly from the pan or inverted and served in wedges.

Note: This can be prepared ahead and baked just before serving or it can be baked ahead and reheated in a water bath at 350°F/180°C for 20 to 30 minutes.

Pureed Parsnips

Although this a very easy, straightforward recipe, it is elegant and delicious. Serve with any plain roast or grilled dish. You can also make this with carrots or turnips. Try the curried variation for a change — it's absolutely spectacular.

2 lb	parsnips, peeled and trimmed	1 kg		½ tsp	ground cinnamon	2 mL
3 tbsp	unsalted butter	50 mL		¼ tsp	freshly ground nutmeg	1 mL
½ cup	cream	125 mL				
1 tsp	salt	5 mL				
¼ tsp	freshly ground pepper	1 mL				

Serves 6 to 8

1. Fit work bowl with medium slicing disc. Add parsnips one at a time through small feed tube and slice.
2. Steam or simmer parsnips in boiling water until tender — 10 to 15 minutes. Drain well.
3. Refit work bowl with metal blade. Add cooked parsnips and chop finely using 6 to 10 on/off pulses. Add remaining ingredients and puree. Taste and adjust seasoning if necessary.
4. Serve immediately or transfer to a casserole dish and keep warm in a 200°F/100°C oven.

Note: To make pureed curried parsnips, while the parsnips are steaming, cook 2 cloves minced garlic in the 3 tbsp/50 mL butter until tender but not brown. Stir in 1 tbsp/15 mL curry powder and cook for 30 seconds. Add to puree along with remaining ingredients. No one ever believes parsnips can taste this good!

Potatoes Baked in Cream

This is one of the most delicious potato dishes of all time. Although it is quite rich, if you just eat a small portion it is enough to satisfy and worth every mouthful. Serve it with any plain foods — roasts, breaded or barbecued meats or poultry.

1	clove garlic, peeled	1	3 lb	baking potatoes (approximately 6 large Idaho potatoes)	1.5 kg
1 tbsp	unsalted butter, at room temperature	15 mL	½ cup	grated Parmesan cheese (if using freshly grated Parmesan, grate cheese before proceeding with rest of recipe — see page 14)	125 mL
2 cups	whipping cream	500 mL			
1½ tsp	salt	7 mL			
¼ tsp	freshly ground pepper	1 mL			
¼ tsp	freshly ground nutmeg	1 mL	**Serves 8**		

1. Rub a 2-qt/2-L gratin dish with cut garlic and then butter heavily. Preheat oven to 425°F/220°C.
2. Heat cream and stir in salt, pepper and nutmeg.
3. Fit work bowl with medium or thin slicing disc. Just before cooking, peel potatoes and cut to fit large feed tube — potatoes should be standing up rather than lying flat. Cut off ends so that flat edge of potato rests on blade. Pack tube tightly and slice potatoes. Repeat until all potatoes are sliced.
4. Arrange potatoes in prepared baking dish and pour cream over all. Sprinkle with cheese. Bake 20 minutes. Reduce heat to 375°F/190°C and continue to bake 25 to 35 minutes or until potatoes are very tender when pierced with knife. Top should be golden and cream thickened. Allow to rest 10 to 15 minutes before serving.

Roesti Potatoes

This is an old recipe of Swiss origin. These potatoes taste good with just about anything and sometimes I just make a meal out of the potatoes so I can eat as much as I want without feeling guilty. The Cuisinart® makes this recipe a delight to prepare.

4	large Idaho baking potatoes (approximately 2 lb/1 kg)	4	¼ tsp	freshly ground pepper	1 mL
½ cup	unsalted butter	125 mL		Handful fresh parsley	
1 tsp	salt	5 mL	**Serves 6**		

1. Fit work bowl with shredding disc or julienne disc. Peel potatoes or scrub well. Cut in half to fit the large feed tube. Process until all are grated or julienned.

2. Melt about 3 tbsp/50 mL butter in a non-stick pan that is about 10 in/25 cm in diameter.

3. Add half the potatoes and press into bottom of pan. Season with salt, pepper and a few pieces of butter cut into bits. Cover with remaining potatoes and press down well. Butter a flat lid that fits into pan directly on surface of potatoes and press down. Weigh down lid if possible. A brick or heavy tin will work. Cook on medium heat for 20 minutes.

4. Remove lid and gently run a spatula under potatoes to loosen. Place a flat plate over pan and invert potatoes. Add remaining butter to pan and melt. Slide potatoes into butter. Cover again and cook other side 20 minutes longer. Potatoes should be nicely browned on both sides. If not, turn up heat and cook a little longer.

5. Meanwhile, wipe work bowl clean. Fit with metal blade. Add parsley and chop with 5 or 6 on/off pulses until finely chopped.

6. When potatoes are ready slide onto a serving platter and sprinkle with parsley. Serve at once.

Stir-fried Broccoli with Oyster Sauce

With the rising popularity of Chinese cooking in North America, stir-fried vegetable dishes have become very popular.

5	black, dried oriental mushrooms (shiitake)	5	Sauce:			
			½ cup	chicken stock, homemade (see page 46) or commercial, or water	125 mL
2 lb	broccoli	1 kg			
3	cloves garlic, peeled	3			
1	piece fresh ginger root, size of a quarter and ½ in/1 cm thick, peeled	1	2 tbsp	oyster sauce	25 mL
			2 tbsp	soy sauce	25 mL
			1 tbsp	rice wine or vodka	15 mL
			1 tsp	sugar	5 mL
2	green onions, cut into 2-in/5-cm lengths	2	1 tbsp	cornstarch	15 mL
			½ tsp	oriental sesame oil	2 mL
3 tbsp	peanut oil or vegetable oil	50 mL			
			Serves 6		

1. Soak black mushrooms in enough warm water to cover for 30 minutes. Remove from water, squeeze dry and cut out tough stems. Slice mushrooms. Reserve.

2. While mushrooms are soaking, trim tough ends off broccoli and peel skin from bottom end of stem if especially tough or stringy. Cut florets off stems and reserve. Fit work bowl with medium or thick slicing disc. Place stems in small feed tube and slice. Steam or boil stems and florets 3 to 5 minutes or until barely tender but still crisp and bright green. Remove from heat, drain and reserve.

3. Meanwhile, refit work bowl with metal blade. Add garlic and ginger and chop finely using 4 or 5 on/off pulses. Remove from bowl and reserve. Add green onions and chop using 3 or 4 on/off pulses. Remove and reserve with garlic.

4. Add all ingredients for sauce to work bowl still fitted with metal blade. Blend together briefly.

5. Heat wok or large frying pan over high heat for 1 minute. Add peanut oil and heat again. Add garlic/ginger/green-onion mixture and cook 30 seconds until very fragrant but do not brown. Add mushrooms and stir-fry 30 seconds longer. Add precooked broccoli and toss until thoroughly heated.

6. Blend sauce ingredients again (cornstarch sometimes settles on bottom) and add to wok. Stir and cook until liquid thickens. Serve immediately.

Tomatoes Stuffed with Duxelles

This duxelle stuffing can also be used as an omelet filling or for crepes. If you are only serving one vegetable serve two stuffed halves per person but if you are serving other vegetables, just serve one half.

6	medium-sized tomatoes, firm but ripe	6
½ tsp	salt	2 mL

Duxelle Stuffing:

	Half handful fresh parsley	
6	slices French or Italian bread	6
1	onion, peeled and quartered	1
3 tbsp	unsalted butter	50 mL

1 lb	fresh mushrooms, cleaned	500 g
½ cup	whipping cream	125 mL
	Salt and freshly ground black pepper to taste	

Topping:

⅓ cup	fresh breadcrumbs from above	75 mL
1 tbsp	unsalted butter, melted	15 mL

Serves 6

1. Cut core from tomatoes. Cut tomatoes in half. Scoop out seeds and discard. Cut out pulp (a grapefruit knife or spoon is good for this) and save for soups or sauces. Sprinkle inside of scooped-out tomatoes with ½ tsp/2 mL salt and invert to drain on paper towels.
2. Fit work bowl with metal blade. Add parsley and chop using 5 or 6 on/off pulses. Remove and reserve.
3. Cut bread into cubes and add to work bowl still fitted with metal blade. Blend continuously until finely chopped. Remove from bowl and reserve.
4. Add onion to work bowl still fitted with metal blade. Process with 3 or 4 on/off pulses until onion is coarsely chopped.
5. Melt butter in skillet and add onions. Cook gently until tender and fragrant but do not brown.
6. Meanwhile refit work bowl with shredding disc. Process mushrooms through large or small feed tube. They will come out grated-chopped and perfect for duxelles. Add to onions and cook until nearly all mushroom liquid has evaporated from skillet.
7. Add whipping cream and continue cooking on medium-high heat until cream thickens and reduces quite a bit – about 5 minutes.
8. Remove from heat and stir in all but ⅓ cup/75 mL breadcrumbs (reserve this amount for topping). Stir in all but 1 tbsp/15 mL parsley (reserve with extra breadcrumbs). Taste mushroom mixture and season with salt and pepper.
9. Place tomatoes side by side in a flat casserole dish and divide mushroom filling evenly among them. Combine reserved breadcrumbs and parsley with 1 tbsp/15 mL melted butter and sprinkle over filling.
10. Just before serving, bake tomatoes in a preheated 350°F/180°C oven for 10 to 15 minutes or until heated through. Do not overcook or tomatoes may become mushy.

Vegetable Rice Pilaf

The pilaf method is one of the best ways to cook rice. Many different types of vegetables can be used, but this combination is particularly delicious and colorful.

2	onions, peeled and cut into quarters	2	¼ tsp	freshly ground pepper	1 mL
1	carrot, peeled and trimmed	1	1	bay leaf	1
1	rib celery	1		Handful fresh parsley	
8 oz	mushrooms	250 g	3 tbsp	unsalted butter	50 mL
3 tbsp	unsalted butter	50 mL	½ cup	grated Parmesan (if using freshly grated Parmesan, grate cheese before proceeding with rest of recipe — see page 14)	125 mL
1½ cups	long-grain rice	375 mL			
3 cups	chicken stock, homemade (see page 46) or commercial, hot	750 mL			
1 tsp	salt	5 mL	**Serves 6**		

1. Fit work bowl with metal blade. Add onions and chop coarsely using 3 or 4 on/off pulses. Remove and reserve.

2. With work bowl still fitted with metal blade, cut carrots into 1-in/2.5-cm lengths and add to work bowl. Chop using 5 or 6 on/off pulses. Remove to another bowl and reserve. Cut celery into 1-in/2.5-cm lengths and add to work bowl. Chop using a few on/off pulses. Reserve with carrots. Add mushrooms and chop using 2 or 3 on/off pulses (process mushrooms in 2 to 3 batches depending on size of your machine). Add to carrots.

3. Melt 3 tbsp/50 mL butter in a large saucepan and add onions. Cook until fragrant and wilted — about 5 minutes. Add remaining vegetables. Continue cooking until any juices from mushrooms have evaporated. Stir in rice and coat well with vegetables. Add hot chicken stock and bring to a boil. Add salt, pepper and bay leaf. Cover, reduce heat and cook 20 to 25 minutes or until all liquid has been absorbed.

4. Fit work bowl with metal blade that has been wiped dry. Add parsley and chop using 4 or 5 on/off pulses.

5. When rice is ready, stir in parsley, butter and cheese. Taste and reseason if necessary. Serve immediately.

Note: If the rice has absorbed all the liquid after only 10 or 15 minutes, your heat was too high. Add more liquid and cook longer. If after 30 or 35 minutes the liquid has not yet been absorbed, the rice will be overcooked and slightly mushy. Next time use a slightly higher heat. You can also make a rice pilaf in a casserole baked in a preheated 350°F/180°C oven for 30 minutes after the vegetables are wilted and the stock comes to a boil.

Wild Rice Pilaf with Wild Mushrooms

Wild rice is actually a grass rather than a grain, but when the long black needles are cooked and puff open, they resemble rice. The wild mushrooms add a wonderful taste to the rice, but if you can't find them, just use fresh mushrooms and 2 cups / 500 mL more chicken stock. Although wild rice has always been very expensive, the price is coming down because of new harvesting methods. Different qualities (usually determined by the length of the needle) also determine the price. In Toronto many large grocery stores sell generic wild rice for half the usual cost, and I've found it to be very good.

1	½-oz / 15-g package dried wild mushrooms (preferably Italian porcini)	1	2 cups	wild rice	500 mL	
2 cups	warm water	500 mL	3 cups	chicken stock, homemade (see page 46) or commercial, hot	750 mL	
1	clove garlic, peeled	1	1 tsp	salt (or more to taste)	5 mL	
2	onions, peeled and quartered	2	¼ tsp	freshly ground pepper	1 mL	
3 tbsp	unsalted butter	50 mL		Handful fresh parsley		
8 oz	fresh mushrooms, cleaned	250 g	**Serves 8**			

1. Place dried wild mushrooms in a bowl and cover with warm water. Allow to soak for 30 minutes. Drain mushrooms through a cheesecloth-lined strainer and reserve liquid with chicken stock. Rinse any extra sand off mushrooms carefully. Reserve.
2. Fit work bowl with metal blade. With machine running, drop garlic through feed tube and process until chopped. Add onions and process with 5 or 6 on / off pulses until finely chopped.
3. Melt butter in a Dutch oven or large saucepan and cook onion mixture gently until fragrant and tender.
4. Refit work bowl with medium or thin slicing disc. Fill small feed tube with fresh mushrooms and slice. Continue until all are sliced. Add to onions and cook until dry.

5. Add wild mushrooms and combine well.
6. Rinse wild rice with cold water, shake dry and add to mushroom-onion mixture. Stir to combine well. Add chicken stock / wild mushroom liquid mixture, salt and pepper. Bring to a boil. Cover, lower heat and cook gently 50 to 60 minutes or until rice is tender and has puffed open.
7. Meanwhile, refit work bowl with metal blade and add parsley. Chop with 5 or 6 on / off pulses until finely chopped. When rice is ready, stir in parsley and taste. Reseason if necessary.

Note: To serve this in a ring, butter a 1½ qt / 1.5-L ring mold well and pack cooked rice in firmly. Invert on a serving platter and lift off ring. The center can be filled with another vegetable.

Risotto

Risotto is an unusually textured dish that results from a unique cooking method. The rice should be creamy when it is finished, but you should be able to taste each grain distinctly. Unfortunately, to achieve this texture the rice must be stirred constantly as the stock is added and eaten immediately when it is finished. That is why not very many restaurants bother to serve risotto and why it is not more widely known even in home cooking. However, once you taste it you will certainly agree it is well worth the trouble.

Risotto is usually served as an appetizer in place of a pasta course in Italian cuisine and can be made with any number of sauces and ingredients. This plainer version can be served as an appetizer or with osso bucco (see page 84).

	Handful Italian parsley	
2	onions, peeled and quartered	2
¼ cup	unsalted butter	50 mL
2 cups	short-grain Italian rice (preferably Arborio)	500 mL
6 cups	chicken stock, homemade (see page 46) or commercial	1.5 L
1 tsp	salt	5 mL

¼ tsp	freshly ground pepper	1 mL
2 tbsp	unsalted butter	25 mL
½ cup	grated Parmesan cheese (if using freshly grated Parmesan, grate cheese before proceeding with rest of recipe — see page 14)	125 mL

Serves 8

1. Fit work bowl with metal blade. Add parsley to work bowl and chop with 6 to 8 on/off pulses until finely chopped. Remove and reserve. Add onions to work bowl and chop finely with 4 or 5 on/off pulses.

2. Melt butter in a large saucepan that is about 8 in/20 cm in diameter and about 5 in/12 cm deep. Add onions and cook gently about 10 minutes or until very fragrant and wilted. (This can be done ahead and removed from heat. Reheat just before adding rice.)

3. Add rice to onions and stir well to coat each grain with butter. Place chicken stock on the heat near the rice and bring to a boil.

4. Add about ½ cup/125 mL boiling stock to rice and, stirring constantly, cook until liquid is absorbed or evaporated. Heat should be medium to medium-high. When rice is dry, add another ½ cup/125 mL stock. Cook again as above, stirring constantly. Continue until all liquid is used or until rice is tender. The whole procedure should take approximately 30 minutes and the rice should be creamy but not mushy. If you have used all the liquid but the rice is not tender, simply add some boiling water and next time, use a slightly lower heat.

5. Stir in the salt, pepper, butter, reserved parsley and cheese. Taste and adjust seasoning if necessary. Serve immediately.

Pasta

The Cuisinart® DLC-8 and DLC-7 have a pasta attachment available and the recipe that accompanies the attachment is the best I have found. Therefore I will not repeat it here. This recipe is for use with a hand-cranked pasta machine (see page 112). You can also roll the dough by hand with a large rolling pin but it is much easier by machine. This pasta can be used where any egg noodle is called for — see Pasta Primavera (page 34), Pasta with Lemon and Garlic Sauce (page 35) and Pasta with Hazelnut Sauce (page 37).

3	extra-large eggs	3		2 cups	all-purpose flour or hard, unbleached white flour, or more	500 mL
1 tbsp	olive oil (see page 18)	15 mL				
½ tsp	salt	2 mL		Makes approximately 1 lb/500 g		

1. Fit work bowl with metal blade. Add eggs, oil and salt. Blend for 3 seconds. Add 1½ cups/375 mL flour and process on/off until dough comes together. If dough is too sticky to gather together, add extra flour by the spoonful until dough cleans sides of bowl.

2. Process 30 to 40 seconds to knead dough. Dough should be soft but not sticky. Add a few more spoonfuls flour if necessary. Use remaining flour for rolling out dough.

3. Cut dough in half. Keep the half you are not using wrapped in plastic or under a bowl. Set the rollers on the pasta machine to the widest width. Dip piece of dough in flour and pass through rollers. Fold pasta in thirds, dip in flour, turn sideways and pass through machine. Repeat this 5 or 6 times or until dough is very smooth. Set rollers one notch closer together. Dip dough in flour, do not fold, and pass through rollers. Only pass through rollers once at each notch from now on. Keep adjusting rollers so they are closer and closer together. When pasta is as thin as possible, cut into approximately 8-in/20-cm lengths and allow to dry while working with second piece.

4. With the pasta in these pieces you can prepare lasagna, cannelloni, tortellini and various other shapes. If you want fettucine (same as tagliatelli) or linguine (same as tagliarini) use the cutters that come with the machine. After the pieces of pasta are cut, toss with flour to prevent sticking.

5. The pasta is best if cooked in lots of boiling, salted water right away. It only takes 1 or 2 minutes after the water has returned to the boil. Otherwise you can dry it at room temperature for a few hours and cook it when you are ready. Even though it can be frozen or refrigerated, it loses texture if kept this way. It is better to dry it.

Spinach Pasta

When Giuliano Bugialli comes to teach at our school he prepares all sorts of pastas with different vegetables in the dough. He has made pasta with wild mushrooms, green peppers, garlic and red peppers, and these all change the flavor of the pasta dramatically. To make vegetable pastas, puree the vegetables and use them as part of the eggs in the recipes — see Bugialli's books, The Art of Italian Cooking *(Times Books) and* Classic Techniques of Italian Cooking *(Simon and Schuster) for recipes.*

When you prepare the pasta with spinach it very seldom alters the flavor but the color is sensational. This dough can be used for lasagna, cannelloni or fettucine.

4 oz	fresh spinach	125 g	3 cups	all-purpose flour or unbleached, hard white flour	750 mL
2	extra-large eggs	2			
1 tbsp	olive oil (see page 18)	15 mL			
½ tsp	salt	2 mL	**Makes approximately 1 lb/500 g**		

1. Wash spinach very well in several changes of water if necessary. Trim off coarse stems. Place in a Dutch oven or saucepan with just the water clinging to the leaves. Cover and cook until wilted. Cool and wring dry.

2. Fit work bowl with metal blade. Add spinach, eggs, oil and salt. Process until well blended and spinach is finely pureed. Add 1¾ cups/425 mL flour and process on/off until dough comes together and cleans sides of bowl. You may have to add more flour. If so, add it by spoonfuls.

3. Process for 30 to 40 seconds to knead. Dough should be smooth and soft but not sticky. Add more flour if necessary. Use remaining flour when rolling out dough.

4. See page 111 for rolling out instructions.

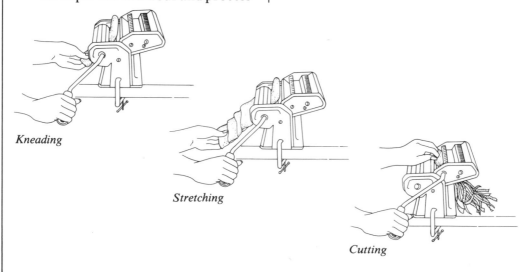

Kneading

Stretching

Cutting

Salads, Salad Dressings and Sauces

Although many food trends have come and gone, some, such as the salad craze, have come and stayed. Many of my students have suggested that salads first became popular when the exercising fad began and people became so concerned with calorie-watching. Others suggested that home cooks became interested in the possibilities of salad making after experimenting at restaurant salad bars. Some suggested that salads have become a more tempting menu item because of all the different kinds of oils and vinegars that are now available.

Simple salads are usually served after the main course because they cleanse the palate before the dessert, and the dressing does not then interfere with the taste of the wine. However, you can serve salads before the main course if you prefer. A new trend in menu planning is to serve salads as an appetizer, and actually many of the salads included in this chapter are meant to be served this way, or even as light main courses.

There are some dressings and sauces included in this chapter as well, and there are also many other dressings and sauces described in other recipes throughout the book. Check the list on page 115 for a complete selection.

Salmon and Pasta Salad with Lemon Dill Mayonnaise

This is a hearty salad that can be served as a light supper dish, first course or for brunch. I find that commercial, dried pasta stands up the best in pasta salads and in this recipe I prefer shell-shaped pasta or macaroni.

1	onion, peeled and quartered	1
1	carrot, peeled and trimmed	1
1	rib celery	1
	Small handful fresh parsley	
4 cups	water	1 L
½ cup	dry white wine	125 mL
1 tsp	salt	5 mL
¼ tsp	freshly ground pepper	1 mL
2 lb	salmon steaks or fillets	1 kg
4	green onions	4
1	ripe avocado	1
3	hard-cooked eggs	3
8 oz	shell-shaped pasta or macaroni	250 g

Lemon Dill Mayonnaise:
Small handful fresh parsley

	Large handful fresh dill	
1	egg, room temperature	1
1 tsp	dry mustard	5 mL
1 tsp	salt	5 mL
3 tbsp	lemon juice (or more to taste)	50 mL
¼ tsp	freshly ground pepper	1 mL
pinch	cayenne pepper	pinch
¾ cup	vegetable oil (I use corn oil)	175 mL
½ cup	olive oil (see page 18)	125 mL

Garnish:
Lettuce leaves
Lemon twists (see page 23)
Tomato roses (see page 22)

Serves 8

1. Fit work bowl with metal blade. Add onion and chop coarsely with 5 or 6 on/off pulses. Place chopped onion in saucepan.
2. Cut carrot into 1-in/2.5-cm chunks and add to work bowl still fitted with metal blade. Chop with 5 or 6 on/off pulses. Add to onions. Repeat with celery and then parsley.
3. Add water, wine, salt and pepper to saucepan. Bring to a boil and then simmer 15 minutes. Strain liquid, discard vegetables and transfer liquid to a large, heavy skillet.
4. Add salmon, in one layer if possible, and cover with a buttered piece of parchment paper, waxed paper or foil. Poach over medium heat 10 minutes per 1 in/2.5 cm of thick-

ness. Salmon should be barely cooked through. Remove from broth and cool. Break salmon into chunks. Save the cooking liquid for another purpose where a strong fish stock is required.

5. Prepare Lemon Dill Mayonnaise.

6. Add mayonnaise to salmon.

7. Refit work bowl with medium slicing disc. Cut green onions into thirds and pack tightly into small feed tube. Slice. Add green onions to salmon mixture.

8. Cut avocado in half and remove pit. Scoop out pulp and dice. Add to salmon. Cut hard-cooked eggs into wedges and add to salmon.

9. Bring large pot of water to a boil. Add approximately 1 tbsp/15 mL salt along with pasta. Cook 8 to 12 minutes or until just tender. Drain and rinse with cold water to stop cooking. Shake out excess moisture and cool. Combine with salmon and other ingredients and toss well.

10. Line a large serving dish with lettuce and mound salad on top. Surround with lemon twists and garnish with tomato roses. Refrigerate until ready to serve.

Lemon Dill Mayonnaise:

1. Fit work bowl with metal blade. Add parsley and dill and chop with 7 or 8 on/off pulses or until herbs are finely chopped. Remove from bowl and reserve.

2. Put egg, mustard, salt, lemon juice, pepper and cayenne in work bowl still fitted with metal blade. Add ¼ cup/50 mL oil. Blend 3 or 4 seconds. Add remaining vegetable oil and olive oil slowly through the feed tube as the machine is running. When oil has been added the mixture should be the consistency of mayonnaise. If it isn't, see page 123.

3. Add dill and parsley mixture. Blend. Taste and adjust seasoning with salt, pepper or lemon juice. Combine with salmon.

Dressings and Sauces from Other Chapters

Marinated Eggplant Salad

My friend Ruthie Ladovsky runs her family's restaurant, the United Bakers Dairy Restaurant. It is an institution in Toronto and serves some of the most delicious Jewish dairy meals. Ruthie passes on some wonderful recipes to me and this is one of her favorites. I like to serve it with lamb or with other salads for brunch.

2	large eggplants	2
1 tbsp	salt	15 mL
	Vegetable oil for deep-frying	
3	cloves garlic, peeled	3
	Large handful fresh parsley	
	Large handful fresh dill	
2	green peppers, halved and seeded	2

2	red peppers, halved and seeded	2
3	hot banana peppers, fresh or preserved	3
	Salt to taste	
½ tsp	freshly ground pepper	2 mL
½ cup	white vinegar	125 mL
½ cup	water	125 mL
¼ tsp	Tabasco sauce	1 mL

Serves 8

1. Trim base and stem ends of eggplants. Cut into ½-in/1-cm thick slices crosswise. Sprinkle eggplant with salt and place in a colander. Allow to drain at least 30 minutes. Rinse off salt and pat dry with paper towels.

2. Heat at least ¾ in/2 cm oil in a large skillet. Add a few eggplant slices at a time and cook approximately 4 minutes on each side until cooked through and golden brown. Drain on paper towels and repeat until all eggplant is cooked. Add more oil between batches if necessary.

3. Fit work bowl with metal blade. Add garlic through feed tube with machine running. Process until chopped. Add parsley and dill and process with 8 to 10 on/off pulses until herbs are finely chopped. Remove from bowl and reserve.

4. Refit work bowl with medium slicing disc. Cut green and red peppers into large cubes. Pack tightly in small feed tube and slice. Repeat until all are sliced. Leave in machine.

5. Carefully halve the hot peppers. If you have sensitive skin use rubber gloves. Remove seeds and ribs and cut into cubes. Pack into small feed tube and slice. Remove peppers, combine well and reserve.

6. In a large, flat casserole dish arrange a layer of eggplant, peppers, herbs and some salt and pepper. Repeat layers until all vegetables are used.

7. Combine vinegar, water and Tabasco sauce and pour over vegetables. Cover and allow to marinate overnight in the refrigerator.

Cold Rice Salad with Lime and Ginger Dressing

This is a refreshing, different salad that tastes wonderful with a cold main course.

1 tbsp	salt	15 mL	2	green onions, cut into 1-in/2.5-cm lengths	2	
1½ cups	raw, long-grain rice	375 mL	2 tbsp	lemon juice	25 mL	
2 tbsp	corn or vegetable oil	25 mL	2 tbsp	lime juice	25 mL	
4	carrots, peeled and trimmed	4	1 tsp	salt (or more to taste)	5 mL	
8 oz	snow peas	250 g	¼ tsp	freshly ground pepper	1 mL	

Lime and Ginger Dressing:

1	clove garlic, peeled	1
1	piece fresh ginger root, size of a quarter and ½ in/1 cm thick, peeled	1

1 tsp	Dijon mustard	5 mL
⅔ cup	olive oil (see page 18) or vegetable oil	150 mL

Serves 6 to 8

1. Bring a large pot of water to the boil. Add salt. Add rice in a thin stream and cook at a gentle boil, with water constantly rotating around rice, 12 to 15 minutes or until rice tastes tender. Drain in a fine sieve and rinse with cold water to stop the cooking. Shake dry and toss with 2 tbsp/25 mL vegetable oil so that it will not stick. Reserve in a large bowl.

2. Fit work bowl with medium or thin slicing disc. Fit carrots into small feed tube and slice. Boil 2 to 4 minutes until just barely tender, drain and refresh with cold water. Pat dry and add to rice.

3. Trim snow peas and cut into halves on the diagonal. Blanch in boiling water 30 seconds and drain. Refresh with cold water and pat dry. Add to rice.

4. Prepare Lime and Ginger Dressing.

5. Combine dressing with rice and vegetables and toss well. Allow to marinate in the refrigerator until ready to serve.

Lime and Ginger Dressing:

1. Wipe work bowl dry and fit with metal blade. With machine running, add garlic and ginger through feed tube.

2. Add green onions and process until well chopped. Add lemon and lime juice, salt, pepper and mustard. Blend.

3. With machine running, slowly add oil through the feed tube. Taste dressing and adjust seasoning if necessary.

Fiddlehead and Radish Salad

This is a delicious and unusual salad to serve as an appetizer or side salad. The fiddleheads are available fresh in the spring, but can be purchased frozen in specialty grocery stores all year round. If you cannot find fiddleheads, use green beans cooked for 3 minutes, cooled and cut into 1½-in/3-cm lengths.

1	10-oz/300-g package frozen fiddleheads, defrosted	1	½ cup	olive oil (see page 18) or vegetable oil	125 mL
2	large bunches radishes	2		Salt and freshly ground black pepper to taste	
4	green onions	4	¼ tsp	hot, red pepper flakes, optional	1 mL
1	clove garlic	1			
½ tsp	Dijon mustard	2 mL			
2 tbsp	fresh lemon juice	25 mL		Serves 6	

1. Cook fiddleheads in enough boiling water to cover for 2 minutes. Drain and refresh under cold water to stop the cooking. Pat dry with paper towels.
2. Fit work bowl with shredding or julienne disc. Place radishes in small feed tube and grate. Combine with fiddleheads.
3. Refit work bowl with medium or thin slicing disc. Cut green onions into thirds and pack tightly, standing up, in the small feed tube. Slice. Add to fiddleheads.
4. Wipe work bowl dry and refit with metal blade. Add garlic through feed tube with machine running. Add mustard and lemon juice and blend.
5. Slowly add oil through the feed tube. Add salt, pepper and hot pepper flakes. Taste dressing on a fiddlehead and adjust seasoning if necessary.
6. Combine dressing with vegetables and marinate until ready to serve.

Note: If you are using fresh fiddleheads, wash them well in 3 or 4 changes of cold water to clean out all the grit. Cook 8 to 12 minutes in boiling water until they are tender. Drain and refresh with cold water. Pat dry and use as above.

Spinach Salad with Blue Cheese Dressing

I like to serve this salad as an appetizer or light supper dish, as I think it is too hearty for a side salad. The dressing is one I use in our "Eat and Run" course because it is easy to prepare and very low in fat. You can use all spinach or combine spinach with lettuce. The dressing is also good over sliced avocados, cold poached chicken breasts or tomatoes.

1 lb	fresh spinach	500 g		¾ cup	cottage cheese	175 mL
8 oz	fresh mushrooms	250 g		2 tbsp	lemon juice	25 mL
3	tomatoes, cut into chunks	3		½ cup	unflavored yogurt	125 mL
				1 tsp	dried tarragon	5 mL
½ cup	black olives	125 mL		½ tsp	dried chervil	2 mL
Blue Cheese Dressing:					Salt and freshly ground black pepper to taste	
1	clove garlic, peeled	1				
2	green onions	2				
	Handful fresh parsley					
3 oz	blue cheese	100 g		**Serves 6**		

1. Wash spinach well in several changes of water. Break off and discard tough stems. Dry spinach thoroughly. Place in a large salad bowl.
2. Fit work bowl with medium slicing disc. Clean mushrooms with wet paper towels and trim. Arrange mushrooms on their sides in small feed tube. Pack tightly to the top and slice. Repeat until all mushrooms are sliced. Sprinkle mushrooms over the spinach. Arrange tomatoes and olives around outside edge.
3. Prepare Blue Cheese Dressing.
4. Just before serving pour dressing over salad and toss well.

Blue Cheese Dressing:

1. Fit work bowl with metal blade. Add garlic, green onions (cut into 1-in/2.5-cm lengths) and parsley. Chop with 9 or 10 on/off pulses until herbs are finely chopped.
2. Add blue cheese and blend with 2 or 3 on/off pulses.
3. Add cottage cheese and lemon juice and process until cheese is smooth.
4. Add yogurt and remaining ingredients. Taste dressing and adjust seasoning if necessary.

Note: The salad and dressing can be prepared ahead of time but should not be combined until just before serving as the leaves will wilt slightly if dressed too far in advance.

Vegetable Slaw

Cabbage is one of the most difficult vegetables to cut in any food processor (see page 14). After much experimentation, I have decided that I like it best coarsely chopped. In this recipe I use all the different blades — it's a great way to learn what they do. This is a large salad but it will keep well for a few days.

1	small cabbage	1
4	green onions	4
	Handful fresh parsley	
	Handful fresh dill	
2	carrots, peeled and trimmed	2
2	dill pickles	2
1	apple, cored (peeled or not to suit your taste)	1
1	red onion, peeled and halved	1
2	ribs celery	2
1	green pepper, halved and seeded	1

1	red pepper, halved and seeded	1
1	clove garlic, peeled	1
1½ cups	mayonnaise, homemade (see page 123) or commercial	375 mL
2 tbsp	Dijon mustard	25 mL
3 tbsp	red wine vinegar	50 mL
dash	Tabasco sauce	dash
½ cup	sour cream	125 mL
	Salt and freshly ground pepper to taste	

Serves 12

1. Cut cabbage in half and cut out core. Cut each half into 4 wedges and then each wedge in half crosswise. Fit work bowl with metal blade. Place 2 to 5 pieces (half wedges) in work bowl at one time, depending on size of your machine. Chop cabbage coarsely with only 3 or 4 on/off pulses. Remove from work bowl to a large bowl and repeat until all cabbage is chopped.

2. Cut green onions into 2-in/5-cm pieces and add to work bowl still fitted with metal blade. Add parsley and dill. Chop using 5 or 6 on/off pulses and add chopped herbs to cabbage.

3. Refit work bowl with shredding disc, French-fry or julienne disc. Cut carrots in half lengthwise and stand them up in small feed tube. Process so that carrots are grated but in short strands. Repeat with pickles and apples. Add to cabbage.

4. Refit work bowl with medium or thin slicing disc. Cut onion into quarters to fit small feed tube and slice. Pack celery ribs in small feed tube and slice. Cut peppers into 2-in/5-cm cubes and pack into small feed tube and slice. Add vegetables to cabbage.

5. Wipe the work bowl dry and refit with metal blade. Drop garlic through feed tube with machine running, and process until chopped.

6. Add remaining ingredients and blend thoroughly. Taste and season with salt and pepper if necessary. Dressing should be well seasoned as you are combining it with a lot of unseasoned ingredients.

Note: If you prefer to slice the cabbage, a trick for slicing the outer leaves is to roll individual leaves tightly and stack vertically in large feed tube as shown.

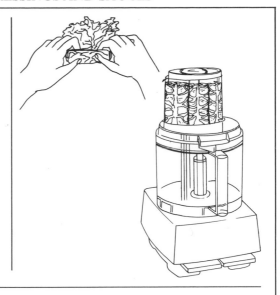

Mushroom Salad with Dill Dressing

This is a lovely salad to serve as an appetizer or a side salad. If you can't find watercress, serve the mushrooms on a leaf of Boston lettuce.

	Handful fresh parsley		¾ cup	olive oil (see page 18) or corn oil	175 mL
	Handful fresh dill		1½ lb	fresh mushrooms, cleaned and trimmed	750 g
¼ cup	red wine vinegar	50 mL	2	bunches watercress, washed, dried and trimmed	2
1 tsp	dry mustard	5 mL			
1 tsp	salt	5 mL			
¼ tsp	freshly ground pepper	1 mL	**Serves 6 to 8**		

1. Fit work bowl with metal blade. Add parsley and dill and chop with 8 or 9 on/off pulses. Add wine vinegar, mustard, salt and pepper. Blend.

2. With machine running, add oil through feed tube. Taste dressing on a mushroom and adjust seasoning with salt, pepper or oil.

3. Leave dressing in work bowl and refit bowl with slicing disc (thin or medium). Arrange mushrooms on their sides in small feed tube and

slice into dressing. Repeat until all mushrooms are sliced. Transfer to a bowl and allow to marinate in the refrigerator until ready to serve. (If work bowl becomes too full while slicing mushrooms, transfer dressing to a bowl first and add sliced mushrooms to it as they are processed.)

4. To serve, arrange a bed of watercress on each serving plate. Spoon mushrooms on the watercress and serve.

Cucumber and Tomato Raita

This yogurt salad is wonderful served with hot, spicy foods. Raitas (yogurt salads) are traditionally served as an accompaniment to curries and really do help cool your mouth after a hot bite. Raitas can be made with fruits, cooked vegetables or raw vegetables.

If you take the trouble to salt and drain the cucumbers before combining them with a dressing, they will not water down the dressing. Also, if raw onions are soaked in cold water, their sting is removed and they become much more digestible.

1	English cucumber	1		Handful fresh parsley		
2 tsp	salt	10 mL				
1	onion, peeled	1	2 cups	unflavored yogurt	500 mL
1 cup	ice water	250 mL	1 tsp	ground cumin	5 mL
2	tomatoes	2				
	Handful fresh coriander, if available (there is no substitute)			**Serves 6 to 8**		

1. Peel cucumber and cut in half lengthwise. Scoop out any seeds. Fit work bowl with thin or medium slicing disc. Cut cucumber in half crosswise, fit tightly into small feed tube and slice. Place cucumber slices in a colander and toss with salt. Allow to drain 30 minutes.

2. Meanwhile wipe out work bowl and refit with slicing disc. Cut onion to fit small feed tube and slice. Soak onions in ice water for about 20 minutes.

3. Cut tomatoes in half across and scoop out seeds. Cut into quarters. Refit work bowl with metal blade and add tomato quarters. Process with 3 or 4 on/off pulses until tomatoes are coarsely chopped. Drain.

4. Drain and pat cucumbers and onions dry and combine them in a serving bowl with tomatoes.

5. Wipe work bowl dry and refit with metal blade. Add fresh coriander and parsley and chop with 5 or 6 on/off pulses. Add yogurt and cumin and blend briefly. Combine with vegetables and refrigerate until ready to serve. Taste and adjust seasoning if necessary.

Homemade Mayonnaise

It is always a surprise to many people that mayonnaise is virtually just egg and oil. There really isn't anything "creamy" about it. When prepared by hand, the egg yolks must be whisked continuously as the oil is added drop by drop to form an emulsion. With a food processor, it is so easy to make and so much more delicious than commercial products, which often contain too much sugar and preservatives.

The flavor of homemade mayonnaise can vary in many ways. You can use a whole egg or two yolks — the mayonnaise will taste "eggier" with the two yolks. You can use lemon juice, which is my favorite, or you can use wine vinegar. The oil can also change the flavor of the mayonnaise, so be sure to taste the oil first to make sure you like it (peanut, safflower, corn and olive oil all taste completely different) and to make certain it is not rancid. I usually use extra virgin or first pressing olive oil, combined with corn oil.

When making mayonnaise, the more oil you add, the thicker the mayonnaise becomes. For example, if you want to decorate with it, you may want to add a little more oil. However, if you have added 1½ cups/375 mL and it hasn't thickened at all, then stop. This means it hasn't "caught," but this is very easy to fix (see below).

1	egg (or 2 yolks), room temperature	1
3 tbsp	lemon juice or wine vinegar	50 mL
1 tsp	dry mustard	5 mL
pinch	cayenne pepper	pinch
½ tsp	salt	2 mL
¼ tsp	freshly ground pepper	1 mL
1½ cups	vegetable oil (I use corn oil)	375 mL

Makes 1½ cups/375 mL

1. Fit work bowl with metal blade. Add egg, lemon juice, mustard, cayenne, salt, pepper and 3 tbsp/50 mL oil. Blend for 3 seconds.

2. With machine running, slowly drizzle the remaining oil through the opening in the feed tube. When all the oil has been added the consistency should be similar to commercial mayonnaise. Taste and adjust seasoning if necessary with salt, pepper or lemon juice.

3. Transfer to a jar and store in the refrigerator (I don't like to keep this longer than 4 or 5 days). It can also be frozen — to defrost, return to work bowl fitted with metal blade and process with 1 tbsp/15 mL boiling water until smooth.

Note: If mayonnaise has not thickened after adding the 1½ cups/375 mL oil, transfer the thin sauce to a container with a pouring spout. Wash and dry work bowl and add another egg at room temperature to bowl fitted with metal blade. With machine running, slowly drip thin sauce through feed tube into the egg. Mixture should now thicken.

Vinaigrette Dressing

This is the easiest but most important salad dressing of them all. A basic vinaigrette is suitable for any lettuce or marinated vegetable dish, so it is essential to have it in your repertoire. There are many variations — so try them all and decide on your favorite. You can make this dressing ahead of time and store it in the refrigerator. If it separates, just return it to the work bowl fitted with the metal blade and blend.

3 tbsp	red wine vinegar or lemon juice or other vinegar of your choice	50 mL	1 tsp	salt	5 mL
			¼ tsp	freshly ground pepper	1 mL
1 tsp	dry mustard or Dijon mustard	5 mL	¾ cup	olive oil (see page 18) or vegetable oil	175 mL

Makes approximately 1 cup/250 mL

1. Fit work bowl with metal blade and add vinegar, mustard, salt and pepper.
2. Blend ingredients together.
3. With machine running, add oil through the feed tube. This will form a temporary emulsion and dressing will thicken.

Variations:

Garlic Vinaigrette:

Before adding vinegar, add one clove peeled garlic through the feed tube while the machine is running. Proceed as above. As dressing stands, the garlic flavor will increase.

Herb Vinaigrette:

If you are using fresh herbs such as tarragon, dill, basil or chervil, add half a handful to the work bowl with half a handful of parsley before the vinegar. Chop using 6 or 7 on/off pulses and proceed as above. (Fresh herbs will chop better if some parsley is also used, and the fresh parsley usually adds to the flavor.) If you are using dried herbs, use approximately 1 tsp/5 mL (total measure) and add at the end.

Shallot Vinaigrette:

Peel and halve one shallot. Fit work bowl with metal blade. While machine is running add shallot through feed tube. Add vinegar and proceed as above.

Tarragon Salad Dressing

This creamy dressing is great on most lettuce salads and is especially good with spinach. I also love it served over cooked, cold asparagus.

1	clove garlic, peeled	1	¼ tsp	freshly ground pepper	1 mL
1	egg yolk	1	1 tsp	dried tarragon (1 tbsp/15 mL fresh)	5 mL
1 tbsp	Dijon mustard	15 mL			
2 tbsp	lemon juice	25 mL	¾ cup	olive oil (see page 18) or vegetable oil	175 mL
1 tbsp	red wine vinegar	15 mL			
1 tsp	salt	5 mL			

Makes approximately 1½ cups/375 mL

1. Fit work bowl with metal blade. With machine running, drop garlic through feed tube and process until chopped.
2. Add egg yolk, mustard, lemon juice, wine vinegar, salt, pepper and tarragon. Blend together well.
3. With machine running, drip oil through feed tube. Dressing should be thick. Taste and adjust seasoning if necessary.

Mustard Dressing

This is great on cold roast beef, cold chicken and anytime you want a rich mustard flavor. Whenever I have leftover roast beef I cut it into julienne strips and toss it with cooked green beans or asparagus, hard-cooked eggs, cooked potatoes, tomatoes, Romaine lettuce and this dressing.

This is a creamy dressing similar to mayonnaise but not as stable. If you do not use it immediately, store it in a covered container in the refrigerator. If it separates, just return it to the work bowl and process until blended again.

2 tbsp	Dijon mustard	25 mL	¼ tsp	freshly ground pepper	1 mL
¼ cup	red wine vinegar	50 mL	¾ cup	olive oil (see page 18) or corn oil	175 mL
1 tsp	Worcestershire sauce	5 mL			
½ tsp	salt (or more to taste)	2 mL			

Makes 1 cup/250 mL

1. Fit work bowl with metal blade. Place mustard, vinegar, Worcestershire sauce, salt and pepper in work bowl and blend.
2. With machine running, slowly add oil through the feed tube until dressing thickens. Taste and adjust seasoning as necessary.

Tomato Sauce

Although I have tried many different tomato sauces, this is still my favorite all-purpose recipe. Unless tomatoes are in season, I prefer to use the canned plum tomatoes as they seem to give a more consistently flavored sauce. This freezes well — when reheating, simply whisk if it separates.

2	cloves garlic, peeled	2		2 cups	chicken stock, homemade (see page 46) or commercial	500 mL
2	onions, peeled and quartered	2		1 tsp	salt	5 mL
1	carrot, peeled and trimmed	1		½ tsp	freshly ground pepper	2 mL
1	rib celery	1		1	bay leaf	1
1	leek, white and light green part only, cleaned	1		1 tsp	dried thyme	5 mL
				1 tsp	dried oregano	5 mL
¼ cup	olive oil (see page 18) or unsalted butter	50 mL		1 tsp	dried basil	5 mL
¼ cup	all-purpose flour	50 mL			Half handful fresh parsley	
½ cup	tomato paste	125 mL				
1	28-oz/796 mL can plum tomatoes, undrained	1				

Makes approximately 4 cups/1 L

1. Fit work bowl with metal blade. With machine running, drop garlic through feed tube and process until chopped. Add onions to work bowl and process with 5 or 6 on/off pulses until finely chopped. Remove and transfer to a bowl.

2. Cut carrot into 2-in/5-cm pieces and add to work bowl still fitted with metal blade. Chop with 5 or 6 on/off pulses until coarsely chopped. Add to onions. Repeat with celery and leek.

3. Heat oil or butter in a large saucepan or Dutch oven. Add vegetables and cook over medium heat until wilted and very fragrant. Add flour and cook at least 5 minutes.

4. Add tomato paste, tomatoes with juice and chicken stock. Bring to a boil, stirring constantly, as tomatoes tend to burn easily. Add salt and pepper. Reduce heat.

5. Make a bouquet garni (spice bag) by placing the herbs in a piece of cheesecloth and tying firmly. Add to sauce. Cook gently for 1½ hours, stirring occasionally.

6. Remove bouquet garni. Fit work bowl with metal blade. Puree sauce in 3 or 4 batches depending on size of your machine. Taste and season as necessary.

Note: If tomatoes are in season use 8 large peeled tomatoes instead of the canned tomatoes and increase chicken stock to 3 cups/750 mL.

Pickles, Preserves, Jams and Condiments

When I was a child I liked everything absolutely plain–and that included hot dogs and hamburgers. Mustards, relishes and pickles were all out! Even when I started to love food, pickles and preserves were still not high on my list of food priorities. But after meeting Linda Stephen (my associate teacher at the cooking school), Loni Kuhn (cooking teacher in San Francisco) and Gwen Fargeon (excellent cook and good friend in Mont Rolland, Quebec), I came under their influence and now I love pickles, preserves, mustards, jams and jellies. But I have to admit that I still prefer to eat them rather than prepare them!

Because I think students can tell if a teacher really loves what he or she is teaching, I do not teach the pickling and preserving classes myself. Linda Stephen, who was born and raised on a farm near Coburg, Ontario, loves pickling and preserving, so she teaches these classes at my school. Therefore in this chapter there are some of Linda's recipes and some from Loni and Gwen as well. I have also included a recipe for homemade almond paste (page 135) as I think that most commercial brands contain too much sugar.

Bread and Butter Pickles

I was never that fond of different types of pickles, but between Linda Stephen, who teaches our pickling and preserving courses, and friends who can't seem to pickle enough, I've become quite an addict. This recipe from Gwen Fargeon of Mont Rolland, Quebec, was one of the first that won me over. And now that the Cuisinart® is involved, the whole job is far easier.

2	cloves garlic, peeled	2
2	green peppers, halved and seeded	2
3	large onions, peeled and quartered	3
20 to 25	pickling cucumbers (approximately 4 in/10 cm long) or 4 English cucumbers, unpeeled (should be 10 cups/2.5 L after slicing)	20 to 25

⅓ cup	coarse salt	75 mL
4	trays ice cubes	4
3 cups	white vinegar	750 mL
4 cups	sugar	1 L
1½ tsp	turmeric	7 mL
1½ tsp	celery seed	7 mL
1½ tsp	mustard seed	7 mL

Makes 6 (1 pint/500 mL each) jars

1. Fit work bowl with metal blade. With machine running, drop garlic through feed tube and process until chopped. Remove ribs from green peppers and cut into 2-in/5-cm cubes. Add to work bowl and chop with 4 or 5 on/off pulses. Remove to large mixing bowl.

2. Refit work bowl with medium slicing disc. Fit onions into small feed tube and slice. Add to peppers in large bowl.

3. Trim ends off unpeeled cucumbers and slice through small feed tube. As the work bowl becomes filled, remove slices to large bowl. When all cucumbers have been sliced, combine vegetables well.

4. Add salt and ice cubes to bowl of vegetables and combine well. Allow to rest 4 hours. Drain well and discard any ice cubes that are left.

5. In a large stainless-steel saucepan or Dutch oven combine remaining ingredients. Bring to a boil. Stir until sugar is completely dissolved. Add vegetables and bring to a boil again.

6. Immediately remove from heat and spoon into hot, sterilized jars. Place a sterilized knife in each jar to remove any air bubbles. Seal immediately.

Note: If you are using English cucumbers, make sure that you buy cucumbers that will fit the small feed tube.

Opposite: *Salmon and Pasta Salad with Lemon Dill Mayonnaise (see page 114).*
Overleaf: *Braided Spiced Challah (see page 142).*

Chili Sauce

Homemade chili sauce is far superior to the commercial varieties, and with the Cuisinart® it really isn't too time consuming to prepare.

30	medium-sized tomatoes	30
6	onions, peeled and quartered	6
6	ribs celery	6
1	red pepper, halved and seeded	1
1	green pepper, halved and seeded	1
4 cups	white vinegar	1 L

2 cups	sugar	500 mL
2 tbsp	coarse salt	25 mL
1 tsp	mustard seed	5 mL
1 tsp	celery seed	5 mL
½ tsp	cinnamon	2 mL
¾ tsp	hot, red pepper flakes (more or less to taste)	4 mL

Makes 14 to 16 cups/3.5 to 4 L

1. Cut core from each tomato and make a cross in the opposite end. Bring a large pot of water to a boil and add tomatoes, about 6 at a time. Cook for 1 minute only. Remove and peel off skin. Cut peeled tomatoes in quarters. Place in a large stainless-steel pot.

2. Fit work bowl with metal blade. Add 2 quartered onions at a time and chop with 4 or 5 on/off pulses. Add to tomatoes and continue until all onions are chopped. If you have the DLC-8, DLC-7 or DLC-X, you can chop 3 onions at a time.

3. Cut celery into 2-in/5-cm pieces and add 2 or 3 ribs at a time to machine still fitted with metal blade. Chop with 3 or 4 on/off pulses and add to tomatoes. Repeat until all celery is chopped.

4. Remove ribs from peppers and cut into 2-in/5-cm chunks. Add to work bowl still fitted with metal blade and with 3 or 4 on/off pulses chop coarsely. Add to tomatoes.

5. Add remaining ingredients to pot and bring to a boil. Reduce heat and simmer gently, uncovered, 2 to 2 ½ hours or until mixture is quite thick. Stir occasionally and break up tomatoes. Towards the end of the cooking time stir more frequently as mixture tends to stick.

6. Pour hot sauce into hot, sterilized jars and seal.

Opposite: *Apricot Mousse in Chocolate Cups* 129 *(see page 172).*
Overleaf: *Hazelnut Cheesecake with Chocolate Glaze (see page 156).*

Carrot Marmalade

This is a wonderful variation on traditional marmalades. It is not expensive to pre-pare and makes great presents.

10	medium-sized carrots, peeled and trimmed (1½ lb/750 g)	10
2	oranges	2
2	lemons	2

2	red cooking apples	2
3 cups	water	750 mL
2 cups	sugar	500 mL
1 cup	honey	250 mL

Makes 6 (1 cup/250 mL each) jars

1. Fit work bowl with shredding disc. Fit carrots individually into small feed tube and grate. If the machine gets too full, transfer grated carrots to a large stainless-steel bowl (you should have about 5 cups/1.25 L packed carrots).
2. Refit work bowl with thin or medium slicing disc. Cut oranges and lemons into quarters, remove as many seeds as possible and slice standing up through small feed tube. Add to carrots in bowl.
3. Refit work bowl with metal blade. Cut apples in half and remove cores and seeds. Cut into quarters and add to work bowl. Process with 5 or 6 quick on/off pulses to chop coarsely. Add to carrots and combine ingredients well. Add water. Cover bowl and allow to rest overnight.
4. Transfer mixture to large stainless-steel pot and bring to boil. Reduce heat and simmer 20 minutes.
5. Stir in sugar and honey and bring to a boil again. Cook gently over medium heat until mixture reaches the jelly stage – about 30 minutes. It should be 225°F/110°C on a candy thermometer.
6. Pour into hot, sterilized jars and seal with melted paraffin.

Nectarine-Ginger Jam

This is one of Linda Stephen's favorite jams, which she developed for the pickling and preserving course at the school. It is also good made with peaches.

2½ lb	nectarines, washed, halved and pitted	1.25 kg	2¾ cups	sugar	675 mL
⅓ cup	lemon juice	75 mL			
3 tbsp	candied ginger in syrup	50 mL			

Makes 6 (3/4 cup/175 mL each) jars

1. Cut unpeeled nectarines into approximately 1-in/2.5-cm pieces and combine with lemon juice.

2. Fit work bowl with metal blade and add ginger. Process with 3 or 4 on/off pulses until ginger is coarsely chopped. Add to nectarines and combine.

3. In 4 to 6 batches, depending on the size of your machine, add nectarines to work bowl fitted with metal blade and process with 6 or 7 on/off pulses until you have a rough mixture of pulp and coarse chunks.

4. Measure out 5 cups/1.25 L nectarine pulp (should be almost everything). Place in a large stainless-steel pot and bring to the boil. Boil steadily 25 minutes, partially covered. Stir often.

5. Remove from heat and stir in sugar. Bring to a boil again and cook at a gentle boil for 15 minutes or until mixture reaches the jelly stage — 225°F/110°C on a candy thermometer.

6. Pour into hot, sterilized jars and seal with melted paraffin.

Mincemeat

Linda Stephen recommends serving this in tiny baked tart shells, as it is very rich.

	Rind of 2 lemons	
1 cup	brown sugar	250 mL
1¾ cups	currants	425 mL
1¾ cups	golden raisins	425 mL
1¼ cups	dark, seedless raisins	300 mL
1 cup	mixed candied fruit peel	250 mL
½ cup	candied citron	125 mL
¼ cup	candied ginger in syrup	50 mL
1 lb	suet	500 g

3	apples, peeled, halved and cored	3
½ cup	lemon juice	125 mL
1 cup	Cognac or brandy	250 mL
1 tsp	allspice	5 mL
1 tsp	cinnamon	5 mL
½ tsp	mace	2 mL
½ tsp	nutmeg	2 mL

Makes 5 pints/2.5 L

1. Fit work bowl with metal blade. Pat lemon peel dry and add through feed tube with machine running. Add brown sugar and continue processing until peel is finely chopped. Remove from bowl and place in a large mixing bowl.
2. Add currants to work bowl still fitted with metal blade. Chop with 3 or 4 on/off pulses. Add to bowl with sugar. Repeat with each batch of raisins. Add candied peel, citron and ginger to work bowl still fitted with metal blade. Chop with 3 or 4 on/off pulses. Remove to large mixing bowl.
3. Wipe work bowl dry and refit with metal blade. If suet is not already chopped, cut it into 1-in/2.5-cm cubes and chop finely in 2 batches. Add to bowl of fruit.
4. Refit work bowl with shredding disc. Grate apples and add to fruit and suet.
5. Add remaining ingredients to fruit and suet and combine thoroughly.
6. Spoon into hot, sterilized jars and seal. Store in the refrigerator for 4 weeks before using.

Orange Chutney

I first tasted this chutney at Loni Kuhn's cooking class in San Francisco. It tastes great with roast chicken or pork.

7	large oranges	7	2	green peppers	2
1	large lemon	1	2	red peppers	2
2½ cups	dark brown sugar	625 mL	¾ cup	golden raisins	175 mL
3	large onions, peeled and quartered	3	1½ tsp	freshly ground pepper	7 mL
6	cloves garlic, peeled	6	1 tsp	salt (or more if necessary)	5 mL
5	pieces fresh ginger root, size of a quarter and ½ in/1 cm thick, peeled	5	1 tsp	cayenne pepper	5 mL
			1 tsp	hot, red pepper flakes	5 mL
5	Granny Smith apples, peeled and cored	5	2 tbsp	turmeric	25 mL
			4 cups	malt vinegar	1 L

Makes about 6 pints/1.5 L

1. Remove peel from oranges and lemon with a vegetable peeler (colored part only – no white pith). Pat dry with paper towels. Fit work bowl with metal blade. In 2 batches, add peel with half the brown sugar in each batch. Process continuously until peel is finely chopped. Remove to a large, heavy preserving kettle.
2. Remove white pith from oranges and lemon. Cut fruit into sections and discard seeds. In 3 batches, chop orange and lemon pulp using a few on/off pulses. Add chopped fruit to preserving kettle.
3. Wipe bowl dry and refit with metal blade. Add onions, garlic and ginger to work bowl in 2 batches and chop using 6 or 7 on/off pulses. Add finely chopped mixture to kettle. Cut apples into chunks and chop in 2 batches using 4 or 5 on/off pulses. Add to kettle.
4. Cut green and red peppers in half and discard ribs and seeds. In 2 batches add to work bowl and chop coarsely using 4 or 5 on/off pulses. Add peppers and any accumulated juices to kettle.
5. Add raisins and all remaining ingredients to kettle. Simmer gently 1½ hours. Stir frequently to prevent sticking. Continue cooking until mixture is thickened and well blended. Taste and adjust seasoning (usually salt and/or sugar).
6. Pour into sterilized jars and seal. Process in a water bath for 10 minutes.

Pralines and Praline Powder

Pralines are caramel-coated nuts. They're wonderful to have on hand for last-minute ice cream toppings and snacks. They also make nice presents. You can leave the chunks whole and eat it like a sophisticated peanut brittle, you can chop it up to use in icings, ice creams and toppings, or you can leave it in chunks and eat it coated with melted chocolate. I like the combination of almonds and hazelnuts but many people love them made with pecans or walnuts. If shelled hazelnuts are not available at your supermarket, try a health food store or specialty nut store.

1½ cups	white, granulated sugar	375 mL	1 cup	shelled, toasted hazelnuts, with skins removed	250 mL
⅓ cup	water	75 mL			
1 cup	shelled, toasted whole almonds, blanched or unblanched	250 mL			

Makes approximately 2½ cups/625 mL

1. Have a buttered cookie sheet close by. Also have a small bowl of cold water and a pastry brush at hand.

2. Place sugar and water in a heavy saucepan. Cook, stirring until mixture reaches a boil and sugar dissolves.

3. Continue to cook, watching closely without stirring, until mixture turns a deep caramel color. Every now and then brush any sugar crystals from the side of the pot down into the mixture with the pastry brush dipped in cold water. The caramel should be a deep golden color, but if it burns it must be discarded as it will be very bitter. (At least that way you are only wasting sugar and not the expensive nuts!)

4. When mixture reaches proper color, remove from heat and stir in nuts quickly. Spread on buttered cookie sheet. Allow to cool at least 1 hour.

5. Break mixture up with a knife into approximately 2-in/5-cm chunks and fit work bowl with metal blade. Add pralines in 2 batches. For pralines chop coarsely. For praline powder process until fine. Repeat with remaining mixture.

6. Store in tightly sealed jars in refrigerator or freeze. Use as directed in specific recipes or sprinkle over desserts, parfaits or ice cream.

Note: To toast and remove skins from hazelnuts, see page 18. Do not worry if little bits of skin remain.

Almond Paste (or Hazelnut Paste)

Sometimes it is very hard to find good almond paste even in the best specialty stores. Most places seem to stock it only around Christmas. The very sweet almond icing is a poor substitute. But it is easy to prepare your own. Hazelnut paste is an excellent variation in most recipes that call for almond paste. It is easy to find blanched almonds but you have to remove the brown skins from the hazelnuts yourself (see page 18).

1½ cups	blanched almonds or hazelnuts	375 mL	1	egg white	1
1¼ cups	icing sugar	300 mL	½ tsp	pure almond extract	2 mL

Makes approximately 1 lb/500 g

1. Fit work bowl with metal blade. Add almonds and sugar. Chop using 9 or 10 on/off pulses until nuts are finely chopped.
2. Run machine continuously until nuts are a fine powder. Add egg white and almond extract and process continuously until a paste is formed.
3. Remove from work bowl and wrap well in plastic. Store in the refrigerator or freeze.

Breads, Muffins and Biscuits

After all these years of cooking and teaching students to cook exotic foods, I still have not found anything more rewarding than baking bread.

For some reason people seem to be intimidated by yeast. This is probably because it is alive and yes, you can kill it. But if you treat it gently and keep it warm and cosy–not too hot or not too cold–it is very easy to work with. And I can assure you that your first successful loaf of bread will thrill you more than making a sophisticated recipe that takes days to prepare. I remember a student once telling me of her first bread-baking experience: "The bread smelled wonderful. From the outside, it looked like a perfect loaf. But when I sliced it, and it was actually bread on the *inside*, I was ecstatic. I felt like an earth mother."

Bread is very easy to make in the Cuisinart®, and if you have one of the large models you can make as much bread at one time as you can in a heavy-duty electric mixer. But even if you have the DLC-10 you can make three separate loaves in the time it would take a mixer to prepare the three loaves at once. If you are making bread and using less than 4 cups/1L of flour in the DLC-X or less than 3 cups/750 mL in the DLC-7, DLC-8 or DLC-10, you should use the metal blade. For larger quantities use the plastic blade.

When making yeast breads, add most of the flour called for in the recipe to the work bowl and add the liquid as directed. In most cases the mixture will be very sticky, as it is always easier to add more flour to a sticky dough than water to a dry dough. However, the dough should not be so sticky that it strains and/or stops the machine. Add flour until the dough cleans the sides of the work bowl but is still soft and manageable.

Whole Wheat Honey Bread

This bread is wholesome and delicious. It is light in texture but has a wonderful whole-grain flavor. It's great for sandwiches and toast and can also be shaped into hot dog or hamburger buns.

1 tsp	sugar	5 mL		1 tsp	salt	5 mL
¼ cup	warm water	50 mL		1 cup	unflavored yogurt	250 mL
1	envelope dry yeast	1		2 tbsp	oil or unsalted butter, melted	25 mL
1 cup	hard whole-wheat flour	250 mL		2 tbsp	honey	25 mL
2 cups	all-purpose flour or hard, unbleached white flour	500 mL		**Glaze:**		
				1	egg	1
¼ cup	bran, optional	50 mL		½ tsp	salt	2 mL
¼ cup	wheat germ, optional	50 mL				

Makes 2 medium-sized loaves

1. Dissolve sugar in warm water and sprinkle yeast over the top. Allow mixture to rest 10 minutes or until mixture has bubbled up and doubled in volume.

2. Meanwhile fit work bowl with metal or plastic blade. Add whole-wheat flour and 1½ cups/375 mL all-purpose flour. Add bran and wheat germ if you are using them and salt. Blend together a few seconds.

3. When yeast has bubbled up, stir it down and combine with yogurt, oil and honey. With machine running, slowly pour liquid ingredients through the feed tube. Continue running until blended. Add enough extra white flour until the dough comes away from the sides of the bowl. This may take more or less than the remaining ½ cup/125 mL flour – do not worry. The dough should be moist and easy to handle but not sticky to the touch. Run the machine 40 seconds to knead the dough and then remove from work bowl.

4. Butter a large bowl and turn dough around in bowl until it is completely greased. Cover bowl with buttered plastic wrap and place in a warm place (no hotter than 80°F/30°C) to rise until doubled in volume – 1 to 2 hours.

5. When dough has doubled, punch it down and shape into loaf or loaves. Butter pans and line with a strip of parchment paper if you wish. Fit loaf or loaves into pan(s) and cover loosely with buttered plastic wrap. Allow to rise again about 1 hour or until doubled.

6. Preheat oven to 400°F/200°C. Combine egg and salt with a fork or in work bowl fitted with metal blade, using 2 on/off pulses. Slash tops of loaves and brush with egg mixture just before baking. Bake 1 large loaf 40 to 45 minutes and 2 smaller loaves 30 to 35 minutes. Remove bread from pans as soon as they are ready and cool on wire racks.

Caraway Sour Rye Bread

A good rye bread is very hard to make because of the nature of rye flour. If you use too much rye flour, the bread will hardly rise because there is not enough gluten in it. This is one of the best homemade rye breads I've ever tasted. Don't worry if the dough is quite moist — if it is too dry the bread will not rise as much.

2 tsp	sugar	10 mL	½ cup	cracked wheat	125 mL
½ cup	warm water	125 mL	¾ cup	water	175 mL
2	envelopes dry yeast	2	¼ cup	white vinegar	50 mL
1½ cups	light rye flour	375 mL	2 tbsp	vegetable oil	25 mL
2 cups	hard, unbleached white flour (or more)	500 mL	¼ cup	yellow cornmeal	50 mL
			1	egg white	1
1 tbsp	salt	15 mL	2 tbsp	cracked wheat	25 mL
2 tbsp	caraway seeds	25 mL	**Makes 2 small oval loaves**		

1. Dissolve sugar in warm water and sprinkle with yeast. Allow to rest 10 minutes or until yeast has bubbled up and doubled in volume.

2. Fit work bowl with plastic or metal blade. Add rye flour, white flour, salt, caraway seeds and cracked wheat. Blend 3 seconds or just until combined. Combine water, vinegar and oil in a measuring cup. When yeast is ready, stir it down and add to water mixture.

3. With machine running, very slowly drip in liquid ingredients through feed tube. Mixture will probably be very wet so add extra white flour by the spoonful until dough is very moist but not too sticky to be handled. Dough should just clean sides of work bowl.

4. Process dough about 30 seconds to knead.

5. Remove dough from work bowl and place in a greased bowl. Turn dough until completely greased. Cover with buttered plastic wrap and allow to rise until doubled —

usually 1½ hours but sometimes up to 2 or 2½ hours as this dough is heavy. Punch dough down and then allow to rise in bowl again until doubled. This time it should only take 1 to 2 hours.

6. When dough is ready punch down a second time and divide in half. Roll out each half into an elongated oval shape (about 10 in/25 cm long). Roll up each loaf tightly lengthwise and pinch seam to close.

7. Sprinkle a large cookie sheet with cornmeal. Place loaves on top of cornmeal with the seam side down. Slash loaves on top at regular intervals. Cover with buttered plastic wrap and allow to rise until doubled — about 1 hour.

8. Preheat oven to 400°F/200°C. Just before baking brush loaves with slightly beaten egg white and sprinkle with cracked wheat. Bake 15 minutes. Reduce heat to 375°F/190°C. Bake 25 to 30 minutes longer. Remove loaves from baking pans immediately after removing from oven and cool on wire racks.

Oatmeal Bread

In this recipe maple syrup is used for sweetening, but honey, corn syrup or sugar can be used if you prefer. One of my students, Dick Dewhurst, gave me an unusual recipe for oatmeal, which calls for apple juice instead of water. It's delicious. So as an experiment I used apple juice instead of the 1½ cups/375 mL water in this recipe. It tastes wonderful — try it as a variation.

¾ cup	uncooked rolled oats	175 mL		2 cups	hard whole-wheat flour	500 mL
3 tbsp	maple syrup	50 mL		2 cups	all-purpose flour or more if necessary	500 mL
3 tbsp	unsalted butter	50 mL		**Glaze:**		
1½ tsp	salt	7 mL		1	egg	1
1½ cups	boiling water	375 mL		2 tbsp	water	25 mL
1 tsp	sugar	5 mL		2 tbsp	uncooked rolled oats	25 mL
3 tbsp	warm water	50 mL		**Makes 2 medium-sized loaves**		
1	envelope dry yeast	1				

1. Combine the oats with maple syrup, butter, salt and boiling water. Stir and allow to cool at least 20 minutes. Mixture should be at room temperature or cooler when you use it.

2. Dissolve sugar in warm water and sprinkle yeast over the top. Allow to rest 10 minutes until mixture has bubbled up. Stir it down and combine with the cool oat mixture.

3. Fit work bowl with plastic or metal blade. Add whole-wheat flour and 1½ cups/375 mL all-purpose flour. Blend together briefly. With machine running, slowly add the yeast-oat mixture. Dough will probably be very sticky. Add additional flour by the spoonful until dough has a soft texture. Dough should just clean sides of work bowl. Don't worry if you need more flour (you want the dough to be moist but not so sticky that you cannot handle it). Then process continuously for 30 seconds to knead.

4. Place dough in a buttered bowl and turn until dough is completely greased. Cover with buttered plastic wrap and set in a warm place to rise until doubled in bulk (about 1 to 2 hours).

5. Punch dough down and divide in half. Pat each half out into a large rectangle (approximately 24 in x 8 in/60 cm x 20 cm). Fold each rectangle into thirds crosswise and then roll up tightly lengthwise. Fit into 2 greased loaf pans approximately 8 in x 5 in/1.5 L. Cover with buttered plastic wrap and allow to rise in a warm place until doubled (about 1 to 1½ hours).

6. Preheat oven to 400°F/200°C. Just before baking combine egg with water. Brush over top of loaves and sprinkle with oats. Slash tops of loaves if you wish.

7. Bake 35 to 40 minutes. Remove from pans immediately and cool on wire racks.

Challah (Braided Egg Loaf)

My maternal grandmother had a large family — eleven children. The family was very poor and lived in Grand Valley, Ontario. She used to make the most fabulous challahs, and every year she'd win first prize at the county fairs. The prize was always enough flour to keep the family in bread for the year! She was a very practical woman.

When I make this bread in my classes I always do it to look like my grandmother's. She used to braid two loaves and bake them together in a large square tin. The braid would bubble up over the top and have straight sides — it looked gorgeous. My grandmother kept a kosher kitchen, so she made this bread with water and oil, but I like it with butter and milk.

1 tsp	sugar	5 mL		3	eggs	3
¼ cup	warm water	50 mL		4 cups	all-purpose flour or more if necessary	1 L
1	envelope dry yeast	1		**Glaze:**		
¾ cup	milk or water	175 mL		1	egg	1
¼ cup	honey or sugar	50 mL		2 tbsp	cream or water	25 mL
¼ cup	unsalted butter or vegetable oil	50 mL		2 tbsp	sesame seeds	25 mL
1½ tsp	salt	7 mL		**Makes 1 large loaf**		

1. Dissolve sugar in warm water and sprinkle yeast over the top. Allow to rest until mixture has bubbled up and doubled in volume – about 10 minutes.

2. Meanwhile combine milk, honey, butter and salt and heat just until butter melts. Cool to room temperature. Beat in eggs. When yeast is ready, stir it down and add it to other liquid ingredients.

3. Fit work bowl with plastic or metal blade. Add 3¾ cups/925 mL flour. With machine running, slowly add liquid ingredients through the feed tube. When all the liquid has been added the dough should be quite sticky. Add more flour by the spoonful until dough reaches proper consistency. Do not worry if you need more flour – you want the dough to be soft and moist but not too sticky to handle. Dough should just clean sides of work bowl. Then run machine for 40 seconds to knead. Remove dough from machine and place in a well-buttered bowl. Turn dough until completely greased. Cover with buttered plastic wrap and set in a warm place to rise until doubled – about 1½ hours.

4. When dough has doubled, punch down and shape. The easiest way is to divide it into 3 and roll out long strands. Braid (see diagram) and place in a buttered 10-in x 6-in/2.5-L loaf pan. This way the top will be braided and the sides will be straight – the best shape for sandwiches and toast. Otherwise you can divide the dough in half. Then divide each half into thirds and form 2 braids. Bake side by side in a deep 8-in/2-L square cake pan as my grandmother did. You can also

divide the dough into ⅓ and ⅔ portions. Make a large braid and a smaller one. Set the large braid on a cookie sheet that has been buttered or lined with parchment paper and "glue" the smaller braid on top in the center using egg wash as glue. Or you can form 4 rope braids (see diagram). To form 6 rope braids, see page 143.

5. Cover the bread with buttered plastic wrap and allow to rise in a warm place until doubled — about 1 hour. Preheat oven to 400°F/ 200°C.

6. Just before baking combine egg with cream and brush on top of braid. Sprinkle with sesame seeds. Bake 45 to 50 minutes. After 40 minutes check bread and if it is browning too much turn oven down to 350°F/180°C to finish cooking.

7. Remove from pan or cookie sheet immediately and cool on racks.

THREE-ROPE BRAID

FOUR-ROPE BRAID

1. Start with 4 strands.

2. Top strand goes down.

3. Bottom strand goes up.

4. Left strand goes to right.

5. Right strand goes to left.

6. Repeat, starting at the top, until all strands are used.

Braided Spiced Challah (only for DLC-7 or DLC-X)

This egg bread has a very different flavor because of the spices in the dough. It is unusual and delicious and if you think the smell of homebaked bread is wonderful, this one smells even more wonderful because of the spices. It can be made into individual loaves, rolls or buns but looks great when baked in one huge braided loaf. If you want to slice it for sandwiches or toast, it is better to bake it in two large loaf pans. This amount of bread can only be done in the DLC-7 or DLC-X, but if you have a smaller machine simply halve the recipe.

1 tbsp	sugar	15 mL		¼ tsp	ground ginger	1 mL
⅓ cup	warm water	75 mL		¼ tsp	ground cloves	1 mL
2	envelopes dry yeast	2		1 tsp	finely grated orange peel	5 mL
1¼ cups	milk	300 mL				
⅓ cup	unsalted butter	75 mL		1 tsp	finely grated lemon peel	5 mL
¼ cup	honey	50 mL		**Glaze:**		
2 tsp	salt	10 mL		1	egg	1
3	eggs	3		1 tbsp	cream	15 mL
5 cups	all-purpose flour (or more if necessary)	1.25 L		1 tbsp	sesame seeds	15 mL
1 tbsp	ground coriander	15 mL				
1 tsp	ground cinnamon	5 mL		**Makes 1 huge loaf or 2 large loaves**		

1. Dissolve sugar in warm water and sprinkle yeast over the top. Allow to rest 10 minutes or until yeast bubbles up and doubles in volume.
2. Combine milk with butter, honey and salt and heat just until butter melts. Cool. Beat in eggs. Mixture should now be about room temperature or cooler.
3. Fit work bowl with plastic or metal blade. Add flour, spices and grated peel. Blend 3 seconds.
4. When yeast has bubbled up, stir down and add to milk mixture. With machine running, slowly add liquid through the feed tube. Dough should come together and be very sticky. Add enough extra flour, a little at a time, to make dough soft but not too sticky. Dough should just come away from sides of the bowl. Knead no longer than 50 seconds. Remove from machine and place dough in a buttered bowl. Turn dough until it is completely greased. Cover with buttered plastic wrap and set in a warm place to rise until doubled. This should take 1 to 1½ hours.

5. Punch dough down and shape according to directions below.

6. Preheat oven to 350°F/180°C. Just before baking combine egg with cream and brush over top. Sprinkle with sesame seeds. Bake the huge loaf 50 to 60 minutes and the 2 large loaves 40 to 50 minutes. Remove loaves from baking pans immediately and cool on wire racks.

Note: If you do not have a supply of peel already grated, cut the peel of half an orange and half a lemon into 1-in/2.5-cm pieces. In a clean work bowl fitted with metal blade, grate peel along with ¼ cup/50 mL sugar. The additional sugar will not affect the recipe greatly.

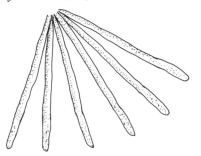

1. Start with 6 strands.

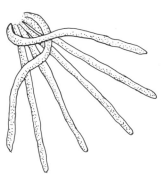

2. Cross outer 2 strands.

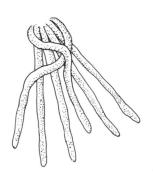

3. Place outer right strand back over 2 strands.

4. Place second strand from left to outer right position.

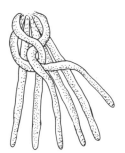

5. Place outer left strand back over 2 strands.

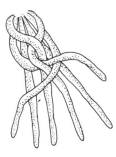

6. Place second strand from right to outer left position.

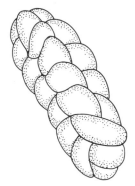

7. Repeat from Step 3 until all strands are used. Tuck ends under.

Cheddar Cheese Muffins with Fresh Parsley

When there is no time to bake bread, try serving muffins for special meals. Any semi-hard or semisoft cheese can be used instead of the Cheddar, and when fresh dill or fresh basil are in season, try using them instead of parsley.

Try using an ice cream scoop to scoop out muffin batter. It gives your muffins nicely rounded tops.

2 oz	old Cheddar cheese	60 g	1 cup	sour cream or unflavored yogurt	250 mL
	Small handful fresh parsley		½ cup	milk	125 mL
2 cups	all-purpose flour	500 mL	¼ cup	unsalted butter, melted	50 mL
1 tbsp	baking powder	15 mL			
¾ tsp	salt	4 mL	1	egg	1
1 tbsp	sugar	15 mL	2 tbsp	cream or milk	25 mL
1	egg	1	**Makes 12 large muffins**		

1. Preheat oven to 400°F/200°C. Butter muffin pan or line with paper baking cups.
2. Fit work bowl with shredding disc. Fit cheese into feed tube and grate. Remove from work bowl and reserve.
3. Refit work bowl with metal blade. Add parsley and chop using 4 or 5 on/off pulses. Add grated cheese, flour, baking powder, salt and sugar. Blend together for 3 seconds.
4. Combine liquid ingredients with a fork. Pour into flour mixture and blend only until mixed. Do not overmix!
5. Scoop mixture into prepared pan. Mix together egg and cream and brush on top of muffins. Bake 20 to 25 minutes. Remove muffins from pan and cool on racks.

Banana Bran Muffins

Use really ripe bananas for a strong banana flavor.

1½ cups	natural bran	375 mL	1	egg	1
1 cup	all-purpose flour	250 mL	2	medium-sized very ripe bananas	2
1 tsp	baking soda	5 mL			
1 tsp	baking powder	5 mL	¾ cup	buttermilk, unflavored yogurt or sour cream	175 mL
¼ tsp	salt	1 mL			
⅓ cup	corn oil or vegetable oil	75 mL	½ cup	raisins	125 mL
⅓ cup	brown sugar	75 mL	**Makes 12 medium-sized muffins**		

1. Preheat oven to 400°F/200°C. Butter muffin pan or line with fluted paper baking cups.
2. Fit work bowl with metal blade. Add bran, flour, baking soda, baking powder and salt. Process for 3 seconds or until blended. Remove from work bowl and reserve.
3. Place oil, brown sugar and egg in work bowl. Blend 2 seconds. Break bananas into pieces and add to mixture. Process until pureed. Add buttermilk and blend.
4. Add flour mixture and blend in with 3 or 4 quick on/off pulses. Add raisins and blend in with 1 on/off pulse. Dry ingredients should be just blended together with liquid — do not overprocess.
5. Spoon mixture (or use an ice cream scoop) into prepared muffin cups (batter will be slightly runny). Bake for 20 minutes. Remove from pan and cool on racks.

Fruit and Nut Bran Muffins

These muffins are rich in fiber. You can use hazelnuts or almonds instead of walnuts, and dates, raisins, dried currants or prunes instead of apricots.

½ cup	toasted walnuts	125 mL	1 tsp	ground cinnamon	5 mL
½ cup	dried apricots	125 mL	½ cup	vegetable oil	125 mL
2 cups	natural bran	500 mL	1 cup	brown sugar	250 mL
1¾ cups	all-purpose flour	425 mL	2	eggs	2
1½ tsp	baking soda	7 mL	1½ cups	buttermilk or unflavored yogurt	375 mL
1½ tsp	baking powder	7 mL			
½ tsp	salt	2 mL			
pinch	freshly ground nutmeg	pinch			

Makes 12 extra-large or 18 large muffins

1. Preheat oven to 400°F/200°C. Butter muffin pan or line with paper baking cups.
2. Fit work bowl with metal blade. Add walnuts. Chop with 3 or 4 on/off pulses until nuts are coarsely chopped. Remove and reserve. Cut apricots into small pieces with kitchen shears and reserve with nuts.
3. Add bran, flour, baking soda, baking powder, salt and spices to work bowl. Process 3 or 4 seconds or just until ingredients are well blended. Remove and reserve.
4. Place oil, sugar, eggs and buttermilk in work bowl. Process a few seconds to blend. Add dry ingredients all at once and blend in with 3 or 4 on/off pulses. Blend in apricots and nuts very quickly. Do not overprocess.
5. Spoon batter into prepared pan with a spoon or ice cream scoop. Bake 20 minutes for large muffins and 25 to 30 minutes for the oversized ones. Remove from pan and immediately cool on racks.

Note: If using DLC-10, batter may run out slightly but do not worry.

Pumpkin Muffins

These delicious morsels are wonderful for breakfast. Sprinkled with cinnamon sugar, they melt in your mouth. If you do not have tiny muffin pans you can just bake them in regular-sized ones or even the new-style extra-large muffin pans. Instead of the cooked pumpkin you can also use cooked winter squash or cooked sweet potatoes.

¼ cup	sugar	50 mL		1 cup	sugar	250 mL
1 tbsp	ground cinnamon	15 mL		2	eggs	2
½ cup	walnut pieces	125 mL		1 cup	cooked, mashed pumpkin (canned or homemade)	250 mL
1½ cups	all-purpose flour	375 mL				
2 tsp	baking powder	10 mL		1 cup	milk	250 mL
1 tsp	ground cinnamon	5 mL		¼ cup	unsalted butter, melted	50 mL
¼ tsp	salt	1 mL				
pinch	ground nutmeg	pinch				
½ cup	unsalted butter, cold	125 mL				

Makes 24 small muffins or 12 large ones

1. Preheat oven to 400°F/200°C. Butter muffin tins well or line with paper baking cups.
2. Fit work bowl with metal blade. Add sugar and 1 tbsp/15 mL cinnamon and blend together about 5 seconds. Remove and reserve.
3. Place walnut pieces in work bowl still fitted with metal blade. Chop using 3 or 4 on/off pulses or until finely chopped. Remove and reserve.
4. Place flour, baking powder, 1 tsp/ 5 mL cinnamon, salt and nutmeg in work bowl still fitted with metal blade. Blend together about 5 seconds. Remove and reserve.
5. Place butter and sugar in work bowl still fitted with metal blade. Process on/off with 5 or 6 pulses until butter is in tiny bits. Process continuously until mixture is creamy and smooth. Beat in eggs and blend until smooth. Add pumpkin and milk and blend. Scrape down sides of work bowl when necessary.
6. Add flour mixture and nuts. Blend in with only 1 or 2 on/off pulses or until just combined. Spoon batter into prepared pans and bake 15 minutes for tiny muffins and 25 minutes for larger ones.
7. Remove from pans and brush with melted butter. Sprinkle tops with cinnamon-sugar.

Hazelnut Quick Bread

While on a trip to British Columbia to see the salmon spawning, I had a chance to visit a hazelnut farm in Rosedale, B.C. I was amazed to see the nuts harvested by helicopter — the downdraft from the helicopter shakes the nuts off the trees. The owners of the farm, Hazel and John Spencer, served this lovely tea bread during our visit.

¾ cup	shelled hazelnuts	175 mL	2	eggs		2
1½ cups	all-purpose flour	375 mL	½ tsp	pure vanilla extract		2 mL
½ tsp	salt	2 mL	¼ tsp	pure almond extract		1 mL
	Peel of ½ lemon		½ cup	7-UP		125 mL
1 cup	sugar	250 mL				
⅓ cup	unsalted butter, cold	75 mL	**Makes 1 loaf**			

1. Preheat oven to 350°F/180°C. Butter an 8-in x 4-in/1.5-L loaf pan.
2. Spread hazelnuts on a cookie sheet and toast for 15 minutes or until browned. To remove skins, see Food Hints, page 18. Do not worry if the skins will not come off completely.
3. Fit work bowl with metal blade. Add hazelnuts and chop, using 4 or 5 quick on/off pulses or until coarsely chopped. Remove from bowl and reserve.
4. Place flour and salt in work bowl still fitted with metal blade. Blend for 5 seconds, remove and reserve.
5. Pat lemon peel dry and cut into 1-in/2.5-cm pieces..With work bowl still fitted with metal blade, drop lemon peel through feed tube with machine running. Add sugar and process until peel is chopped. Cut butter into equal-sized cubes and add to sugar mixture. Process on/off with 4 or 5 pulses until butter is in tiny bits. Process continuously until mixture is creamed.
6. Beat in eggs until smooth and then add extracts and 7-UP. Scrape down sides of bowl when necessary. Process until well mixed.
7. Add flour mixture and blend in 2 quick on/off pulses. Add nuts and blend in with 1 quick pulse.
8. Pour or spoon batter into loaf pan and bake 50 or 60 minutes or until top is firm when lightly pressed. Cool 10 minutes and remove from pan. Cool on wire rack.

Biscuits

This is a delicious dough that can be used for many different purposes. These biscuits can be served plain for tea or they can be made with raisins or currants. They can also be made into strawberry shortcake by serving with whipped cream and berries. They are easy to make in the Cuisinart® — just be careful not to overmix once the yogurt has been added.

	Peel of 1 orange	
2 tbsp	sugar	25 mL
2 cups	all-purpose flour	500 mL
1 tbsp	baking powder	15 mL
½ tsp	baking soda	2 mL

¼ tsp	salt	1 mL
½ cup	unsalted butter, cold	125 mL
1¼ cups	unflavored yogurt or sour cream	300 mL

Makes 6 to 10 biscuits

1. Preheat oven to 425°F/220°C. Line a cookie sheet with parchment paper or tin foil.
2. Pat orange peel dry with paper towels. Cut into 1-in/2.5-cm pieces. Fit work bowl with metal blade and add peel through small feed tube with machine running. Add sugar and continue to process until peel is finely chopped. You will probably have to scrape down the sides of the work bowl a few times.
3. Add flour, baking powder, baking soda and salt and blend briefly. Add butter and process with 5 or 6 on/off pulses until the butter is cut into the dry ingredients in tiny pieces.
4. Add yogurt or sour cream. Process as briefly as possible using 3 or 4 on/off pulses just until the dough is completely moistened. Turn dough out onto a floured board and knead only once or twice. Pat or roll dough 1 in/2.5 cm thick and cut out with round cutters. The dough may be sticky, but don't worry. For shortcakes I usually use a 4-in/10-cm cutter and for biscuits a 2-in/5-cm cutter.
5. Place biscuits on prepared cookie sheet and bake 15 minutes. Serve warm or at room temperature.

Cakes, Crisps, Tarts and Cookies

The recipes included in this chapter are sweets that can be easily made and are nice to have in the house for family desserts or unexpected company. They are not as elaborate as the dishes in the Pastries and Mousses chapter, but they tend to keep better and many can be frozen. That is, if no one eats them first!

Although I adore sweets of all kinds and I never pass up a dessert (I say it's for research!), like an increasing number of people I am very particular about what I eat. Even with cakes and cookies, nutrition is important as well as flavor. None of the recipes in this chapter are especially low in calories, but neither are they excessively rich (with the exception of the truffles). I like cakes, crisps and cookies to have a wonderful flavor but not a lot of sugar. I hope you'll like them, too.

Almond Cake with Raspberry Sauce

This cake tastes great with or without the sauce. The sauce can also be used over ice cream.

2 tbsp	shelled almonds	25 mL		1 tsp	pure vanilla extract	5 mL
1½ cups	all-purpose flour	375 mL		1 tsp	pure almond extract	5 mL
1 tsp	baking soda	5 mL		**Raspberry Sauce:**		
	Peel of 1 orange			2	15-oz/425-g packages frozen raspberries, defrosted	2
1½ cups	sugar	375 mL				
1 cup	unsalted butter, cold	250 mL				
8 oz	almond paste, homemade (see page 135) or commercial	250 g		3 tbsp	orange liqueur	50 mL
4	eggs	4		**Makes 1 Bundt cake**		

1. Preheat oven to 350°F/180°C. Butter a 9-cup/2-L Bundt or tube pan well.
2. Fit work bowl with metal blade. Add almonds and chop finely with on/off pulses. Dust buttered pan with almonds. Add flour and baking soda to work bowl and process 3 seconds. Remove and reserve.
3. Pat orange peel dry, cut into 1-in/2.5-cm pieces and with machine running, add through feed tube. Add sugar and process until peel is finely chopped. Scrape down sides of work bowl when necessary.
4. Cut butter into cubes, add to work bowl and process with on/off pulses until finely chopped. Process continuously until mixture is creamed. Cut almond paste into cubes, add to mixture and blend together. Scrape down sides of bowl again if necessary.
5. Add eggs and extracts and process until blended. Add flour mixture and process with 3 or 4 quick on/off pulses, or until just blended.
6. Transfer batter to prepared pan and bake 50 minutes or until cake springs back when lightly pressed. Cool 10 minutes. Invert onto wire rack and cool completely.
7. Prepare Raspberry Sauce.
8. Spoon a circle of sauce on each serving plate and place a slice of cake on top.

Raspberry Sauce:

1. Strain juice from berries and reserve.
2. Fit clean work bowl with metal blade and add berries. Puree. Press through a sieve if you want raspberry seeds removed.
3. Add liqueur and enough juice to make a medium-thick sauce.

Apple Cake

For those who love apple desserts, this cake can't be beat. It's very moist. At first it may look as if you have too many apples, but don't worry. It all bakes together beautifully.

4	apples (Spy or Golden Delicious)	4	1½ cups	sugar	375 mL	
⅓ cup	sugar	75 mL	3	eggs	3	
1 tbsp	ground cinnamon	15 mL	⅔ cup	vegetable oil	150 mL	
2 cups	flour	500 mL	3 tbsp	orange juice	50 mL	
2 tsp	baking powder	10 mL	2 tsp	pure vanilla extract	10 mL	
¼ tsp	salt	1 mL				
	Peel of 1 orange					

Makes 1 cake (8 in/20 cm)

1. Preheat oven to 375°F/190°C. Butter an 8-in/2-L springform pan.

2. Fit work bowl with medium or thin slicing disc. Peel, halve and core apples. Cut thin slices off the tops and bottoms to form flat ends. Pack apples into large feed tube with flat end sitting on disc and slice. Repeat until all apples are sliced. Remove apples to a bowl and toss with sugar and cinnamon. Reserve.

3. Wipe work bowl dry and fit with metal blade. Add flour, baking powder and salt. Process for 3 seconds or until mixed. Remove and reserve.

4. Pat orange peel dry and cut into 1-in/2.5-cm pieces. Add to work bowl with machine running. Process until chopped. Add sugar and process until peel is finely chopped.

5. Add eggs and process until blended. Scrape down sides of bowl. Add oil, juice and vanilla.

6. Add flour mixture all at once and quickly blend into batter using only 3 or 4 quick on/off pulses.

7. Spoon a thin layer of batter on the bottom of the pan. Put a layer of apples on top. Spread more batter on apples and repeat layers until apples and batter are used (end with a layer of batter). Bake 1 hour. Cake will be very moist. Cool before removing from pan.

Sour Cream Coffee Cake

This is an old-time favorite that was adapted very easily to the food processor. Do not taste the raw batter; it's so delicious that the cake may never make it to the oven!

Filling and Topping:

⅓ cup	brown sugar	75 mL
1 tbsp	cocoa	15 mL
⅓ cup	shelled, toasted hazelnuts or walnuts	75 mL
2 tsp	ground cinnamon	10 mL

Batter:

2 cups	all-purpose flour	500 mL
2 tsp	baking powder	10 mL
1 tsp	baking soda	5 mL
	Peel of 1 orange	
1 cup	sugar	250 mL
½ cup	unsalted butter, cold	125 mL
2	eggs	2
1 tsp	pure vanilla extract	5 mL
1 cup	sour cream	250 mL

Makes 1 Bundt cake

1. Preheat oven to 350°F/180°C. Butter 9-cup/2-L Bundt or tube pan.

2. Fit work bowl with metal blade. Add brown sugar, cocoa, nuts and cinnamon. Blend together until nuts are finely chopped — 6 to 8 on/off pulses. Remove from work bowl and reserve.

3. Wipe work bowl clean with paper towel and refit with metal blade. Add flour, baking powder and baking soda. Blend together for 3 or 4 seconds. Remove from work bowl.

4. Refit work bowl with metal blade. Pat orange peel dry, cut into 1-in/2.5-cm pieces and drop through feed tube with machine running. Add sugar and process until peel is finely chopped.

5. Cut butter into cubes and add to sugar. Process with 5 or 6 on/off pulses or until butter is chopped evenly and finely into sugar. Continue to run machine until butter and sugar cream together. Add eggs and vanilla and blend. Blend in sour cream. Batter should be smooth. Scrape down sides of bowl as necessary.

6. Add flour mixture all at once to ingredients in work bowl. With only 2 or 3 quick on/off pulses, blend in dry ingredients.

7. Sprinkle a third of the brown sugar topping mixture into the bottom of the Bundt or tube pan. Spoon in ⅓ of the batter and spread as evenly as possible. Sprinkle with another ⅓ of the topping and another ⅓ of the batter. Sprinkle with the remaining topping mixture and spread remaining batter over it.

8. Bake cake 40 to 50 minutes or until the center of cake springs back when lightly touched. Allow cake to cool in pan about 10 minutes. Run a knife around the edge of cake to loosen it and then invert onto cooling rack.

Note: This can also be prepared in a 9-in/2.5-L square cake pan. Start with a layer of batter, then alternate with filling, and end with layer of topping. Either serve directly from the pan or invert onto cooling rack and then turn it right side up again.

Plum Coffee Cake

Plums are a true treat of summer and fall, and this recipe shows them off well. I prefer using purple plums in this cake but have also used yellow or red ones and it has come out well. If plums are not in season you can use apples, pears or peaches. Serve it with whipped cream.

	Peel of 1 orange	
½ cup	sugar	125 mL
2 cups	all-purpose flour	500 mL
1 tbsp	baking powder	15 mL
⅓ cup	unsalted butter, cold	75 mL
⅔ cup	cottage cheese	150 mL
1	egg	1

3 tbsp	orange juice	50 mL
3½ lb	plums, halved and pitted	1.5 kg
¼ cup	sugar	50 mL

**Makes 1 cake
(9 in x 13 in / 23 cm x 33 cm)**

1. Preheat oven to 400°F/200°C. Butter a 9-in x 13-in/3.5-L casserole dish well.

2. Fit work bowl with metal blade. Cut peel into 1-in/2.5-cm pieces and pat dry. With machine running, drop peel through feed tube and chop. Add sugar and process until peel is finely chopped. Add flour and baking powder and process 2 seconds or until blended.

3. Cut butter into 1-in/2.5-cm pieces and add to flour. Process with 5 or 6 on/off pulses or until butter is finely chopped. Remove to a bowl and reserve.

4. Place cottage cheese, egg and orange juice into work bowl still fitted with metal blade. Process 3 or 4 seconds or until blended.

5. Add flour mixture to cheese mixture in work bowl. Process on/off 5 to 10 times or until mixture is just blended. Pat into prepared pan.

6. Arrange plums cut side up over dough. Sprinkle with sugar.

7. Bake cake 40 to 45 minutes or until dough can be lifted off the sides of the pan if you insert a knife.

Note: If you make this in a glass pan, reduce oven temperature to 375°F/ 190°C.

Lemon Cheesecake with Fresh Strawberries

This is a simple, elegant cheesecake with a rich, lemony flavor. It freezes very well but can also be made up to three days in advance and kept refrigerated. This cake can be easily made in the DLC-8, DLC-7 and DLC-X, but it is the largest mixture that the DLC-10 can hold, so if you are using a DLC-10, after everything is in the work bowl, transfer it to the prepared baking dish quickly.

In the late summer you can also top this cake with fresh raspberries and blackberries, for a dramatic appearance.

	Peel of 1 lemon				
1 cup	sugar	250 mL	3	eggs	3
1½ lb	cream cheese	750 g	**Garnish:**		
1 tsp	pure vanilla extract	5 mL	2 cups	fresh strawberries	500 mL
2 tbsp	fresh lemon juice	25 mL			

Makes 1 cake (8 in/20 cm)

1. Preheat oven to 325°F/160°C. Butter an 8-in/2-L deep round cake pan very well and line the bottom with a circle of parchment paper or waxed paper. Butter well again. If you are using a springform pan, prepare it as above but wrap it well in foil so that batter cannot leak out and the water from the water bath will not seep into the cake.

2. Pat lemon peel dry, cut into 1-in/2.5-cm pieces and fit work bowl with metal blade. With machine running, drop peel through feed tube. Add sugar and process until peel is finely chopped. This may take 30 seconds or longer.

3. Cut cheese into cubes and add to sugar. Process on/off until cheese is chopped and then process continuously until smooth. Add remaining ingredients and process 5 seconds, scrape down bowl and process only until smooth. Do not overbeat.

4. Pour cheese mixture into prepared pan and place in a larger pan, adding enough boiling water to form a water bath that comes at least halfway up the sides of the pan. Bake 50 to 60 minutes or until the center is firm but not brown or cracked. Cool cake completely at room temperature, run a knife around edge of cake to loosen, and turn out of pan onto a serving dish. Serve right side up or upside down – it makes no difference. (If you are using a springform pan, simply release the outside ring.) Cut berries in half and arrange around outside edge of cake just before serving, or if you want to decorate the cake ahead of time, glaze the berries with strained raspberry or strawberry jam. Chill thoroughly.

Note: This cake is usually served in thin wedges but it can also be baked in an 8-in/2-L square baking dish, then cut into squares, topped with strawberry halves and served in pretty paper baking cups.

Cheesecake

Although this cheesecake is quite old-fashioned next to all the different-flavored cheesecakes you find these days, it is still one of the best. If you haven't grown up on it as I have, you are in for a treat. For a "diet" version I use creamed cottage cheese (the solid curd variety) for the filling and yogurt for the topping. It's still pretty good, although obviously not nearly as rich.

Crust:

1½ cups	Graham wafer crumbs	375 mL
1 tsp	ground cinnamon	5 mL
¼ cup	unsalted butter, melted or softened	50 mL

Filling:

1 lb	cream cheese, cold	500 g
2	eggs	2
½ cup	sugar	125 mL
1 tsp	pure vanilla extract	5 mL

Topping:

1½ cups	sour cream	375 mL
2 tbsp	sifted icing sugar	25 mL
¼ tsp	pure vanilla extract	1 mL
2 cups	fresh strawberries, washed, hulled and halved	500 mL

Makes about 25 squares

1. Preheat oven to 350°F/180°C. Butter an 8-in/2-L square baking dish.

2. Place crumbs and cinnamon in work bowl fitted with metal blade. Add butter and blend in until crumbs are moistened. Remove and pat into the bottom of the buttered pan.

3. Clean work bowl and refit with metal blade. Cut cheese into cubes and process until very smooth. Add eggs and blend until smooth. Blend in sugar and vanilla.

4. Pour filling over crust and spread evenly. Bake 30 to 35 minutes or until filling starts to set. Do not overbake but it should not be runny.

5. Just before cake is ready fit clean work bowl with metal blade. Add sour cream, icing sugar and vanilla and blend for 2 or 3 seconds. When cake is ready, remove from oven and spread sour cream over the top. Return to oven for 5 minutes to spread sour cream evenly. Remove from oven and cool.

6. When cake is cool refrigerate overnight to chill thoroughly. Cut into squares. Remove from pan carefully and fit into paper cups. Top each square with a strawberry half.

Hazelnut Cheesecake with Chocolate Glaze

Hazelnuts add an unusual flavor to this cheesecake and make it a pleasant change from more traditional cheesecakes. It is moist, rich and nutty. This cake also freezes very well. This chocolate glaze is the most practical and delicious one I've ever found and can be used on brownies, mousses and cakes. It can also be used on any cheesecake that cracks after it has been baked. The glaze seeps into the cracks and produces an ingenious chocolate marble cheesecake.

Crust:					
½ cup	shelled, toasted hazelnuts	125 mL	3	eggs	3
			1 tsp	pure vanilla extract	5 mL
4 oz	chocolate wafer cookies	125 g	½ tsp	pure almond extract	2 mL
3 tbsp	unsalted butter, at room temperature	50 mL	2 tbsp	Frangelico (hazelnut liqueur), Amaretto or rum	25 mL
Filling:			**Chocolate Glaze:**		
	Peel of 1 orange		6 oz	bittersweet or semisweet chocolate	175 g
1 cup	sugar	250 mL	⅓ cup	whipping cream	75 mL
1 cup	shelled, toasted hazelnuts	250 mL	2 tbsp	Frangelico, Amaretto or rum	25 mL
1½ lb	cream cheese, cold	750 g	**Makes 1 cake (9 in/23 cm)**		

1. To prepare crust, preheat oven to 350°F/180°C. Have a 9-in/2.5-L springform pan ready.

2. Fit work bowl with metal blade. Add nuts and process with 8 to 10 on/off pulses or until coarsely chopped. Add cookies and process on/off again until the cookies and nuts are finely chopped.

3. Cut butter into 4 or 5 pieces and process until crumbs are all moistened. Pat mixture into the bottom of springform pan.

4. To prepare filling, wash or wipe work bowl and refit with metal blade. Pat orange peel dry. Cut into 1-in/2.5-cm pieces and drop through feed tube while the machine is running. Add sugar and process continuously, scraping down sides as necessary, until peel is finely chopped.

5. Add 1 cup/250 mL hazelnuts and process on/off 8 to 10 times and then continuously until nuts are finely chopped. Remove mixture from work bowl and reserve.

6. Cut cream cheese into cubes and add to work bowl still fitted with metal blade. Process on/off until cheese is in small pieces and then process continuously until smooth.

7. Add all eggs at once and process into cheese. Scrape down sides once or twice. Add vanilla, almond extract and liqueur.

8. If you have the DLC-10 transfer cheese mixture to large bowl with nuts and sugar and stir to blend. If you have the DLC-8, DLC-7 or DLC-X add the nut-sugar mixture back into the work bowl and process into the cheese. Transfer cheese into crust and spread

smoothly. Bake for 40 to 50 minutes or just until filling is set. Remove from oven and cool. Before refrigerating cake, run a knife around the outside edge between cake and pan to help stop cake from cracking. Refrigerate overnight.

9. To prepare glaze, place chocolate in clean work bowl fitted with metal blade. Chop chocolate with about 20 on/off pulses or until finely chopped.

10. Bring cream to a boil and add through feed tube. Process about 1 minute or until chocolate is smooth. Blend in liqueur.

11. Remove outside ring of springform pan and spread chocolate glaze over the cake. Swirl with a knife or run a decorating comb over the top of the cake to create a circular pattern. Refrigerate until ready to serve.

Note: To toast hazelnuts, spread them on a cookie sheet and toast lightly in a 350°F/180°C oven for 15 minutes or until browned. To remove skins, see Food Hints, page 18. Remove as much of the skins as possible but do not worry if bits remain.

Rhubarb and Apple Crisp

Rhubarb is plentiful in many North American gardens, but if you cannot find fresh rhubarb use 4 cups/1 L frozen, sliced rhubarb. You can also make this with all rhubarb or all apple, but if you are using all apple, cut back on the sugar.

3	apples (preferably Spy or Golden Delicious)	3	½ cup	white sugar	125 mL
			½ cup	brown sugar	125 mL
1 lb	fresh rhubarb, trimmed	500 g	1 tsp	ground cinnamon	5 mL
			½ cup	unsalted butter, cold	125 mL
1 cup	all-purpose flour	250 mL	**Serves 8**		

1. Preheat oven to 400°F/200°C. Lightly butter a 9-in x 13-in/3.5-L baking dish.

2. Fit work bowl with medium or thick slicing disc. Peel apples and cut in half. Remove cores. Fit apples tightly into large feed tube and slice. Repeat until all 6 apple halves are sliced. Arrange in bottom of casserole.

3. With work bowl still fitted with slicing disc, pack either large or small feed tube (if the rhubarb is very thick use large feed tube but if the rhubarb is thin and delicate use small) and slice. Repeat until all rhubarb is sliced. Spread on top of apples.

4. Wipe work bowl dry and refit with metal blade. Add flour, white and brown sugars and cinnamon. Blend. Cut butter into cubes and add. Process butter into dry ingredients using 6 to 8 on/off pulses or until mixture is crumbly. Spread over fruit.

5. Bake 45 to 55 minutes or until apples and rhubarb are very tender. Cool and serve plain or with vanilla ice cream.

Fruit Tartlets with Lemon Cream

Maureen Lollar, the manager of our cooking school, dreamed up this wonderful filling and we've used it for many things ever since. As well as being a luscious filling for tarts, it's great in crepes and makes a terrific filling for the hazelnut roulade on page 182. I usually top these tarts with sliced strawberries, sliced kiwi fruit, blueberries or raspberries. Sliced fresh figs also make a delicious and different fruit topping.

Although these tarts taste best the same day they are made, because of the chocolate on the bottom of the tarts, they do not get soggy when kept overnight.

Crust:		
	Peel of ½ lemon	
2 tbsp	sugar	25 mL
1½ cups	all-purpose flour	375 mL
½ cup	unsalted butter, cold	125 mL
3 tbsp	ice water	50 mL
3 oz	bittersweet or semisweet chocolate	125 g

Lemon Cream Filling:		
	Peel of 1 lemon	
½ cup	sugar	125 mL
3	egg yolks	3
⅓ cup	lemon juice	75 mL
⅓ cup	unsalted butter, melted	75 mL
1½ cups	whipping cream, very cold	375 mL

Topping:		
2 cups	strawberries	500 mL
2	kiwi fruit, peeled	2

Glaze:		
½ cup	apricot jam	125 mL
2 tbsp	Cointreau or other orange liqueur	25 mL

Makes 24 tarts

1. Fit work bowl with metal blade. Pat lemon peel dry and cut into 1-in/2.5-cm pieces. With machine running, drop peel through feed tube. Add sugar and process until finely chopped. Scrape down sides of bowl when necessary. Add flour and process with sugar and peel.

2. Cut butter into cubes and process with 10 or 12 on/off pulses or until fat is in tiny pieces.

3. With machine running, drip cold water through feed tube and process until flour is moistened and dough starts to come together. Remove from work bowl and gather dough together with your hands. Wrap with plastic wrap and refrigerate at least 30 minutes.

4. Prepare Lemon Cream Filling.

5. Cut dough in half and roll each half to ⅛-in/3-mm thickness. Cut out circles approximately 2 in/5 cm in diameter and fit into tart pans. Reroll extra dough and cut as well. Prick with a fork. Refrigerate while oven preheats to 425°F/220°C. Bake tarts 5 minutes. If they bubble up, press down with a fork. Reduce heat to 350°F/180°C and bake 5 to 8 minutes longer or until browned lightly. Cool.

6. Melt the chocolate and brush lightly over bottom of baked tarts. Allow to dry.

7. Fit work bowl with medium or thin slicing disc. Wash and hull strawberries. Place in small feed tube and slice using gentle pressure. Remove from work bowl. Cut bottoms and tops off kiwi fruit, leaving a flat surface. Place in small feed tube with the flat end on the slicing blade. Slice using gentle pressure. (If strawberries or kiwi fruit are not very firm, slice by hand.)

8. Assemble tarts by spooning a little of the filling into baked shells. Top with slices of strawberries or kiwi. Heat apricot jam and strain. Stir in liqueur. Brush on top of fruit to glaze. Refrigerate until ready to serve. Eat any extra filling and fruit.

Lemon Cream Filling:

1. Wash or wipe work bowl clean. Fit with metal blade. Pat lemon peel dry and cut into 1-in/2.5-cm pieces. With machine running, drop peel through feed tube. Process until chopped. Add the sugar and process until peel is chopped fine.

2. Beat in egg yolks. Scrape down sides of work bowl. Add lemon juice and butter and process until blended.

3. Transfer to a heavy saucepan and cook until mixture thickens. Remove from heat, transfer to a bowl and cool to room temperature.

4. With machine running, add whipping cream through feed tube and process until thickened. Fold gently into lemon base. Refrigerate.

Pear Custard Tart

This pastry is rich and very short. If you have trouble rolling it out, simply pat it into the pan. It's worth any amount of trouble.

Pastry:		
1 cup	all-purpose flour	250 mL
¼ tsp	salt	1 mL
2 tbsp	sugar	25 mL
½ cup	unsalted butter, cold	125 mL
1 tbsp	white vinegar, cold	15 mL
Filling:		
3 tbsp	apricot jam	50 mL
4	large pears, ripe but firm (preferably Bosc or Bartlett)	4

	Peel of ½ lemon	
⅓ cup	sugar	75 mL
3	egg yolks	3
pinch	ground cardamom, optional	pinch
½ tsp	pure vanilla extract	2 mL
¾ cup	whipping cream	175 mL
2 tbsp	sliced almonds, toasted	25 mL

Makes 1 tart (9 in/23 cm)

1. Fit work bowl with metal blade. Add flour, salt, sugar and blend 1 or 2 seconds.
2. Cut butter into small chunks and add to flour. Process on/off 12 to 15 times or until butter is in tiny bits.
3. With machine running, drizzle vinegar slowly through feed tube. Process until flour is moistened but not in a ball. Remove mixture from machine. Gather together and knead lightly. Wrap in plastic wrap and refrigerate 30 minutes.
4. Preheat oven to 425°F/220°C. Roll out dough to fit a 9-in/1.5-L pie plate. Flute or even off edges. Save extra pastry. Line pastry with parchment paper, waxed paper or foil. Weigh down with beans, dried legumes or special pie weights. Bake 15 minutes. Remove weights and paper. Patch with reserved pastry if necessary.
5. Spread pastry with apricot jam.
6. Peel pears and cut in half. Remove cores with a melon baller for a professional look. Cut the elongat-ed portion off pears and add these portions to work bowl still fitted with metal blade. Chop extra pieces of pear coarsely using only 3 or 4 on/off pulses. Spread chopped pears in bottom of crust.
7. Refit work bowl with medium slic-ing disc. Insert pears in large feed tube, packed tightly in 1 layer with flat edges at bottom. Slice. Repeat with remaining pears. Arrange slices neatly over chopped pears.
8. Wipe work bowl dry. Refit with metal blade. Pat lemon peel dry and cut in 1-in/2.5-cm pieces. Drop through feed tube with ma-chine running. Add sugar and process until peel is finely chopped.
9. Beat in egg yolks, cardamom and vanilla. Blend briefly. Beat in cream, but do not whip. Pour mix-ture over pears. Sprinkle with nuts.
10. Reduce heat to 375°F/190°C. Place tart back in oven. Bake tart 45 to 55 minutes or until set. Allow to rest at least 20 minutes. I like to serve this very cold.

White Chocolate Mousse with Raspberry Sauce (see page 174).

Custard Tarts (Dim Tat)

Every year, Chinese cooking expert Nina Simonds comes to my cooking school to teach. She always brings interesting specialties and these custard tarts were immensely popular with all the students. Nina, however, felt our Canadian ingredients worked a little differently so I have adapted her recipe as follows. The tarts are traditionally served as part of a dim sum meal and make wonderful snacks with tea. They are delicious warm or cold.

Pastry:

1½ cups	all-purpose flour	375 mL
½ tsp	salt	2 mL
1 tbsp	sugar	15 mL
¼ cup	unsalted butter, cold	50 mL
¼ cup	lard or shortening, cold*	75 mL
3 tbsp	ice water	50 mL

Filling:

3	egg yolks	3
2	whole eggs	2
⅔ cup	sugar	150 mL
1 cup	half and half cream	250 mL
½ cup	whipping cream	125 mL
2 tsp	pure vanilla extract	10 mL

* See note on metric, page 12 re conversion.

Makes 24 tarts

1. To prepare pastry, fit work bowl with metal blade. Add flour, salt and sugar. Blend for 2 or 3 seconds.
2. Cut butter and lard into small cubes and add to flour mixture. Process with 5 or 6 on/off pulses or until fat is in tiny bits.
3. With machine running, drizzle water in through the feed tube. Process continuously until all dough is moistened but not yet in a ball. Remove from bowl and gather dough together. Wrap in plastic wrap and refrigerate at least 30 minutes.
4. Meanwhile wipe work bowl clean and refit with metal blade. To prepare filling, add egg yolks, whole eggs and sugar and blend until combined. Scrape down sides and blend again.
5. Add both creams and vanilla and blend into egg mixture until smooth.
6. Preheat oven to 325°F/160°C. Divide dough in half and roll out each half to a circle approximately ⅛ in/3 mm thick. Cut with a 2-in/5-cm cutter or to fit tart pans. Roll out extra dough and cut again. Line tart pans with pastry.
7. Divide filling among the 24 tarts and bake 25 minutes. Filling should just be set. Do not overbake. Cool 10 minutes before serving.

Pistachio Roulade (see page 178).   161

Butter Tarts

Butter tarts are a truly Canadian sweet. Every cook has a different recipe, but here's my favorite. This particular version is based on a long-time family recipe of Cuisinart® demonstrator Dorothy Orr.

Pastry:		
1½ cups	all-purpose flour	375 mL
½ cup	unsalted butter, cold	125 mL
3 tbsp	ice water	50 mL

Filling:		
½ cup	walnut pieces	125 mL
1 cup	boiling water	250 mL
⅓ cup	raisins	75 mL
¼ cup	unsalted butter, at room temperature	50 mL

½ cup	brown sugar	125 mL
1 cup	corn syrup	250 mL
1 tsp	pure vanilla extract	5 mL
1 tsp	ground cinnamon	5 mL
2	eggs	2

Makes 18 tarts

1. Preheat oven to 400°F/200°C.
2. To prepare pastry, fit work bowl with metal blade. Add flour. Cut butter into small cubes. Add to flour and process on/off with 4 or 5 pulses or until fat is completely cut into flour.
3. With machine running, slowly dribble water through feed tube and process until dough is moistened and almost comes together. Remove dough from work bowl and gather together into a ball. Wrap in plastic wrap and refrigerate about 30 minutes.
4. Wipe bowl clean and fit again with metal blade. To prepare filling, add walnuts and chop with 2 or 3 on/off pulses or until coarsely chopped. Remove from work bowl.
5. Pour boiling water over raisins and allow to plump 10 minutes. Drain well and pat raisins dry. Reserve with nuts.
6. Place butter, brown sugar and corn syrup in work bowl still fitted with metal blade. Blend. Add vanilla, cinnamon and eggs. Blend as briefly as possible but ingredients should be combined.
7. Divide dough in half. Roll out each half to about ⅛-in/3-mm thickness. Cut out 2-in/5-cm circles and fit into tart pans. Press firmly into pans. Spoon a little nuts and raisins into the bottom of each and then divide the filling evenly among them. Bake 20 minutes.

Nut Torte

I originally learned this recipe from Darlene Byers, a friend in California who bakes desserts for the Hotel Mack. It's delicious! However, when I started making my own hazelnut paste, I decided to try this torte made with hazelnut paste. It was great. So you can make this with commercial almond paste, or homemade almond or hazelnut paste (see page 135).

Pastry:		
1¼ cups	all-purpose flour	300 mL
2 tbsp	sugar	25 mL
½ cup	unsalted butter, cold	125 mL
1	egg yolk	1
1 tbsp	rum or Amaretto	15 mL
Filling and Topping:		
8 oz	hazelnut paste or almond paste	250 g
½ cup	unsalted butter, at room temperature	125 mL
¼ cup	sugar	50 mL
2	eggs	2
2 tbsp	all-purpose flour	25 mL
¾ cup	sugar	175 mL
1 tbsp	corn syrup	15 mL
¼ cup	unsalted butter	50 mL
¼ cup	whipping cream	50 mL
2½ cups	toasted walnut halves	625 mL

Serves 8 to 12

1. To prepare pastry, fit work bowl with metal blade. Add flour and sugar to work bowl.
2. Cut butter into cubes and add to flour. Process with 3 or 4 on/off pulses or until butter is in tiny bits.
3. Combine egg yolk with liqueur and pour through feed tube with machine running. Process only until all dough is moistened and begins to come together. Remove from work bowl and gather into a ball. Wrap and refrigerate 30 minutes.
4. Preheat oven to 400°F/200°C. Roll out pastry and line 9-in/2.5-L springform pan with pastry coming 1½ in/4 cm up sides of pan. Cover with parchment paper and fill with dried legumes or pie weights. Bake 15 minutes. Reduce oven temperature to 375°F/190°C. Carefully remove weights and paper and bake 10 minutes longer.
5. To prepare filling, add hazelnut or almond paste to work bowl still fitted with metal blade. Cut butter into pieces and add. Process with a few on/off pulses and then continuously for 5 seconds or until nut paste and butter are well combined.
6. Add sugar and eggs and blend in. Quickly blend in flour. Pour into slightly cooled baked shell.
7. Bake 25 to 30 minutes or until filling is set but not brown. Cool on a rack approximately 2 hours.
8. When torte is cool heat sugar and corn syrup in a heavy saucepan until golden brown. Remove from heat and carefully stir in butter and cream (mixture may bubble up). Return to heat and cook 1 minute or until smooth. Stir in nuts and combine to coat well. Quickly spread over top of torte. Cool completely before serving.

Lemon Tart

This is one of my favorite desserts. It's easy to prepare but looks classical and elegant. Although it is rich, because of its tart flavor it tastes wonderful even after a heavy meal. The pastry is quite delicate and because it consists of a high proportion of butter, it can be difficult to roll. If you have trouble, simply pat it into the pan. You can make this in a regular pie dish but it looks sensational when made in a removable-bottom flan pan and presented with the fluted pastry edge showing.

Pastry:

	Peel of ½ lemon	
2 tbsp	sugar	25 mL
1 cup	all-purpose flour	250 mL
pinch	salt	pinch
½ cup	unsalted butter, cold	125 mL
1 tbsp	lemon juice, cold	15 mL

Filling:

	Peel of ½ lemon	
1½ cups	sugar	375 mL
4	eggs	4
1	egg yolk	1
1 cup	fresh lemon juice (from 4 or 5 lemons)	250 mL
½ cup	whipping cream	125 mL

Makes 1 tart (10 or 11 in/25 or 28 cm)

1. To prepare pastry, fit work bowl with metal blade. Pat lemon peel dry and cut into 1-in/2.5-cm pieces. With machine running, drop through the feed tube. Add sugar and process until peel is finely chopped. This may take 10 to 20 seconds.

2. Add flour, salt and butter cut into cubes and process with 4 or 5 on/off pulses or until butter is cut into flour in tiny bits.

3. With machine running, add lemon juice slowly through feed tube and process until all dough is evenly moistened and just barely begins to stay together. Remove from work bowl, wrap in plastic wrap and refrigerate 30 minutes.

4. Preheat oven to 425°F/220°C. Remove dough from refrigerator and roll out to fit tart pan. If you are using a traditional pie dish, flute edges slightly. If you are using a flan pan, double over the edge so that the outside crust is slightly thicker. Save extra pastry to patch shell after prebaking if necessary. Line shell with parchment paper, waxed paper or tin foil and weigh down with dried legumes, rice or special pie weights. Bake 15 minutes. Carefully lift out weights and lift off paper. (If any pastry is removed when lifting paper just pat back into place or patch with extra dough.)

5. To prepare filling, rinse and dry bowl thoroughly. Fit with metal blade. Dry lemon peel well, cut into 1-in/2.5-cm pieces and drop through feed tube while machine is running. Add sugar and process until peel is finely chopped. This may take 10 to 20 seconds.

6. Add eggs and egg yolk and mix together well – about 10 seconds. Add lemon juice and blend. Add cream and blend.

7. Place prebaked crust on a cookie sheet and pour in filling. Reduce oven temperature to 350°F/180°C and bake tart 25 to 35 minutes or until set. Remove and cool. I like this best served at room temperature but it is also good cold. Serve ungarnished for a simple, elegant effect or if you wish decorate it with a few rosettes of whipped cream piped around the outside edge and topped with candied violets or chopped crystallized ginger.

Old-Fashioned Refrigerator Cookies

Refrigerator cookies will never go out of fashion. This recipe is from one of my favorite Canadian cooks, Gwen Fargeon, whose recipes always have a wonderful, full flavor.

1¾ cups	all-purpose flour	425 mL	1 cup	brown sugar	250 mL
1 tsp	baking soda	5 mL	1	egg	1
¾ cup	shelled, toasted almonds, sliced	175 mL	1 tsp	vanilla	5 mL
½ cup	unsalted butter, cold	125 mL			

Makes 30 to 36 cookies

1. Combine the flour, soda and almonds in work bowl fitted with metal blade. Blend using 2 or 3 on/off pulses. Do not worry if nuts get chopped. Remove from bowl and reserve.

2. Cut butter into 1-in/2.5-cm cubes and add to work bowl still fitted with metal blade. Add sugar and process on/off in 5 or 6 pulses or until butter is finely chopped. Process continuously until butter and sugar are smoothly creamed. Beat in egg and vanilla. Blend well.

3. Add flour mixture all at once and blend into batter using 6 or 7 quick on/off pulses. Remove dough from bowl and shape into cylinders — approximately 6 in/15 cm long and 1½ in/4 cm in diameter. Wrap in waxed paper and freeze for a few hours or overnight.

4. Before baking preheat oven to 350°F/180°C. Butter cookie sheets well or line with parchment paper. Slice cookies very thin (approximately ¼ in/3 mm) and arrange on sheets. Bake 8 to 10 minutes until golden or until very crisp. Cool on cookie racks.

Oatmeal Shortbread Cookies

These cookies were the trademark of my Aunt Reba who used to bake them for every family gathering. And with a family of a hundred close relatives, that was quite a job. I once made these cookies for an office party when I was working for my father one summer. All the partners wanted the recipe and naturally I gave it to them. Some years later, my mother went to one of their homes for tea and was served these cookies. She commented that they were just like the ones her oldest sister used to make. My mother was then told that they were called Aunt Reba's Oatmeal Cookies, but the hostess couldn't remember who had given her the recipe. That's how recipes get around!

½ cup	walnut pieces	125 mL	½ cup	white sugar	125 mL
2 cups	uncooked rolled oats	500 mL	¾ cup	light brown sugar	175 mL
1½ cups	all-purpose flour	375 mL	1	egg	1
½ tsp	salt	2 mL	½ tsp	pure vanilla extract	2 mL
1 tsp	baking soda	5 mL	½ tsp	pure almond extract	2 mL
1 cup	unsalted butter	250 mL		Makes approximately 60 cookies	

1. Preheat oven to 350°F/180°C. Butter cookie sheets or line with parchment paper.
2. Fit work bowl with metal blade. Add walnuts and chop with 5 or 6 on/off pulses or until very finely chopped. Add oats and blend together with nuts – about 3 seconds. Remove from work bowl and reserve.
3. Add flour, salt and baking soda to work bowl still fitted with metal blade. Process just until mixed – about 3 seconds. Remove and reserve.
4. Cut butter into 1-in/2.5-cm cubes and add to work bowl with white and brown sugar. Process on/off with 8 to 10 on/off pulses or until butter and sugar are mixed and then process continuously until mixture is creamed.
5. Add egg and extracts. Blend in. Scrape down sides of bowl when necessary. Add flour mixture all at once and combine with a few on/off pulses or just until blended. Add oatmeal mixture and blend in with 1 or 2 on/off pulses.
6. Roll dough into small balls – about 1 tbsp/15 mL each. Place balls on prepared cookie sheets and press down very flat with a fork or flat bottom of a glass dipped in flour. Cookies should be very thin and crisp. Bake 8 to 12 minutes. Remove from baking pans and cool on wire racks.

Mandel Broidt

This almond bread is a dry cookie with a wonderful flavor. Although this is the Jewish version, usually served with tea, there are also many Italian, French and Spanish variations often served with wine.

1 cup	shelled almonds	250 mL	¾ cup	sugar	175 mL
2 cups	all-purpose flour	500 mL	1 cup	unsalted butter, cold	250 mL
1 cup	cake flour	250 mL	2	eggs	2
2 tsp	baking powder	10 mL	3 tbsp	orange juice	50 mL
¼ tsp	salt	1 mL	1 tsp	pure vanilla extract	5 mL
	Peel of ½ orange				
	Peel of 1 lemon				

Makes approximately 36 cookies

1. Preheat oven to 350°F/180°C. Butter a large cookie sheet with unsalted butter.
2. Fit work bowl with metal blade. Add almonds. Process on/off 10 to 12 times or until nuts are coarsely chopped. Remove from work bowl and reserve.
3. Add flours, baking powder and salt to work bowl fitted with metal blade. Process 5 seconds or until well blended. Remove and reserve.
4. Pat orange and lemon peels dry and cut peels into 1-in/2.5-cm pieces. With machine running, drop peels through feed tube and process until chopped. Add sugar and process until finely chopped.
5. Cut butter into cubes and add to work bowl. Process on/off about 6 or 7 times or until butter is in tiny bits and then process continuously until mixture is creamed. Add eggs. Process until blended. Scrape down sides of bowl. Add orange juice and vanilla and process 2 seconds.
6. Add flour mixture all at once and blend in with 3 quick on/off pulses. Add almonds and process with another 1 or 2 pulses.
7. Remove dough from work bowl and divide into thirds (see diagram). Shape each piece into a loaf that is about 1½ in/4 cm high and 3 in/8 cm wide. Place on cookie sheet. Leave room for expansion between loaves. Bake 15 to 20 minutes until somewhat firm.
8. Lower oven temperature to 300°F/ 150°C. Slice loaves crosswise into ½-in/1-cm slices. Arrange slices on another cookie sheet with cut sides up. Bake another 15 to 20 minutes or until firm and dry. Remove from baking pans and cool on racks.

Poppy Seed Cookies

This is an old family recipe. These cookies keep in an airtight canister for at least three weeks. They are not too sweet and taste wonderful with a cup of tea.

3 cups	all-purpose flour	750 mL	3	eggs	3
2 tsp	baking powder	10 mL	¾ cup	vegetable oil or unsalted butter, melted	175 mL
¼ tsp	salt	1 mL			
⅓ cup	poppy seeds	75 mL	1 tsp	pure vanilla extract	5 mL
	Peel of 1 orange				
½ cup	sugar	125 mL			

Makes approximately 60 cookies

1. Preheat oven to 350°F/180°C. Line cookie sheets with parchment paper or butter heavily.
2. Fit work bowl with metal blade. Add flour, baking powder, salt and poppy seeds. Process approximately 3 seconds or just until blended. Remove and reserve.
3. Pat orange peel dry with paper towels and cut into 1-in/2.5-cm pieces. With machine running, drop peel through feed tube into work bowl still fitted with metal blade. Process until coarsely chopped, add sugar and process until finely chopped.
4. Add eggs and process until well blended. Add oil and vanilla and process about 5 seconds.
5. Add flour mixture all at once to work bowl and process into egg mixture using 8 to 12 on/off pulses or until batter is well combined. Do not overprocess.
6. Break off balls of batter (approximately 1 tsp/5 mL each) and arrange on cookie sheets. With a fork or bottom of a glass dipped in flour, press cookies flat. Bake 8 to 12 minutes or until cookies are crisp and light brown. Cool on racks.

Chocolate Chestnut Truffles

Linda Stephen developed this delicious candy for our Gifts from the Kitchen course that we teach every November and December.

1 lb	fresh chestnuts	500 g
4 oz	bittersweet or semisweet chocolate	125 g
½ cup	unsalted butter	125 mL
2 tbsp	instant coffee powder	25 mL
¾ cup	icing sugar	175 mL

Makes approximately 36 truffles

1. Slit round side of chestnut with a small, sharp knife (see diagram). Cover with boiling water and cook 30 minutes or until tender. Or bake in a preheated 450°F/230°C oven for 20 minutes or until tender. Peel while still warm.
2. Fit work bowl with metal blade. Add shelled chestnuts and puree just until smooth — do not overprocess.

3. In the top of a double boiler over gently simmering water, melt the chocolate with butter and coffee powder. Cool slightly and blend into chestnuts with icing sugar.

4. Line an 8-in/2-L baking dish with foil and spread chestnut mixture in it. Cover and refrigerate overnight. Cut into small squares or roll into balls. Keep refrigerated or freeze until ready to use or give away.

Chocolate Hazelnut Truffles

For chocolate addicts there is nothing like homemade chocolate truffles. They get their name from the black, expensive fungus found deep in the roots of oak trees in France. Of course, these truffles have nothing to do with chocolate, but because they are so expensive and highly prized, the best chocolates that any chocolatier has to offer are called chocolate truffles. Usually they are irregular shapes and rolled in cocoa to resemble the true truffle. They can be served for dessert, after dessert, or given away as wonderful gifts from the kitchen.

6 oz	shelled hazelnuts	175 g	3 tbsp	orange liqueur, rum or Cognac	50 mL
	Peel of ½ orange		1 cup	sifted Dutch process cocoa (see page 15)	250 mL
3 tbsp	sugar	50 mL			
12 oz	bittersweet or semisweet chocolate	350 g			
½ cup	unsalted butter	125 mL	**Makes approximately 60 truffles**		

1. Preheat oven to 350°F/180°C. Spread nuts on a cookie sheet and bake 10 minutes. Rub nuts in a tea towel to remove as much husk as possible. Do not worry if all is not removed. Cool.

2. Fit work bowl with metal blade. Pat orange peel dry and cut into small pieces. Drop through feed tube while machine is running. Add sugar. Continue processing until peel is finely chopped. Add nuts and process by chopping on/off until a fine texture is achieved.

3. Melt chocolate with butter in the top of double boiler over barely simmering water. Add to nuts in work bowl along with liqueur. Blend well. Transfer to a bowl and refrigerate until firm enough to shape. Roll into small balls about the size of small cherry tomatoes. Roll in cocoa and set in tiny paper cups. Keep refrigerated or freeze.

Pastries, Mousses, Roulades and Frozen Desserts

In 1973 when I first opened the cooking school, people loved the dessert courses. They were always the first courses to be completely booked and everyone wanted to practice what they had learned!

But shortly after, for a period of about five years, desserts seemed to fall by the wayside. Salads became very popular, and stir-fried, low-calorie foods took over. People seemed to be pretending that they really didn't like desserts anymore.

Now I'm happy to say that desserts are again the rage. Maybe because everyone is exercising so much, they feel they need a treat as a reward for working so hard. Dessert restaurants and cafés have sprung up all over, and restaurants are now realizing that they must offer delicious desserts, worth their calories, in order to compete.

The desserts in this chapter are all worth the calories and are very special. I really started to love cooking by making and eating desserts, so I have a special place in my heart for them and I always give them a lot of attention. My personal diet philosophy is if there is something good to eat, eat it and enjoy. Then when there is nothing really great around, eat fruit or yogurt, but don't eat just for the sake of eating. And never pass up something wonderful for the sake of a diet.

So, join your local "Y" as I did, and enjoy desserts without guilt!

Cold Lime Mousse

This mixture is very versatile. I have served it in individual chocolate cups, layered it with berries for a parfait, or spooned it into small baked tart shells. I have also served it as a pie in a chocolate or vanilla wafer crust. This dish is always refreshing and tastes great even after a heavy meal. It can also be served frozen, or defrosted for a few hours in the refrigerator before serving.

1	envelope unflavored gelatin	1	1 tbsp	rum	15 mL
¼ cup	cold water	50 mL	1 tbsp	icing sugar	15 mL
	Peel of 2 limes		¼ cup	shelled pistachio nuts, lightly toasted	50 mL
¾ cup	sugar	175 mL			
4	egg yolks	4			
⅔ cup	fresh lime juice	150 mL			
2½ cups	whipping cream	625 mL	Serves 6 to 8		

1. In a heavy, medium-sized saucepan, sprinkle gelatin over cold water and allow to soften 5 minutes. Heat very gently just until gelatin has dissolved.

2. Fit work bowl with metal blade. Pat lime peel dry with paper towels, cut into 1-in/2.5-cm pieces and add through feed tube with machine running. Add sugar and process until peel is finely chopped. Add egg yolks and immediately blend until smooth. Scrape down sides once or twice to be sure you are incorporating all the yolks. Blend in juice and gelatin mixture.

3. Return mixture to saucepan and cook gently until slightly thickened. The yolks are thickening the mixture at this point (the gelatin only works as it cools) so it won't be too thick. Transfer to a bowl and cool over a larger bowl of ice cubes, stirring occasionally to be sure mixture is not setting too much. (When you fold in the cream, the gelatin mixture should be at room temperature but not yet set.)

4. Wipe or wash out work bowl and fit with metal blade. With machine running, add cream through the feed tube. Watch carefully and process only until cream is thick and light.

5. Stir about ½ cup/125 mL cream into gelatin base to lighten it and then fold in about 1½ cups/375 mL more cream. Reserve the remaining cream in the work bowl for the garnish. Transfer lime mixture to a serving bowl and refrigerate until firm – at least 2 hours.

6. Meanwhile, return work bowl with the cream to machine and add rum and sugar. Process a few seconds until cream is slightly stiffer and ingredients are very well blended. Spoon or pipe cream on top of mousse.

7. Fit clean work bowl with metal blade. Add pistachio nuts and chop with 2 or 3 on/off pulses until nuts are coarsely chopped. Sprinkle over top of mousse.

Apricot Mousse in Chocolate Cups

This dessert can be made in large chocolate cups (2½ in/6 cm) or it can be made in smaller cups (1½ in/4 cm) and served as part of a sweet table with other desserts. If you have never made chocolate cups before, you are in for a treat because they look so elegant and yet are easy to prepare. Foil cups, are a little easier to use but after some practice you will be able to make them just as easily in the paper ones. The mousse can also be served on its own in individual soufflé dishes or can be used to fill chocolate crepes (page 180), cookie cups (page 174), small tart shells, or the hazelnut roulade (page 182).

Chocolate Cups:		
8 oz	bittersweet or semisweet chocolate	250 g

Apricot Mousse:		
1½ cups	dried apricots	375 mL
1 cup	whipping cream (or a little more if necessary)	250 mL

2 tbsp	dark rum or Amaretto	25 mL
2 tbsp	icing sugar	25 mL

Garnish:		
8	dried apricots	8
3 oz	bittersweet or semisweet chocolate	100 g

Makes 8 large or 16 small desserts

Chocolate Cups:

1. Melt chocolate in the top of double boiler over gently simmering water. With a spoon or brush, paint the inside of 8 large or 16 small fluted foil muffin cups. If the chocolate is too hot, it tends to drip down into the bottom of the cup. If this happens, just cool the chocolate for a few minutes and then recoat the cups. Place the cups on a cookie sheet and freeze for at least 30 minutes (see diagram).

2. Remove cups from freezer one at a time. Because the chocolate is so thin and your hands are warm, they tend to melt easily, so keep the rest in the freezer while you are working with one. Gently peel the foil from the chocolate and then store the cups in the refrigerator or freezer until ready to fill.

Apricot Mousse:

1. Place apricots in a saucepan and barely cover with cold water. Allow to soak 1 hour. Then cook apricots 30 to 40 minutes or until tender.

2. Fit work bowl with metal blade and add apricots and any remaining liquid. Process until apricots are pureed. If you want the mixture completely smooth, you can press the puree through a sieve, but it is not necessary. Measure mixture and transfer to a bowl. (Use the same amount of whipping cream as you have puree.)

3. Wash and dry work bowl and refit with metal blade. With machine running, add the whipping cream through the feed tube and process, watching very carefully, until it starts to thicken. Add rum and icing sugar. Process until thick but do not overprocess or you may inadvertently make butter.

4. Fold cream into apricot mixture and taste. Fold in more sugar or more rum if necessary. Mixture should be fairly stiff. If not, refrigerate 15 minutes and beat with a whisk until it becomes slightly thicker — 1 minute at most.

To Assemble:

1. Spoon mousse into chocolate cups, or use a piping tube. Refrigerate.

2. For garnish, use 1 whole apricot for large desserts or cut them in half for the small ones. Melt chocolate in a double boiler over gently simmering water and dip half of each piece of apricot into chocolate. Place on a piece of waxed paper to dry. Place 1 dipped apricot into the top of each mousse so that chocolate and apricot are showing. Refrigerate until ready to serve.

Note: Some people use coating (couverture, enrobing, summer coating) chocolate to make the cups and although it is very easy to work with, the flavor is not nearly as nice as good imported chocolate.

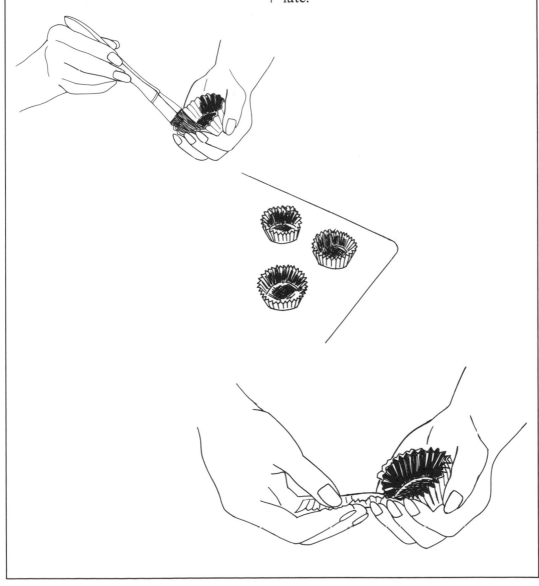

White Chocolate Mousse with Raspberry Sauce

This is a stunning dessert that tastes as good as it looks. The mousse can be used to fill chocolate cups, roulades or crepes or can be eaten on its own. The cookie cups can be used for any mousse or ice cream or can be served as cookies without shaping them into cups. The raspberry sauce is great over ice creams, pound cakes and mousses.

Cookie Cups:		
½ cup	sugar	125 mL
⅓ cup	all-purpose flour	75 mL
2	egg whites	2
¼ cup	unsalted butter, melted	50 mL
2 tsp	water	10 mL
1 tsp	pure vanilla extract	5 mL

White Chocolate Mousse:		
10 oz	white chocolate	300 g
2 cups	whipping cream	500 mL

½ cup	coarsely chopped pralines (see page 134) or chopped hazelnuts or almonds	125 mL

Raspberry Sauce:		
2	15-oz/425-g packages frozen raspberries	2
2 tbsp	orange liqueur	25 mL

Serves 8

Cookie Cups:

1. Preheat oven to 400°F/200°C. Butter and flour 2 cookie sheets. (If you are using a jelly roll pan, turn it upside down first.)

2. Fit work bowl with metal blade. Add sugar and flour and process just until mixed. Add remaining ingredients for dough and process just until mixed.

3. Spoon batter onto prepared cookie sheets, using 2 or 3 spoonfuls for each cookie. Do not try to make more than 3 cookies at one time. Spread batter until you have a thin circle about 6 in/15 cm in diameter.

4. Bake 4-7 minutes or just until cookies begin to brown around the edges. While cookies are baking prepare the second sheet.

5. When cookies are ready, allow to cool 10 to 30 seconds and then carefully lift off sheet with a spatula while they are still hot and malleable. Gently press cookies into the inside of 3 custard cups, individual soufflé dishes or individual brioche molds. Cookies will take the shape of the mold. Do not worry if the bottoms are not flat as the desserts look just as nice presented on their sides – maybe better. After a few minutes cookies can be removed from molds. If cookies harden before you can form them properly, return them to the oven for 30 seconds to soften and try again (eat any that break!). If you are not using them that day, store in an airtight container or freeze.

White Chocolate Mousse:

1. Break chocolate into chunks. Fit clean work bowl with metal blade. Add chocolate and chop using 5 or 6 on/off pulses or until coarsely chopped. Remove ⅓ cup/75 mL and reserve.

2. Heat ½ cup/125 mL whipping cream. Process remaining chocolate in work bowl until finely chopped and then add hot cream through feed tube. Process until chocolate is smoothly melted. Remove from work bowl and cool to room temperature.

3. Wash and dry work bowl. Add remaining 1½ cups/375 mL cold whipping cream through the feed tube while the machine is running. Whip until thick. Do not overprocess. Fold cream into cooled chocolate mixture along with reserved chopped chocolate and pralines or nuts. Reserve.

Raspberry Sauce:

1. Drain almost all juice from raspberries. Pick out 8 berries, pat dry and reserve. Fit clean work bowl with metal blade. Add berries and liqueur. Puree. Strain through a sieve to remove seeds. For thinner sauce, add some of the strained juice. Refrigerate until ready to serve.

To Assemble:

1. Fill cookie cups with mousse. Top each mousse with a reserved raspberry. Refrigerate. Just before serving spoon a circle of sauce on each dessert plate and place a cookie cup in the center of each.

Chocolate Mousse

Although there are many, many recipes for chocolate mousse, most people settle on one favorite after trying them all. This is mine — it's deep, dark, rich and luscious. Chocolate mousse is sometimes served with a rosette of whipped cream, but this really is not necessary because it is so rich. A few candied roses or violets, or slivered ginger or orange peel would be lovely on top of each serving.

6 oz	bittersweet or semisweet chocolate	175 g	1 tsp	pure vanilla extract	5 mL
¼ cup	boiling water	50 mL	¼ cup	Cognac, Cointreau or strong coffee	50 mL
⅓ cup	unsalted butter, at room temperature	75 mL	1½ cups	whipping cream	375 mL
4	egg yolks	4	Serves 6		

1. Fit work bowl with metal blade. Break chocolate into 1-in/2.5-cm chunks and add to work bowl. Chop chocolate using 10 to 12 on/off pulses or until finely chopped.

2. With machine running, add boiling water through feed tube and process 1 minute or until mixture is smooth. Cut butter into cubes and add to chocolate with egg yolks. Process about 30 seconds or until smooth. Add vanilla and liqueur. Transfer to a mixing bowl.

3. Without cleaning work bowl, add cream through feed tube. Process until thickened but do not overprocess. Fold cream into chocolate base.

4. Spoon mousse into individual soufflé dishes or custard cups or use mousse to fill chocolate cups (see page 172). If you want to pipe mousse into cups, refrigerate 30 minutes or until it begins to set and then it can be easily piped.

Cognac Mousse with Pralines and Strawberries

Although you can prepare this dessert with Cointreau, Amaretto or your favorite liqueur, Cognac adds a very sophisticated touch. In most recipes that call for Cognac, you can get away with substituting a less expensive brandy. However, in this recipe, use real Cognac. It is the dominant flavor and the alcohol is not evaporated by cooking, so brandy would taste rough.

2 cups	fresh strawberries	500 mL		1 tsp	pure vanilla extract	5 mL
¼ cup	Cognac	50 mL		1¾ cups	whipping cream	425 mL
¼ cup	unsalted butter, cold	50 mL		1 cup	praline powder (see page 134)	250 mL
6 oz	cream cheese, cold	175 g				
⅓ cup	creamed honey or ½ cup/125 mL sugar	75 mL				
⅓ cup	Cognac	75 mL		**Serves 8**		

1. Fit work bowl with medium slicing disc. Reserve 8 berries for a garnish. Hull remaining berries. Place them in small feed tube and, using gentle pressure, slice. Place berries in a bowl and add Cognac. Mix well.

2. Wipe work bowl clean. Refit with metal blade. Add butter and cheese and process on/off until finely chopped and then process continuously until creamed. Add honey and process until blended. Add Cognac and vanilla and process in. Do not overprocess, or mixture may become too liquid. Transfer mixture to a bowl.

3. Refit work bowl with metal blade (it is not necessary to wash bowl). With machine running, add cream through feed tube and process until thickened. Do not overprocess. Gently fold into cheese base. Mixture should be fairly stiff — if not, refrigerate 1 hour. (If mixture is not firm, it could be that you warmed the butter and cheese too much by overprocessing or did not beat the cream stiff enough.)

4. To assemble, spoon marinated strawberries into the bottom of 8 brandy snifters or wine glasses. Spoon or pipe in a layer of the mousse. Sprinkle with the praline powder. Top with another layer of mousse. Place a reserved whole berry on each dessert and dust with praline powder. Refrigerate at least 2 hours or until ready to serve.

Crème Brûlée

Bite for bite, this may be the most decadently rich dessert I make, and I have to admit it's one of my all-time favorites. Serve it in small quantities and don't make it too often, as it is very, very rich.

1	vanilla bean	1	2 tbsp	sugar	25 mL
2 tbsp	sugar	25 mL	1 cup	brown sugar (or more if necessary)	250 mL
3 cups	whipping cream	750 mL			
8	egg yolks	8	**Serves 6 to 8**		

1. Preheat oven to 325°F/160°C. Fit work bowl with metal blade. Cut vanilla bean into 1-in/2.5-cm lengths and add to work bowl with machine running. Add 2 tbsp/ 25 mL sugar and process until chopped.

2. Place cream and vanilla-sugar in a saucepan and heat but do not boil. Turn heat off and allow cream to absorb vanilla flavor for 5 minutes.

3. Beat egg yolks with remaining sugar and slowly beat in vanilla-flavored cream. Strain mixture to remove pieces of vanilla.

4. Divide custard into ½-cup/125-mL individual soufflé dishes or ramekins or a 6-cup/1.5-L soufflé dish. Place in a water bath (a larger pan filled with enough boiling water to come halfway up sides of custard dish) and bake 20 to 25 minutes for the small custards, or 40 to 45 minutes for the larger one, or until a knife inserted into custard comes out reasonably clean. Cool and refrigerate overnight.

5. Make sure brown sugar is not hard (see page 20) and place in work bowl fitted with metal blade. Process until sugar is smooth and free of lumps.

6. Preheat broiler. Arrange cold custards on cookie sheet. Spoon about ¼ in/5 mm sugar on each custard and smooth evenly. Place approximately 6 in/15 cm from broiler. Watching carefully, broil until sugar melts and just begins to brown. If you like an even thicker, smoother layer, repeat with more sugar and broil once again.

7. Refrigerate until ready to serve.

Note: If you do not have a vanilla bean, simply add 2 tsp/10 mL pure vanilla extract to the custard after beating the hot cream into the sugared egg yolks.

Pistachio Roulade

This pistachio cake is quite unusual and a pretty pale green color. If you cannot find shelled pistachio nuts (try specialty nut stores or Middle Eastern grocery stores), you may want to substitute pine nuts, hazelnuts, walnuts or almonds rather than shelling the nuts yourself. There are different ways to roll roulades (see page 182), but this one is very different and visually stunning.

Cake:		
1½ cups	shelled pistachio nuts	375 mL
¾ cup	sugar	175 mL
1 tsp	baking power	5 mL
5	eggs	5
2 tbsp	icing sugar	25 mL
Filling:		
2 cups	whipping cream	500 mL
3 tbsp	sifted icing sugar	50 mL
3 tbsp	Cointreau or other orange liqueur	50 mL
Topping:		
2 cups	fresh strawberries	500 mL
¾ cup	raspberry jam or jelly	175 mL
2 tbsp	Cointreau or other orange liqueur	25 mL

Serves 6 to 8

1. Preheat oven to 350°F/180°C. Butter a jelly roll pan approximately 9 in x 15 in x ¾ in/26 cm x 38 cm x 2 cm. Line with parchment paper or waxed paper and butter again. Dust lightly with flour.

2. Spread another pan with nuts and bake 10 minutes. Cool.

3. Fit work bowl with metal blade. Add cooled nuts and ¼ cup/50 mL sugar. Process nut mixture with 6 to 10 on/off pulses or until finely ground. Add baking powder and blend in. Remove from work bowl to a mixing bowl.

4. Separate eggs and reserve whites. Add yolks to work bowl still fitted with metal blade. Add another ¼ cup/50 mL sugar and process until mixture is light and lemon-colored. Scrape down sides of bowl several times. Transfer yolk mixture to bowl of nuts and mix together.

5. In a copper, stainless-steel or glass bowl, beat egg whites until light. Slowly beat in remaining sugar until stiff. Stir a quarter of egg-white mixture into nut base to lighten it and then fold in remaining whites lightly. Spread evenly over prepared jelly roll pan and bake 15 to 20 minutes or until cake is firm to the touch but not dry. Cool about 10 minutes.

6. Sprinkle the top of cake with 2 tbsp/25 mL icing sugar and invert onto a tea towel. Cool completely.

7. To prepare filling, fit clean work bowl with metal blade. With machine running, add cream through feed tube and process until lightly thickened. Add icing sugar and liqueur and process until stiff. Do not overbeat. Reserve about a third of the cream for a garnish. Spread the remaining cream over the flat, cooled cake.

8. Cut the flat cake into 1-in/2.5-cm strips crosswise (see diagram). Have a large round serving platter ready and line with a large doily. Take a strip and roll up tightly. Place in center of doily with the cut side (spiral) facing up. Take a second strip and roll up around the outside of the first roll. Continue until all strips are used. You should end up with a spiral that is approximately 12 in/30 cm in diameter.

9. To prepare topping, wash and hull berries. Pat dry and halve. Arrange all over top of cake. Strain jam or jelly and heat if necessary to use as glaze. Add liqueur. With a pastry brush, brush glaze over fruit. Place remaining whipped cream in a piping tube fitted with a star nozzle and pipe around the edge of fruit. Refrigerate until ready to serve.

Note: Other fruits such as kiwi, orange segments, raspberries or blueberries can also be used for a topping.

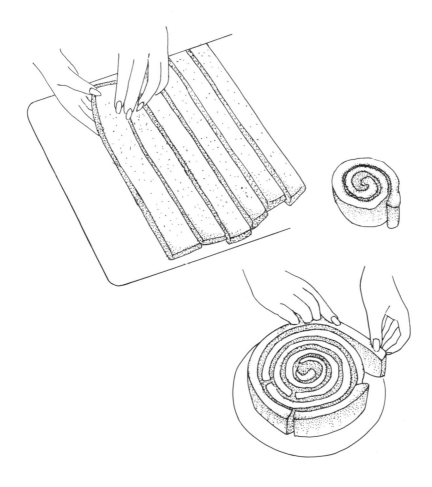

Chocolate Crepes with Coffee Ice Cream and Hot Chocolate Sauce

These crepes can be filled with any number of frozen or mousse-like mixtures. Almost any flavor ice cream tastes wonderful with the chocolate crepes — try the recipes on pages 184 - 186 or any good-quality commercial ice cream. If you prefer mousse-type fillings, try the white chocolate mousse on page 174, dark chocolate mousse on page 175, lime mousse on page 171 or the apricot mousse on page 172. I've tried them all and have had no trouble eating any of them. The crepes can be filled ahead of time and stored frozen if filled with ice cream, or refrigerated if filled with mousse. The sauce can be made ahead of time and reheated just before serving.

Chocolate Crepes:

½ cup	all-purpose flour	125 mL
3 tbsp	cocoa, preferably Dutch process	50 mL
1 tbsp	sugar	15 mL
4	eggs	4
3 tbsp	unsalted butter, melted	50 mL
½ cup	milk	125 mL
2 tbsp	unsalted butter or clarified butter for cooking	25 mL

2 cups	good-quality coffee ice cream	500 mL

Hot Chocolate Sauce:

½ cup	cocoa, preferably Dutch process, sifted	125 mL
1 cup	sugar	250 mL
1 cup	corn syrup	250 mL
½ cup	cream	125 mL
3 tbsp	unsalted butter	50 mL

Serves 6

Chocolate Crepes:

1. Fit work bowl with metal blade. Add flour, cocoa and sugar. Process for a few seconds until ingredients are blended together and free of lumps.

2. Add eggs, melted butter and milk. Process until batter is smooth. Transfer to a mixing bowl, cover with plastic wrap and allow batter to rest at room temperature at least 1 hour before making crepes.

3. Heat 2 tbsp/25 mL butter in an 8-in/20-cm crepe or omelet pan. Add ¼ cup/50 mL batter and swirl in pan. This is a test crepe. If pan sticks badly in a certain spot simply rub spot with oil and salt and try again.

4. When pan is ready, add another ¼ cup/50 mL batter and swirl in pan, but this time pour excess back into batter bowl so you only have a thin coating on the bottom of the pan. The pan should be hot enough that the batter sticks to the bottom almost instantly but not so hot that all the batter runs back into the bowl. Because of the butter in the batter you should not have to grease the pan after the first test crepe. If you do, simply brush the pan lightly with butter. Cook crepe about 1 minute on each side. Stack crepes as they are made. You should have at least 12 crepes.

5. Prepare Hot Chocolate Sauce.
6. Cut ice cream into sticks (approximately 6 in x 1½ in/15 cm x 4 cm). If you are using ice cream that comes in small tubs, cut off the container and cut out wedges, or fill crepes with 2 small scoops. Roll crepes around ice cream and freeze until ready to serve.

7. Just before serving, pour warm sauce over crepes and serve immediately. Serve 1 or 2 per person, depending on the occasion (after a heavy or light meal) and the person.

Hot Chocolate Sauce:
1. Combine all sauce ingredients in a heavy saucepan and bring to a boil. Boil for 3 minutes. Sauce should be thick and fudgy.

Apple or Pear Sauce

Sometimes a simple, homey dessert tastes best. If you always prepare apple sauce, try pear sauce for a great change.

3 lb	apples (such as Spy or Golden Delicious) or pears (such as Bosc or Bartlett)	1.5 kg	2 tsp	ground cinnamon, optional	10 mL
¼ cup	unsalted butter	50 mL	1 tsp	ground cardamom, optional	5 mL
¾ cup	white sugar	175 mL	2 tbsp	Calvados or pear liqueur, optional	25 mL
2 tbsp	lemon juice	25 mL			

Serves 8

1. Fit work bowl with medium slicing disc. Peel apples or pears and cut in half. Remove cores. Pack large feed tube lightly and slice apples or pears. Repeat until all fruit is sliced.
2. Melt butter in a heavy saucepan and add sugar. Stir to dissolve. Add fruit and stir well. Add lemon juice and spices. Bring mixture to a boil, reduce heat and cook gently, uncovered, for approximately 30 minutes or until fruit is very tender. If

there is a lot of liquid in saucepan, turn up heat and, stirring constantly, reduce until thickened.
3. Refit work bowl with metal blade. Add sauce and puree as smooth as you wish. If the sauce is hot, remember to remove the small pusher.

Note: If you wish, add 2 tbsp/25 mL Calvados to the apple sauce or the same amount of pear liqueur to the pear sauce as you puree it.

Hazelnut Roulade with Apricot-Amaretto Cream

This is a cake that is gorgeous to look at and tastes as good as it looks. It is not hard to make once you get over the fact that a cake can really be rolled up. It also freezes well. It can be filled with other fillings such as chocolate mousse (page 175), white chocolate mousse (page 174), lemon cream (page 158) or even just whipped cream and fresh berries.

Cake:

1½ cups	hazelnuts (filberts)	375 mL
¾ cup	sugar	175 mL
2 tbsp	all-purpose flour	25 mL
¾ tsp	baking power	4 mL
5	eggs	5
1 tsp	pure vanilla extract	5 mL
2 tbsp	icing sugar	25 mL

Filling:

Apricot mousse
made with Amaretto

instead of rum (see
page 172)

Garnish:

¾ cup	whipping cream	175 mL
1 tbsp	icing sugar	15 mL
2 tbsp	Amaretto	25 mL
8	dried apricots	8

Serves 6 to 8

1. Preheat oven to 350°F/180°C. Butter a jelly roll pan approximately 9 in x 15 in x ¾ in/26 cm x 38 cm x 2 cm. Line with parchment paper or waxed paper. Butter again and dust with flour.

2. Spread hazelnuts on a cookie sheet and toast 15 minutes. To remove skins, see Food Hints, page 18. You will probably not be able to remove them all but don't worry. Set aside to cool.

3. Fit work bowl with metal blade. Add cooled nuts and process on/off with 4 or 5 pulses or until coarsely chopped. Add ¼ cup/50 mL sugar and continue to process on/off until nuts are finely chopped but not at all oily. Add flour and baking powder and blend in. Remove from work bowl to a large mixing bowl.

4. Separate eggs and reserve whites. Add yolks to work bowl still fitted with metal blade. Add another ¼ cup/50 mL sugar and blend until light and lemon-colored. Process in vanilla. Transfer yolk mixture to bowl with nuts and mix together well.

5. In a copper, stainless-steel or glass bowl, beat egg whites until light. Slowly beat in remaining sugar and continue beating until stiff. Stir a quarter of the egg-white mixture into the nut mixture to lighten it. Lightly fold remaining egg whites into nut mixture. Spread as evenly as possible on prepared cookie sheet. Bake 15 to 20 minutes or until cake is firm to the touch but not dry or hard. Remove from oven and allow to cool 10 minutes.

6. Sprinkle top of cake with 2 tbsp/25 mL icing sugar and invert onto a tea towel. Roll up lengthwise gently and leave in towel until cool.

7. Prepare filling (see page 172).

8. Unroll cake and spread with filling. Do not overfill.

9. Roll up gently using tea towel as a guide and roll onto a long serving plate. Cut off about 2 in/5 cm diagonally at each end and turn up so that filling shows (see diagram). Refrigerate while preparing garnish.

10. To prepare garnish, fit clean work bowl with metal blade. With machine running, add whipping cream through the feed tube and process until it begins to thicken. Add icing sugar and Amaretto. Process until stiff but do not over-process.

11. Place cream in bag with a star nozzle and pipe rosettes of cream down the center of the cake. Decorate with apricots.

12. To serve, cut each slice on the diagonal. The cook gets to eat the ends!

Frozen Apricot Yogurt

This is a light dessert that is quite low in calories. You can vary the flavors by using 1½ cups/375 mL of any fruit puree. Taste the mixture before freezing and if it is not sweet enough for you, just add more honey.

1 cup	dried apricots	250 mL	2 cups	unflavored yogurt	500 mL
1½ cups	orange juice	375 mL			
3 tbsp	honey	50 mL			

Makes 3 cups/750 mL

1. Place apricots in a heavy saucepan and add orange juice. Cook gently for 30 minutes or until apricots are very tender. Cool slightly.

2. Fit work bowl with metal blade. Add apricots and any juice and puree until smooth (or leave it slightly chunky if you wish). Add honey. Process 3 or 4 seconds. Add yogurt and process until well blended. Taste and add more honey if necessary.

3. Transfer mixture to ice cream freezer and freeze according to manufacturer's directions. If you do not have an ice cream freezer, place mixture in a flat, metal baking dish (like a cake pan) and freeze approximately 2 hours. Mixture should be partially frozen but not solid. Break mixture up and puree in 2 batches in work bowl still fitted with metal blade. Return mixture to pan and freeze again. Puree again. This is to break up ice crystals as the mixture freezes. Eat immediately or freeze until ready to serve.

Vanilla-Peach Ice Cream

There is nothing like peaches and ice cream to make it feel like summer. In place of the peaches, you can use nectarines, plums or cherries — just peel and pit according to the fruit. In commercial ice creams, artificial vanilla flavor is usually used, as the pure vanilla is very delicate. Using the vanilla bean really increases the vanilla flavor and will also result in the fine black dots you see in most homemade vanilla ice creams. If you do not have a vanilla bean, use double the amount of vanilla extract in the recipe.

1½ lb	peaches, very ripe	750 g		1 cup	milk	250 mL
½ cup	sugar	125 mL		6	egg yolks	6
1	vanilla bean, cut into 1-in/2.5-cm pieces	1		1 tbsp	pure vanilla extract	15 mL
⅓ cup	sugar	75 mL				
3 cups	whipping cream	750 mL				

Makes approximately 6 cups/1.5 L

1. Cut a cross in the bottom end of the peaches. Place in boiling water for 1 minute. Rinse with cold water and peel off skins. Cut peaches in half and remove pits. Then cut into quarters. Sprinkle with ½ cup/ 125 mL sugar and set aside for 30 minutes.

2. Fit work bowl with metal blade. Add vanilla bean and ⅓ cup/ 75 mL sugar. Process using on/off technique until vanilla bean is finely chopped. Place vanilla and sugar in a heavy saucepan with the cream and milk and cook gently 10 minutes.

3. Meanwhile add peach mixture to work bowl still fitted with metal blade and puree as smooth or as coarse as you wish. Reserve.

4. Beat egg yolks and slowly beat in hot cream mixture. Return to heavy saucepan and cook gently, stirring constantly until mixture becomes slightly custardy. Do not overcook or you may scramble the egg yolks. Strain custard to get rid of any larger pieces of vanilla bean. Combine custard with peach puree and add vanilla extract. Cool completely and refrigerate until well chilled.

5. If you have an ice cream machine, freeze according to manufacturer's directions. If not, place mixture in a flat, metal dish or dishes (like a large cake pan) and partially freeze – about 2 hours. Mixture should not be completely solid. Break mixture up and puree in 2 or 3 batches in work bowl still fitted with metal blade. Return to pan and freeze again. Puree again. This is to break up any ice crystals that form in the freezing process. Eat, or freeze until ready to serve. If mixture is solidly frozen, remove ice cream to refrigerator for about 30 minutes before serving to soften slightly.

Prune-Armagnac Ice Cream

I have always been crazy about ice cream but even if you aren't, this one is sure to win you over. And forget any ideas you may have had about prunes — this ice cream is rich, sophisticated and wonderful!

1½ cups	pitted prunes	375 mL	6	egg yolks	6
⅓ cup	water	75 mL	½ cup	sugar	125 mL
½ cup	Armagnac, Cognac or brandy	125 mL	2 tsp	pure vanilla extract	10 mL
¼ cup	sugar	50 mL	¼ cup	Armagnac, Cognac or brandy	50 mL
2 cups	milk	500 mL			
2 cups	whipping cream	500 mL			

Makes 6 cups/1.5 L

1. Place prunes, water, ½ cup/125 mL Armagnac and sugar in a heavy saucepan. Bring to a boil, cook gently for 5 minutes and remove from heat. Allow to cool about 1 hour.

2. Fit work bowl with metal blade. Add prune mixture and puree as coarse or as fine as you wish (I like to leave it slightly coarse). Remove and reserve.

3. Place milk and cream in a heavy saucepan and bring to a boil. Place egg yolks and sugar in work bowl still fitted with metal blade (it doesn't matter if some prune mixture remains in bowl) and blend together until light and lemon-colored. Scrape down sides of work bowl. Take about 1 cup/250 mL of milk-cream mixture and add to egg yolks. Combine and return to remaining milk-cream mixture in saucepan. Cook gently until mixture becomes slightly custardy. Do not overcook or yolks may scramble (just strain if that happens.) Stir in prune mixture, vanilla and ¼ cup/50 mL Armagnac. Cool completely and refrigerate until well chilled.

4. Transfer mixture to ice cream freezer if you have one and follow manufacturer's directions on how to freeze. Or place mixture in a large, flat, metal dish or dishes (like a cake pan) and freeze about 2 hours or until partially frozen but not solid. Break mixture up and puree in 3 batches in work bowl still fitted with metal blade. Return to pan and freeze again until partially frozen. Puree again to break up ice crystals. Freeze until ready to serve.

Chocolate-Ginger Ice Cream

This is a custard-based ice cream that is rich and very chocolaty. Use the best choco-late you can — I like Swiss or Belgian. If you have an ice cream freezer just freeze the mixture according to its instructions, or simply follow the directions below. Ice cream freezers do a better job because they churn the ice cream during the entire freezing time, but you will not have any trouble eating the ice cream even if you only churn once or twice in the Cuisinart® during the freezing process.

¼ cup	dry crystallized ginger (with sugar coating)	50 mL	1 tsp	pure vanilla extract	5 mL
			3 tbsp	orange liqueur	50 mL
½ cup	sugar	125 mL	6 oz	bittersweet or semisweet chocolate	175 g
2 cups	milk	500 mL			
2 cups	whipping cream	500 mL			
4	egg yolks	4			

Makes approximately 4 cups/1 L

1. Fit work bowl with metal blade. Cut ginger in half if pieces are especially large and add to work bowl with sugar. Process on/off carefully until ginger is chopped very fine.

2. Place milk, cream and ginger-sugar mixture in a heavy saucepan and bring to a boil. Remove from heat and allow to steep about 5 minutes.

3. Beat egg yolks with a wire whisk in a bowl and slowly stir in ginger-milk mixture. Return mixture to heavy saucepan and cook gently, stirring constantly, until mixture thickens slightly. Be careful not to boil or overheat or you may have scrambled eggs in your custard (if that happens don't worry — just strain mixture). Add vanilla and liqueur.

4. Cut chocolate into chunks and add pieces to work bowl still fitted with metal blade. Chop chocolate with 14 to 20 on/off pulses or until finely chopped. Add about half the hot custard and process until chocolate is completely melted. Stir chocolate mixture back into the custard in the heavy saucepan and blend well with whisk.

5. Cool mixture and refrigerate for several hours or overnight. Transfer mixture to an ice cream freezer and freeze according to manufacturer's directions. If you do not have an ice cream freezer, place mixture in a flat, metal dish or dishes (like a cake pan) and freeze about 2 hours. Remove from freezer and, in 2 or 3 batches, process until smooth. Return to pan and freeze again for 2 hours. Break mixture up and puree again in 2 or 3 batches until smooth. This is to prevent large ice crystals from forming. (If ice cream base is not completely cold, or if your freezer is very full, mixture may take longer than 2 hours to semi-freeze. When you puree it in the food processor, it should be at least partially frozen but not so hard that you cannot remove it from the dish.)

6. Freeze again for about 1 hour or longer and serve.

Index

Almonds
  Almond cake with
    raspberry sauce, 150
  Almond paste, 135
  Mandel broidt, 167
  Nut torte, 163
  Pralines and praline
    powder, 134
Appetizers, 25-43. *See also*
  Soups.
  Chicken mousse, 70
  Fiddlehead and radish
    salad, 118
  Leek tart, 90
  Marinated eggplant salad,
    116
  Mushroom salad with dill
    dressing, 121
  Pasta shells with zucchini
    and fresh herbs, 87
  Pesto pizza, 92
  Rainbow vegetable terrine,
    96
  Risotto, 110
  Salmon and pasta salad
    with lemon dill
    mayonnaise, 114
  Spinach salad with blue
    cheese dressing, 119
Apples
  Apple cake, 151
  Apple or pear sauce, 181
  Rhubarb and apple crisp,
    157
Apricots
  Apricot-Amaretto cream,
    182
  Apricot mousse, 172
  Frozen apricot yogurt, 183
  Fruit and nut bran muffins,
    145
Armagnac
  Prune-Armagnac ice cream,
    185
Artichoke frittata, 38
Asparagus
  Cream of asparagus soup,
    53

**Baked fennel with Parmesan
  cheese, 97**
Baked mushroom tartlets, 36
Ballotine, 70
  Chicken stuffed with
    chicken mousse, 70
Banana bran muffins, 144
Barbecued dishes
  Chinese barbecued chicken,
    67
  Salmon steaks with butter
    provençale, 64
  Spicy barbecued ribs, 73

Basil. *See also* **Herbs.**
  Pesto pizza, 92
  Soupe au pistou, 60
Beef
  Beef stock, 45
  Brisket, 83
  Spaghetti and meat sauce,
    86
  Spicy barbecued ribs, 73
  Steaks with wild mushroom
    sauce, 85
Belgian endive cups, 32
**Beurre blanc (white butter
  sauce), 28**
Biscuits, 148
Blintzes
  Cheese blintzes with
    strawberry sauce, 88
Blue cheese dressing, 119
Bouquet garni, 13
Braided breads
  Braided spiced challah, 142
  Challah, 140
  Four-strand braid, 141
  Six-strand braid, 143
  Three-strand braid, 141
Bran
  Banana bran muffins, 144
  Fruit and nut bran muffins,
    145
Bread and butter pickles, 128
Breadcrumbs, 13
**Breaded veal cutlets with
  Florentine sauce, 82**
Breads
  Braided spiced challah, 142
  Caraway sour rye bread,
    138
  Challah, 140
  Hazelnut quick bread, 147
  Oatmeal bread, 139
  Whole wheat honey bread,
    137
Brisket, 83
Broccoli
  Cream of broccoli soup
    with curry, 51
  Rainbow vegetable terrine,
    96
  Stir-fried broccoli with
    oyster sauce, 106
Butter, 13
  Clarified, 13
  Salted vs. unsalted, 13
Butter tarts, 162
Butters, compound, 14
  Butter provençale, 64
  Dill butter, 65
  How to shape, 64
  Lime-ginger butter, 79
  Rosemary butter, 76
  Smoked salmon butter, 32
Butterflied leg of lamb, 78

Buttermilk
  Silver dollar buttermilk
    pancakes, 91

Cabbage
  How to chop, 14, 120
  Vegetable slaw, 120
Cakes. *See also* **Crisps.**
  Almond cake with
    raspberry sauce, 150
  Apple cake, 151
  Cheesecake, 155
  Hazelnut cheesecake with
    chocolate glaze, 156
  Hazelnut roulade with
    apricot-Amaretto cream,
    182
  Lemon cheesecake with
    fresh strawberries, 154
  Nut torte, 163
  Pistachio roulade, 178
  Plum coffee cake, 153
  Sour cream coffee cake, 152
Canapés. *See* **Appetizers.**
Candies
  Chocolate chestnut truffles,
    168
  Chocolate hazelnut truffles,
    169
  Nut truffles, 18
  Pralines, 134
Caraway sour rye bread, 138
Carrots
  Carrot and parsnip ring, 99
  Carrot flowers, 24
  Carrot marmalade, 130
  Carrot timbales, 101
  Cold carrot soup with
    ginger, 62
  Rainbow vegetable terrine,
    96
Cauliflower
  Rainbow vegetable terrine,
    96
Celery
  Celery soup, 57
  Iced celery and coriander
    soup, 54
Challah (braided egg loaf)
  Braided spiced challah, 142
  Challah, 140
  How to form 3-strand
    braid, 141
  How to form 4-strand
    braid, 141
  How to form 6-strand
    braid, 143
Cheddar. *See also* **Cheese.**
  Cheddar cheese muffins
    with fresh parsley, 144
Cheese, 14
  Baked fennel with
    Parmesan cheese, 97

Bonnie Stern is one of Canada's leading cooking instructors. She is the founder and director of The Bonnie Stern School of Cooking, which was established in Toronto in 1973 when food in Canada was just beginning to become the high-profile business it is today. As a result of her experience and expertise, she is a frequent guest on radio and television, with her own radio spot on CKFM's "Hour Toronto," and is a well-known food journalist, contributing to the *Globe and Mail* and *Canadian Living.*

The Bonnie Stern School of Cooking was one of the first schools to have been accredited by the International Association of Cooking Schools, and Bonnie herself is a Certified Member. She is also a professional member of the American Institute of Wine and Food and has studied with many international food specialists, including Simone Beck, Jacques Pépin and Marcella Hazan. Her previous best-selling books include *At My Table: Cooking with Bonnie Stern* and *Food Processor Cuisine.*